Introduction of Buddhism to Korea

Studies in Korean Religions and Culture

General Editors:
 Lewis R. Lancaster
 Chai-shin Yu

Introduction of Buddhism to Korea
New Cultural Patterns

edited by
Lewis R. Lancaster
and
C. S. Yu

ASIAN HUMANITIES PRESS
Berkeley, California

ASIAN HUMANITES PRESS/AHP Paperbacks

Asian Humanities Press offers to the specialist and the general reader alike, the best in new translations of major works and significant original contributions, to enhance our understanding of Asian literature, religions, cultures and thought. "Asian Humanities Press" and "AHP Paperbacks" are trademarks of Jain Publishing Company.

Library of Congress Cataloging-in-Publication Data

Introduction of Buddhism to Korea: new cultural patterns/edited by Lewis R. Lancaster and C. S. Yu.
    p.   cm.—(Studies in Korean religions and culture: v. 3)
Bibliography: p.
Includes index.
ISBN 0-89581-877-9: $40.00.—ISBN 0-89581-888-4 (pbk.): $15.00
    1. Buddhism—Korea—History—To 935. I. Lancaster, Lewis R.
II. Yu, C. S., 1932-   . III. Series.
BQ661.I58 1989
294.3′09519′0909 15—dc20   87-71273
                                   CIP

To Mr. & Mrs. Hyun Baek Kim

Contents

Preface

It is an often repeated truism that Korea is an under studied area of Asia, and in no field is this more evident than in Buddhist Studies. While our studies of Japanese and Chinese Buddhism have advanced in the West during the past decades, that of Korea have lagged behind. Given the number of scholars who are dealing with humanistic studies focused on Korea, it is certain that this paucity of literature on Korean Buddhism will continue for some time to come. With this in mind, we have set in motion this project to translate some of the important articles that have been written in Korean, and in some cases Japanese, related to Buddhism on the peninsula. These studies provide us with a glimpse of some of the important aspects of the tradition and can perhaps allow students and interested readers to grasp the basic facts concerning this form of Buddhism. We have attempted to provide articles that go beyond some of the traditional lore about Buddhism and present us with current speculations based on the available data. This volume deals with the early period of Buddhist life in Korea; later volumes will continue to trace the history in the various dynasties that followed the Three Kingdoms period.

Because we have had to make a limited selection of articles to meet the format of this series, the present translations give only a rough outline of the events of those times. In the first article by Prof. Ahn, we have presented a summary account of the period. In the articles which follow it, the reader will find more detail and in some cases disagreement or suggestions of other ways of viewing the material. If the series is able to continue, a second volume on this period can give even more detail. However, it is felt that the contents of this volume are a necessary preliminary to any further study of Korean Buddhism.

There are a number of aids to research contained in the volume which may go beyond the interest of some readers, but since we have so few books on the subject it was decided to put in a full bibliography of all works referenced. In addition, there is a partial glossary of some of the Korean terms. In some cases, articles have been abridged where there is overlap with material found in one of the other articles. In order to give the volume structure, omissions and in some cases additions have been made and noted in the translations. The additions are mainly in the footnotes.

The book is the product of a number of individuals who have contributed in one way or other. Of primary importance were those individuals who did the initial translations:

Kyoko Tokuno who did the work on the articles by Prof. Kamato and Professor Kodama, Robert Buswell did the translation of Prof. Inoue, Rhi Ju-hyung for the articles of Professors Ahn and Kim and Lee Ho-kuen for Prof. Rhi's work. The editing, indexing and proof reading was done by Jeff Seibel, Koh Nishiike, Anna Shtutina, and Cho Sung-taek. Part of the translation was reviewed by Ven. Mujin.

We would not have been able to undertake this project without the donations given by individuals who wished to see this type of publication. Special note of thanks should go to Mr. & Mrs. Hyun Baek Kim and Mr. & Mrs. Kikon Suh who have made certain that funds were sufficient to bring this and other volumes to fruition. Personnel matters and payment to the helpers was handled by the staff of the Center for Korean Studies at the Institute of East Asian Studies of the University of California-Berkeley.

Lewis R. Lancaster
University of California
Berkeley

A Short History of Ancient Korean Buddhism

by Ahn Kye-hyŏn

Introduction of Buddhism to Korea

Koguryŏ

W hen Buddhism was introduced to Korea in the fourth century during the period of the Three Kingdoms, Koguryŏ was the first to receive the new teaching. However, even before this official introduction the *Kao-seng chuan* makes reference to the presence of Buddhism in Korea. The eastern Chin monk Chih-tao-lin (314-366) sent a letter to a Koguryŏ monk, whose name is not given, praising another Chinese monk Chu-ch'ien (268-374).[1] It was, however, only in the reign of King Sosurim (371-384) that Buddhism was officially recognized. The *Samguk sagi* (vol. 18) records that in the second year of his reign (372) Fu Chien, the king of the Former Ch'in, sent a monk named Sundo with images of the Buddha and copies of several texts from the canon, and in the fourteenth year (384) another monk named Ado came from China. In 385 two monasteries, the Sŏngmun Monastery and the Ibullan Monastery were founded for these two monks. This was the beginning of Korean Buddhism.

In China, at that time, the Han Chinese, driven out by northern nomads, had moved into the Chiang-nan region; the north, which served as an area for struggles between the sixteen countries founded by the five northern tribes, fell into confusion. Of those, the Former Yen set itself in opposition to Koguryŏ, though it maintained good relations with another northern kingdom, the Former Ch'in. By the time of King Sosurim's

accession to the throne, the Former Yen had almost been
defeated by the Former Ch'in, which had continually provided
Koguryŏ with advanced cultural developments. Fu Chien, King
of the Former Ch'in, was an ardent Buddhist, as is well known.
However, Buddhism was only understood on an elementary
level at this time and was mostly concerned with simple doctrines
such as causality and karmic retribution; Buddhism was often
integrated through traditional Taoist categories.

Considering the situation in China, the Buddhism introduced into Koguryŏ must also have been of an elementary form,
with much emphasis given to causality and the search for
happiness. In 392, shortly after the arrival of Buddhism, King
Kogugyang proclaimed that his people should believe in
Buddhism and thus attain secular benefits. Buddhism, then,
which was seen to be merely another method for attaining
worldly profit, was incorporated into the indigenous belief
system. Soon, however, after its more profound aspects were
realized, it played a significant role in the development of the
Koguryŏ kingdom into an ancient state.[2]

Paekche

Paekche admitted Buddhism in 384, 12 years later than
Koguryŏ. The *Samguk yusa* says:

> In the first year of King Ch'imnyu's reign (384), an Indian
> monk, Maranant'a, came from Eastern Chin and was
> brought to the court where he received homage. In the
> next year, (385) ten Buddhist monasteries were built in the
> new capital, Hansan, and monks were installed in them.
> This was the beginning of Paekche Buddhism. In the first
> year of King Asin's reign (392) the King ordered the people
> to believe in Buddhism and seek happiness.[3]

The introduction of Buddhism in Paekche, therefore, was
similar to that in Koguryŏ.

After this date there are no pertinent records in the

Samguk yusa or the *Samguk sagi* until the reign of King Sŏng (523-554). During this reign it appears that Buddhism made great strides, activated in large part, by the return of the monk Kyŏmik from India in 526.

Silla

During the reign of King Nulchi (417-457), a Koguryŏ monk, Mukhoja, came to Silla and stayed in a village in the north; there he propagated Buddhism in secret. At that time an envoy from Liang China brought incense to Silla, but no one knew how to use it. Mukhoja instructed them in its use. He also cured the illness of a princess. Buddhism, though known at this time, had very little effect on Silla society. Later, however, during the reign of King Soji (479-499) another Koguryŏ monk, Ado, came to Silla and from this point on the number of followers increased.[4] The name Ado, which was also the name of a monk who appeared in Koguryŏ a century earlier, seems to have been used to mean a tonsured monk.

Buddhism gradually diffused among the general population, and the royal family sought to obtain official recognition for the new religion; this was opposed by aristocrats. Contrary to Silla society, the ancient tribal system remained strong. The clan was still an important social unit, and indigenous beliefs and customs were powerful and deep-rooted; Buddhism could not gain acceptance among the people.

In spite of this, King Pŏphŭng (r. 514-540) and his supporters tried to establish a more powerful monarchy by using the Buddhist Dharma as a spiritual prop and then identifying it with the King's order. This led to the promulgation of a new law by the king, reorganizing the administrative and bureaucratic systems, in 520, and the proclaiming of official recognition for Buddhism in 527 induced by the miraculous martyrdom of Ich'adon, a court official and devout Buddhist. Buddhist belief and practice, initially, in Silla must have been similar to that in Koguryŏ and Paekche.[5].

Buddhism in the Three Kingdoms Period

Koguryŏ

The Building of Buddhist Monasteries

In the second year of King Kwanggaet'o's reign (393), nine monasteries were founded in P'yŏngyang. A monastery site at Ch'ŏngam-ri in P'yŏngyang excavated in 1938 has been identified as the Kŭmgang Monastery founded in 497. There, the remains of an octagonal wooden pagoda was found to have been surrounded by four buildings facing in the four cardinal directions. This plan is similar to the constellation of the five stars referred to in the chapter on astronomy in the *Shih-chi*, which must have influenced its design.[6] At this site the ratio of the areas of the golden hall to the wooden pagoda is 1:0.7, whereas at the Sach'ŏnwang Monastery built during the early Unified Silla period (late seventh century), the ratio is 1:0.4.[7] This may show an earlier concern with the person of Śākyamuni Buddha rather than what was taught by him or Mahāyāna Buddhist teachings in general. The remains of an octagonal, stone pagoda is recorded as having been built at Yŏngt'ap Monastery. Koguryŏ pagodas seem to have been generally octagonal in shape.[8]

Buddhist Studies

During King Kwanggaet'o's reign (391-413), T'an-shih, an Eastern Chin monk, came to Liao-tung province, at that time in Koguryŏ territory, carrying with him a large collection of Buddhist texts.[9] During the reign of King Munja (491-518), the study of Buddhism became popular and many scholar monks investigated the teachings of the San-lun (Three treatises), T'ien-t'ai and *Nirvāṇa Sūtra*. Among them, the scholar-monk Sŭngnang was especially prominent. Born in Liao-tung, Koguryŏ, most probably in the middle of the fifth century, he went to Tun-huang and studied the San-lun: the *Madhyamaka-*

kārikā, the *Dvādaśamukhaśāstra* and the *Śataśāstra* following the interpretation of Kumārajīva and Seng-chao, established a new way of studying the three śāstras which no longer relied on the *Satyasiddhiśāstra*. He also set up a new epistemological methodology for understanding the śūnyatā theory. He argued that the Two Truths—*paramārtha* and *saṃvṛti*—both illuminate the teaching of the *madhyamapratipad* (the Middle Way) together. The distinction of the two truths is a division for convenience which posits two aspects of the Truth. As a result, he was highly esteemed by the followers of Kumārajīva's thought, and was considered greater even than Kumārajīva's more advanced disciples. He was widely respected in the Ho-hsi region (west of the Yellow River), and was called Ho-hsi ta-lang (Great man of Ho-hsi) or Tu-pu Ho-hsi (the Peerless [monk] of Ho-hsi). Later he moved to the Kang-shan Monastery on Mt. Hui-chi and then to the Ts'ao-t'ang Monastery on Mt. Chung in Shen-hsi where he taught the San-lun to Chou-yung. In his later years he stayed at the Ch'i-hsia Monastery on Mt. She in Chiang-su and became the abbot there in 500, succeeding Fa-tu. In 512, Emperor Wu of the Liang dynasty, because of his deep admiration for Sŭngnang, sent ten monks to study under him. One of these, Seng-ch'üan, succeeded Sŭngnang in the lineage. Encouraged by Sŭngnang and Seng-ch'üan, the study of the San-lun in China developed into an independent school, the San-lun-tsung (The Three Treatises School), founded by Chi-tsang (549-623). In this school, Sŭngnang was respected as the fourth patriarch.[10]

Monks known only as Sil and In also studied the San-lun in China and taught Chinese monks, such as Hui-ch'ih, Fa-min and Ling-juei. In, in particular, developed Fa-lang's idea of *ch'ü-ch'ü* (uneven) and *ping-tao* (leveled up) into a dual division of the Buddha's teaching: the uneven teaching and the leveled-up teaching. The former refers, for example, to the teaching of Śākyamuni Buddha as found in the *Nirvāṇa Sūtra;* the latter refers, for example, to the teachings of Vairocana Buddha as found in the *Avataṃsakasūtra.*[11]

There were many other Koguryŏ scholar-monks who

studied in China. Uiyŏn went to Northern Ch'i in 576 and studied under Fa-shang, master of the Ti-lun School (based on the *Daśabhūmikasūtraśāstra*). He fixed the year of the Buddha's *parinirvāṇa* as 889 B.C., which was generally accepted in Koguryŏ, and introduced the study of the Nan-tao sect of the Ti-lun School, in which the ninth *vijñāna*, the *amala-vijñāna*, was not recognized.[12] P'ayak went to Mt. T'ien-t'ai in 596 and studied under Chih-i, the third patriarch of the T'ien-t'ai school.[13] Chihwang arrived in China during the reign of King Yŏngyang (590-618) and became famous for studying the Sarvāstivāda School. During the late Koguryŏ a policy of suppressing Buddhism was instituted; because of this the monk Podŏk moved to Paekche in 650. There he became famous for his lectures on the *Nirvāṇa Sūtra*.[14] Around this time, Hyŏnyu went to T'ang and then to Ceylon, accompanying his teacher Seng-che; he stayed there after the fall of Koguryŏ.[15]

Buddhist Beliefs Reflected in Art

Buddhist themes are found in the wall paintings of more than ten extant Koguryŏ tombs. On the eastern wall of the Ssangyong tomb, built around the middle of the 5th century, there is a scene of a procession of nine people, including a monk and a woman (most likely a lay follower), all of whom seem to be on the way to a Buddhist monastery. The Muyong tomb, dated to the first half of the sixth century, has a mural showing a monk sitting with a man, the latter most likely serving the former. Also in this tomb there are triangular, flame-shaped patterns painted on the girders, an obvious influence from the Yun-kang in Northern Wei.[16] From the latter half of the sixth century on, Buddhist themes were gradually replaced by Taoist motifs, such as the Four Gods of the four directions; this phenomenon reflects the religio-political situation of Koguryŏ, where the government encouraged Taoism.

There are still many Koguryŏ Buddhist statues existing. A gilt, bronze, standing Buddha image is inscribed with the date 7th year of Yŏn'ga (539) and is therefore the oldest known

Buddhist statue in Korea.[17] We are also informed that this statue was made as one of a set of a thousand Buddhas. There is also a triad made of gilded bronze found in Koksan, Hwanghae province, which is dated 571.[18] It has an inscription saying that this image of Amitāyus Buddha was made with the hope that the dead will be able to meet Maitreya; this shows that there was a confusion in the understanding of Buddhist deities. A gilded bronze statue of a meditating bodhisattva, who has one foot touching the floor and the other crossed over his knee, found at P'yŏngch'ŏn-ri in P'yŏngyang is dated to the latter half of the sixth century.[19] This type of image was commonly used in China to depict Prince Siddhārtha, but in Korea it was usually used to represent the bodhisattva Maitreya.

The Espionage Activities of Monks and Monk-Soldiers

Historical records tell us that Koguryŏ monks were used for espionage purposes. Torim, for example, went to Paekche during the reign of King Changsu (413-491) and pretended to be a fugitive who had fled after committing a crime. After being accepted at court and so acquiring information, he had a large construction project undertaken with the purpose of depleting the energy of Paekche; his activities led to the downfall and capture of the capital, Hansan, by Koguryŏ in 475. The Paekche capital was then moved to Ungjin (present-day Kongju). Another monk, Tŏkch'ang, managed to gain timely information concerning an attack planned against Koguryŏ using 10,000 Silla soldiers in 642.[20].

The fact that a monks' army existed is also worth noting. Interestingly, it developed in the late Koguryŏ, just as Buddhism entered into a decline. The emergence of a monks' army was partly due to frequent wars, as well as the effect on the saṅgha brought about by the Buddhists' attempt to keep pace with society in a practical way. In the early days of the reign of King Pojang (642-668), 30,000 monk-soldiers repelled an attack made by T'ang T'ai-tsung.[21] Later, when the allied forces of Silla and T'ang attacked P'yŏngyang castle, monks also participated in the battle.

The Decline of Buddhism and the Rise of Taoism

Taoism was officially introduced to Koguryŏ in the 7th century during the reign of King Yŏngnyu (624). A Taoist monk came from T'ang and gave a lecture on *Lao-tzu* to thousands of people including the king; the next year students were sent to the T'ang to learn Taoism. In the second year of King Pojang (643), Yŏn Kaesomun, a powerful prime minister, told the king:

> None of the three teachings of Buddhism, Confucianism and Taoism should be neglected as each one of them forms the leg of a tripod. In our country, however, Taoism is not yet as popular as Buddhism or Confucianism. Therefore, in order to reign over the whole country, an envoy should be sent to the T'ang (to learn Taoism), and (transmit it to) the people.[22]

The king followed his suggestion. Consequently, in the following year, eight monks came from T'ang bringing with them the *Lao-tzu*. The king lodged them in Buddhist monasteries, and so it was only natural that Buddhism would suffer. Seven years later the famous monk Podŏk moved to Paekche. Unfortunately, the original intention of Koguryŏ to balance the three religions resulted in friction, and spiritual guidance became confused; this was an important factor in the downfall of Koguryŏ.[23]

Monks Active in Japan

Hyep'yŏn, who went to Japan in 584 was the first Koguryŏ monk recorded as having been active in Japan; he was also responsible for the first Japanese women entering the order of nuns in Japan. From the time of King Yŏngyang (r. 590-618) onward, many Koguryŏ monks crossed over to Japan and played important roles in the development of Japanese Buddhism.

Hyeja, who arrived in Japan in 594, taught Prince Shōtoku

a variety of Buddhist texts, including the *San-lun*, the *Lotus Sūtra* and the *Vimalakīrtinirdeśasūtra;* a Paekche monk named Hyech'ong helped him. Thanks to their instruction, the prince brought about many changes in the country based on the wisdom of Buddhism. Twenty years later Hyeja returned to Koguryŏ. Also during the reign of King Yŏngyang, Tamjing traveled to Japan leaving the peninsula by way of Paekche and took the knowledge of making paper, pigments, brushes and millstones to Japan. Legend has it that he is the painter of the murals in the golden hall of Hōryū Monastery. Hyegwan went to Japan in 635, according to Japanese sources, and was active under the name of Sōjō; he is cited as the founder of the Sanron (San-lun) School in Japan.

Japanese monks also came to Koguryŏ to study: Gyojen reached Koguryŏ late in the reign of King Pojang (642-668) and returned to Japan in 718.[24]

Paekche

Buddhist Studies

In the fourth year of King Sŏng's reign (526), the monk Kyŏmik returned to Paekche from India carrying the *Abhidharmapiṭaka* and five versions of the *Vinaya*, although it is not clear which ones they were. With twenty-eight other monks, he translated seventy-two volumes of *Vinaya* and has been regarded as the founder of the Vinaya School of Paekche. Following Kyŏmik's work Tamuk and Hyein wrote thirty-six rolls of commentaries on the *Vinaya* in Paekche. *Vinaya* study was popular in Paekche from its introduction.

Twelve years after Kyŏmik, in 538, Paekche moved their kingdom from Ungjin (present day Kongju) to Sabi (present day Puyŏ). In 588, several nuns, including Zenshinni, came from Japan and studied the *Vinaya* for three years; on their return to Japan they greatly contributed to the development of *Vinaya* study in Japan. Beginning in the middle of the Sabi period much emphasis was diverted to the precepts and manneristic features began to develop: King Pŏp gave an order to the people in his first year (599), not to kill, to release domestic fowl and to burn all hunting and fishing instruments. Contrary to the king's wish, such a policy must have disheartened the people.

T'ien-t'ai, the san-lun and the *Nirvāṇa Sūtra* doctrines were also studied, Hyŏn'gwang from Ungju studied the *Lotus Sūtra* in China under Nan-yueh Hui-ssu (515-557), the second patriarch of the T'ien-t'ai School, and concentrated on the samādhi based on the *Lotus Sūtra* and contemplation of mind. That samādhi was a method of practice mentioned in the "Pu-hsien" (the Encouragement of Samantabhadra) and "An-lo-hsing" (Comfortable Conducts) chapters of the *Lotus Sūtra;* it was emphasized by Hui-ssu as a proper method of meditation. Hyŏn'gwang, on his return to Paekche, propagated this teaching in Ungju. He was distinguished in his studies and was later included in the group of twelve honored in the hall of the masters built by Hui-jang, the great disciple of the sixth patriarch of Sŏn Buddhism, Hui-neng.[25]

Hyehyŏn (570-627) stayed at the Sudŏk Monastery and became famous for his lectures on the *Lotus Sūtra* and the *San-lun.* Because of this, his biography was included in the *Hsü kao-seng chuan* (Further Biographies of Eminent Monks), even though he had never been to China.[26] Kwallŭk who lived during the reign of King Mu (600-641) is famous for having mastered the *San-lun.*

Commentaries on a variety of sūtras, including the *Nirvāṇa Sūtra*, were obtained through an envoy sent to Liang in 541; much research must have been done on these sūtras themselves. Podŏk, mentioned above, from Koguryŏ, was also involved in this work. The *Satyasiddhiśāstra* was studied and Tojang, in particular, wrote a commentary on it, becoming the founder of the Satyasiddhi School in Japan.[27]

Buddhist Monasteries

Hŭngnyun Monastery (a different monastery from the one in Silla) and Taet'ong Monastery were founded in the Ungjin period (475-538) after the founding of the first nine monasteries in Hansan. Many more monasteries were constructed after the moving of the capital to Sabi in 538. Relative peace and stability during the long reigns of King Sŏng (523-554), King Widŏk (544-598), and King Mu (600-641) accelerated this process. In the Sabi (Puyŏ) region, the sites of the Wanghŭng, Chŏngnim, Imgang and Kŭmgang Monasteries are now confirmed; in the Ungjin region the site of the Suwŏn Monastery, and the site of the Mirŭk (Maitreya) Monastery in Iksan, which seems to have been the secondary capital to Sabi. The Wanghŭng Monastery founded in 600 and the Mirŭk Monastery, founded in 634 were enormous projects. Excavations show that the Mirŭk Monastery was the largest monastery in East Asia during this period. Mirŭk Monastery was founded by King Mu and his queen, who was a daughter of King Chinp'yŏng of Silla. The *Samguk yusa* tells an interesting legend about its foundation:

> One day the king and queen were going to Saja Monastery on Mt. Yongwha (dragon flower: a tree, the Nāgā-puṣpa or bodhi tree of Maitreya). When they reached a pond at the foot of the mountain, there arose a Maitreya Buddha triad from the pond. They stopped their carts and paid homage to Maitreya. The queen asked the king to build a monastery there. The king agreed and asked the monk Chimyŏng how to fill in the pond. Chimyŏng broke up the mountain and filled the pond over night by divine power. Then three Maitreya Buddha statues were made, and halls, pagodas and corridors were built in three places; the monastery was founded and it was named the Mirŭk Monastery. King Chinp'yŏng of Silla sent one hundred craftsmen and assisted in the consecration.[28]

Recent excavations revealed that the monastery was made of three parts, each of which consisted of a hall and a pagoda, only one of these, a stone pagoda in the wooden pagoda style, remains standing today.

This tri-partite plan of the Mirŭk Monastery was peculiar, even in Paekche. Usually Paekche monasteries followed a plan which included a central gate, a pagoda, a golden hall and a lecture hall aligned and facing south; they, in turn, were encircled by corridors in the shape of a rectangle.[29] A good example of this particular plan is a monastery site at Kunsu-ri in Puyŏ. Sometimes, however, the buildings were aligned facing east, as in the Kŭmgang Monastery site also located in Puyŏ.[30]

Buddhist Sculpture and Beliefs

There exist to this day a number of Buddhist statues made in Paekche during the sixth and seventh centuries. Early works were mostly small, gilt-bronze images; of these, the bodhisattvas holding a pearl in both hands is particularly interesting. This type of image was popular in Paekche and later appears to have influenced the Asuka period images of Japan, such as the Yumedono Kannon.

By the seventh century many statues were being made of stone. In the Sŏsan region, South Ch'ungch'ŏng Province, there are two famous rock-cut triads, both dating from the beginning of the seventh century: one known as the Sŏsan triad, the other known as the T'aean triad. In the Sŏsan triad, the figures are strangely arranged: in the center is a standing Buddha, on the left a standing bodhisattva and on the right a bodhisattva with one foot on the ground and the other one resting on his knee. They are thought to be Śākyamuni Buddha, Avalokiteśvara and Maitreya Bodhisattvas respectively.[31] In the T'aean triad, there are two Buddhas and a bodhisattva placed between the two. Of these, the Buddha on the left holds a small casket, probably a medicine bowl, and so has been considered the Bhaiṣajyaguru, the Medicine Buddha.[32]

Seven Buddhist steles found in the Yŏn'gi region in South Ch'ungch'ŏng Province were according to the inscriptions, made by former inhabitants of Paekche in the 670's and 680's —shortly after the downfall of their country. The inscriptions also tell us that their cult was based on Amitābha and the thousand Buddhas.[33]

Bodhisattva figures with one foot on the ground and the other resting on a knee, generally considered to be Maitreya, were very popular in Paekche.[34] This indicates how common the cult of Maitreya was, as the story of the Mirŭk Monastery does. In the *Fa-hua chuan-chi* there is a story recorded about the Paekche monk Palchŏng who witnessed a response by Avalokiteśvara to a prayer: this suggests that the Avalokiteśvara cult was known and popular in Paekche.[35] Scriptures were also copied with wishes for security and happiness; this is recorded at the founding of Chesŏk Monastery where the *Diamond Sūtra* was copied and stored in a pagoda.

Influence upon Japanese Buddhism

The Paekche monk, Norisach'igye, carried Buddhist images, scriptures and banners to Japan in the 29th year of King Sŏng's reign (552). Two years later, nine monks replaced the seven earlier sent to Japan as propagators of the Faith; they were well-versed in the *Satyasiddhiśāstra*. From this time on, many monks journeyed from Paekche to Japan, thus contributing to the development of Japanese culture in many respects.

In 530, Illa arrived in Japan invited by the emperor. In 535 Hyech'ong, Yŏnggŭn and Hyesik accompanying an envoy to Japan, took some relics of the Buddha with them. Hyech'ong, in particular, was well versed in the *Vinaya* and gave the rules to Soga no Umako. Kwallŭk, who arrived in Japan in 601, carried books on astronomy, geography, calculation of dates and the art of invisibility with him and taught these subjects to the Japanese. He was a master of the San-lun and established rules for monks and was active as a leader of the saṅgha. He was also well versed in medicine and is regarded as the founder of Japanese medicine.

Craftsmen often accompanied monks in their travel to Japan. Painters and architects who arrived in 577, for example, worked on the construction of Daibetsuō Monastery. In 588, a painter, Paegyŏ, and architects, T'aeryangmal and T'aemun'ga participated in the construction of Hōkō Monastery. The nun Pŏpmyŏng who arrived in Japan in 655, became famous because she cured illness by chanting the *Vimalakīrtinirdeśasūtra*. It is said to be the influence of Pŏpmyŏng that in Japan the sūtras are chanted according to the accent of Wu.[36] In 660, Paekche was destroyed by Silla and the T'ang. Shortly after its downfall, a number of Paekche monks fled to Japan; one of them was Uigak.

Silla

The Encouragement of Buddhism by King Chinhŭng

After its initial acceptance by King Pŏphŭng, Silla Buddhism developed quickly under King Chinhŭng (r. 540-576). In his fifth year, the king completed the building of the Hŭngnyun Monastery, which had been started by King Pŏphŭng, and passed a law allowing men and women to be ordained. Other monasteries were founded including the Hwangnyong, Kiwŏn and Silche Monasteries. The Hwangnyong Monastery in particular, required thirteen years for completion (566) and was constructed with great care. Excavations of the site in Kyŏngju give us an idea of the former magnificence of this monastery. At the center of the complex there was a huge architectural complex including a wooden pagoda about 200 feet in height; unfortunately, the entire monastery was burnt down by the invading Mongols in the 13th century.

Buddhist relics and scriptures were brought in abundance to Silla by monks returning from India and China. In the tenth year of King Chinhŭng (549), Kaktŏk carried relics received from Emperor Wu of Liang back to Silla and in the presence of the king and other officials, enshrined them in the Hŭngnyun Monastery. In 565 Myŏnggwan returned to Silla with seventeen hundred rolls of scripture; unfortunately, we do not know which texts he brought. In 574 a colossal Śākyamuni Buddha triad was made of gilded bronze and enshrined in the

Hwangnyong Monastery. Finally in the last year of King Chinhŭng's reign, another monk, Anhong, brought relics and Mahāyāna sūtras (such as, the *Laṅkāvatārasūtra* and the *Śrīmālādevīsiṃhanādasūtra*) back from Ch'en. He was accompanied by three Indian monks who had travelled to China through Central Asia and stayed there.

King Chinhŭng worked hard to develop his country, and encouraged Buddhism, which he hoped would supply spiritual guidance, in his confrontation with other kingdoms on the peninsula. In 550 he established two administrative departments for Buddhist affairs: the *Taesŏsŏng* and the *Sonyŏnsŏsŏng*. In the following year he appointed Hyeryang, from Koguryŏ, to the position of *Sŭngt'ong* (the head of monks) and had him guide and organize the saṅgha. Under him, the monk Poryang and the nun Ani were appointed to the posts of *Taedoyuna*, for monks, and *Toyunarang*, for nuns, respectively.[37] Hyeryang organized Buddhist ceremonies such as the *Inwang paekkojwahoe* (*Jen-wang ching* assembly with one hundred seats) and the *P'algwanhoe*. The former was a Buddhist assembly for the peace and security of the country, based on the *Inwang hoguk panya paramilgyŏng* (Ch. *Jen-wang hu-kuo pan-jo po-lo-mi ching*), the latter was a ritual in which lay-people practiced the eight precepts for twenty-four hours. *P'algwanhoe* was held for religious as well as practical reasons. This remembrance of those who died in war had been achieved through indigenous religion rituals before they were replaced by the *P'algwanhoe* ritual. In later years, the close relationship between the court and Buddhism was highlighted when King Chinhŭng became a monk and took the name Pŏbun.

Hwarang and Maitreya Cult

The youth organization known as the *hwarang* (flower-boys) was created during the reign of King Chinhŭng and reveals his hope of becoming a *cakravartin*. In this organization, young men were chosen from aristocratic families and appointed as a *hwarang* to lead hundreds or thousands of followers called *nangdo*. The organization was aimed at establishing, through the efforts of its youthful members, the ideal state—the Pure land of Maitreya as described in the *Mi-le hsia-sheng ching*—in their very own country.[38] This accorded with the political ideals of King Chinhŭng, which were firmly based on his belief in Buddhism. According to the *Mi-le hsia-sheng ching*, five billion years after the nirvāṇa of Śākyamuni Buddha, Maitreya Bodhisattva will descend to earth from Tuṣita heaven. After obtaining enlightenment under the dragon flower tree, Maitreya, becoming a Buddha, will purify this world and in doing so create the ideal land of the Buddha. At this time there is to be a *cakravartin* (a ruler whose chariot wheels can go anywhere) who helps the Buddha to achieve this ideal. A *cakravartin* is said to have a gold, silver, bronze or iron wheeled chariot as his attribute, and he is called a golden-wheeled king. King Chinhŭng named his sons Kŭmnyun (golden wheel) and Tongnyun (bronze wheel) as a symbolic representation of this idea.[39]

When Prince Kŭmnyun became King Chinji (r. 576-579), the relationship between the ideal of the *hwarang* and the belief in Maitreya became even more solidified, as can be seen in the *Samguk yusa:* Chinja, a monk at Hŭngnyun Monastery, always prayed to a Maitreya image in the hope that the latter would appear in the form of a *hwarang* in this world. One night he dreamed that a monk told him to go to Suwŏn Monastery in Kongju and see Mirŭk sŏnhwa (Maitreya of the immortal flower). When he reached Suwŏn Monastery, he was greeted by a handsome youth who said he was from Kyŏngju and immediately disappeared. The next day Chinja went to a mountain as instructed by the monks in the monastery. An old man there, actually a mountain spirit, told the monk that he, Chinja, had already met Mirŭk sŏnhwa in Suwŏn Monastery in the person of that youth. Chinja, surprised, hurried back to Hŭngyun Monastery. On hearing the story, King Chinji summoned Chinja and told him to look for Mirŭk sŏnhwa in Kyŏngju, as the boy had said he was from the capital. At last Chinja found a boy named Misi, who was brought before the king and made a *hwarang*. He proved to be outstanding in both wisdom and propriety, but seven years later he suddenly disappeared. Grieving, Chinja practiced according to the teachings of Maitreya for the rest of his life.[40] The people of Silla considered the *hwarang* as incarnations of Maitreya, and the *nangdo* as his followers, as can be seen in the tale told above.[41] The followers of Kim Yu-sin, who became a *hwarang* in 609 at the age of fifteen, were called *Yonghwa hyangdo* (Incense group of the Dragon Flower).[42] Many of the existing, half cross-legged, meditating, bodhisattva statues produced in Silla, of which the representative examples being two large, gilt-bronze statues at the National Museum, in Seoul (National Treasures nos. 78 and 83), are thought to be of Maitreya Bodhisattva in the form of a *hwarang*.

Among the *nangdo* there was always at least one monk assisting the *hwarang* and guiding the *nangdo*s, just as Chinja had done for Misi (rang), or Hyesuk had done for Hose-rang during the reign of King Chinp'yŏng (579-631) and Chŏnmil had done for Munno-rang during the reign of Chindŏk (647-653).[43] The *hwarang* and his followers travelled to famous mountains and rivers, singing and dancing, and thus they contributed to the development and unification of the Silla kingdom, participating in politics and religion as well as in the defense of the realm.

The Silla Royal Family and Buddhism

The name of King Chinp'yŏng was Paekchŏng, meaning white and pure, which is one of the translations of King Śuddhodana, the father of Śākyamuni. King Chinp'yŏng's wife was Lady Māyā, taken from the name of Śākyamuni's mother. King Chinp'yŏng's two brothers, Paekpan (White Food) and Kokpan (Wooden Vessel of Food) came from the names of King Śuddhodana's brothers, Sukkodana and Dhotodana. This shows that the family of King Chinp'yŏng wanted to compare itself to the family of King Śuddhodana of the Kapilavastu kingdom of India. The aim was to present the king as the Buddha. The names taken by Queen Sŏndŏk (Śrīmālādevī)

and Queen Chindŏk (Guṇāmālādevī) also have their origins in
Buddhism. The royal family and the aristocrats in this manner
were able to portray themselves as belonging to the sacred
kṣatriya family of the Buddha Śākyamuni. All kings from
Chinhŭng to Chindŏk had the character "chin" (true) in their
names; this was done for the same reason.[44]

Wŏn'gwang

Throughout King Chinp'yŏng's reign (579-631), monks
continued to go to China, study and return. In the twenty-fourth
year (602) Chimyŏng, and three years later Tamyuk, followed
this path. Most remarkable for this period was Wŏn'gwang
who became a guide to the people of Silla both spiritually and
morally.[45]

Wŏn'gwang (?-630) traveled to China at the age of twenty-
four. At first he stayed in the Chuang-yen Monastery in Chin-
ling, the capital of the Ch'en dynasty, and studied the *Satyasiddhiśāstra* and the *Nirvāṇa Sūtra* under a disciple of Seng-min.
After that he learned the *Āgamas* at the Hu-ch'iu Monastery in
Su-chou. In 589, when the Ch'en dynasty fell, he moved to
Ch'ang-an, the capital of the new Sui dynasty where the study
of the *She-ta-sheng-lun* (*Mahāyānasaṃgraha*) was beginning to
gain popularity; hence, he was also able to study this important
treatise. During his stay in China, Wŏn'gwang was most likely
also influenced by contemporary Chinese masters such as
Hui-yuan, Ling-yu and Hsin-hsing.

Wŏn'gwang returned to Silla in 600, where he was received
with great respect by the king and his ministers. He tried to
improve the study of Mahāyāna Buddhism by writing the
Yŏraejang sagi (Personal Notes on the *Tathāgatagarbha*) and
the *Yŏraejanggyŏng so* (Commentary on the *Tathāgatagarbha-
sūtra*). He often also wrote diplomatic letters for the court.
When an *Inwang paekchwahoe* (*Jen-wang ching* assembly with
one hundred high seats) was held in the Hwangnyong Monastery
for an envoy from Sui in 613, Wŏn'gwang was given the highest
seat of honor.[46] Most importantly, Wŏn'gwang worked towards

building a foundation for an ethics and morality, based on Buddhist teachings, in Silla. He gave the *Sesok ogye* (Five precepts for lay people) to two youths, Kwisan and Ch'uhang, saying:

> In Buddhism there is the *bodhisattvaśīla* of ten rules. However, as a subject or a son, you cannot observe all of it and so I give you five. First, serve the king with loyalty, second, serve your parents with filial piety, third, be faithful to friends, fourth, do not retreat in battle, and fifth, do not kill indiscriminately.[47]

Virtues such as loyalty, filial piety and trust came from the Buddhist sūtras such as the *Jen wang ching*, the *Fu-mu en-chung ching* and the *Āgama Sūtra*. The fifth rule taught that if one could not avoid killing, one should do it with discrimination. Following Wŏn'gwang's teaching, Kwisan and Ch'uhang both died bravely in a battle with Paekche in 602.[48] The *Sesok ogye* became the ethics of the *hwarang* and of the entire Silla people. He also established the *Chŏmch'albo* (Endowment for the Chŏmch'al ritual) using land donated to him.

Chajang

Chajang came from an important aristocratic family whose status was just below that of the royal family itself.[49] After the death of his parents, he formed an aversion to the troubles of the world; he left his wife and children and went into the mountains where he practiced meditation focused on a skeleton. Because of his origins, however, he was called several times to serve the king as high official. Chajang always refused saying: "I would rather die keeping the rules for one day than live breaking them for one hundred years." Thus, he remained a monk, showing his devotion to precepts in his role as a *Vinaya* Master.

In 636 he went to T'ang; by this time, he must have been already in his mid-forties. During his stay of seven years he visited Mt. Wu-t'ai and there paid reverence to the Bodhisattva Mañjuśrī. He also studied at Mt. Chung-nan where Tao-hsüan was propagating the doctrines of the *Dharmagupta Vinaya*. These experiences on Mt. Wu-t'ai and Mt. Chung-nan appear to have had considerable influence on his later activities. He was invited to the T'ang court as a state guest, and there he delivered a lecture on the *Avataṃsakasūtra*. Queen Sŏndŏk entreated the T'ang emperor to allow Chajang to return to Silla and this he did in 643.

On his return, Chajang stayed at the Punhwang monastery where he continued his work of propagating the Dharma. When invited to the court, he delivered lectures on the *She-ta-sheng-lun* (*Mahāyānasaṃgraha*), or when at the Hwangnyong Monastery he taught on the *bodhisattvaśīla* for seven days. He also composed many works during his life, for example: the *Sabunyul kalma sagi* (Notes on the *Su-fen-lu chieh-mo* by Tao-hsüan), the *Sipsongyul mokch'agi* (Notes on the *Prāti-mokṣa* of the Sarvāstivāda *Vinaya*), the *Amit'agyŏng ŭigi* (Commentary on the *Amitābhasūtra*) and the *Kwanhaengbŏp* (Method of Contemplation). Of these, the *Amit'agyŏng ŭigi* has been handed down to us in part, quotations appearing in the *Hokkekyō shigi* by Ryōchū (1199-1287) in Japan.[50]

Vinaya was of special concern as seen in the works mentioned above. When he was appointed *Kuk'tong* (State Monk), Chajang worked for the establishment of the saṅgha and the moral improvement of the Silla people. He ordered monks and nuns to study harder, to hold the *upoṣadha* on the fifteenth day of each month and to take morality tests twice a year, in the spring and winter. Monks were appointed as itinerant inspectors to the principal monasteries to verify that the rules were being maintained, regulations concerning the making and decorating of Buddha statues were also laid down. Due to his efforts, eight or nine out of ten families received *śīla* and the number of monks increased.

Chajang founded T'ongdo Monastery and there made a stone altar named Kŭmgang kyedan (*Vajraśīla* Altar) where he enshrined the Buddha relics given to him by Mañjuśrī at

Mt. Wu-t'ai. This altar, square in form with a bell-shaped stone stūpa at the center, in which the relics were placed, became the main object of worship of the relic cult in Korea.[51]

The nine-story wooden pagoda at Hwangnyong Monastery was erected, following a suggestion by Chajang, in order to repel attacks by the nine hostile neighboring countries, including Japan and China.[52] The site chosen was believed to have been a place where Kāśyapa Buddha taught. This is typical of the tendency of trying to prove that Buddhism was not something new to Silla, and since it was supposed to have existed in Silla since early times, the kingdom as an important Buddhist country had to be protected. The colossal triad of Hwangnyong Monastery said by the *Samguk yusa* to have been cast in 574 using the gold and iron ore sent by King Aśoka, may have actually been made at the time of Chajang, in the middle of the seventh century.[53] The nine-story pagoda and the Buddha triad of the Hwangnyong Monastery, as well as the jade belt received by King Chinp'yŏng from heaven, were regarded as the three treasures of Silla.[54]

Chajang's meeting with Mañjuśrī on Mt. Wu-t'ai in China led to the worshipping of the other Mt. Odae (the Korean pronunciation of Wu-t'ai) located in Silla.[55]

The Popularization of Buddhism and Amitābha Worship

Chajang's influence on the development of Silla Buddhism, though great, in the main focused only on the upper class, i.e., the royal family and the aristocrats. Hyesuk, Hyegong, Taean and Wŏnhyo, however, endeavored to make the Buddha's teaching known to ordinary people as well.

In the reign of King Chinp'yŏng (579-631), while many monks lived in large monasteries in the capital, Hyesuk founded the Mit'a monastery (Monastery of Amitābha) outside the capital and propagated the belief in Amitābha—a faith more easily understandable to ordinary people. In the middle of the seventh century, Hyegong was known as "the monk with the straw basket" as he always carried around a straw basket, even when drunk, singing or dancing.[56] By intermingling with ordinary people, he led them to the Buddha's teaching. Taean, also beating a copper bowl and clad in rags, taught the common people in the market place.[57]

Wŏnhyo (617-688) was one of the great Buddhist scholars of Silla and wrote a great number of excellent scholarly works.[58] He, too, was a great teacher of the ordinary people, especially after marrying Princess Yosŏk and returning to lay-life, when he devoted himself totally to propagating the Dharma. He travelled around the country, teaching people through songs, beating on a gourd-dipper called *Muae* (*Apratihata*—unhindered) which symbolized that every man of *Muae* is invariably released from the wheel of life and death (saṃsāra). The song he sang called *Muae* was also aimed at teaching people the doctrine of Amitābha in a more digestible form, i.e., that there is no *pratihata* (hindrance) in mind and phenomenon, that is there is an integral harmonization between the invisible mind and visible facts. Due to the efforts of Wŏnhyo, everyone in the country learned to chant and came to know the Buddha's teaching, including the poor and the ignorant. He showed that the sacred and the profane are to be harmonized, and there is no discrimination between the two. Also, Wŏnhyo taught people to believe in Amitābha because he considered that being reborn in the Pure Land of Amitābha was easier than being reborn in the Pure Land of Maitreya; the teaching of Amitābha was aimed at ordinary people. This view forms the main stream in the later development of Silla Pure Land Buddhism.[59]

NOTES

1. Vol. 4, "Biography of Chu-ch'ien".

2. Ahn Kye-hyŏn, "Koguryŏ pulgyo ŭi chŏn'gae" (The Development of Koguryŏ Buddhism), *Han'guk sasang* (The Thoughts of Korea), vol. 7 (1964).

3. Vol. 3, "Maranant'a Opens Paekche".

4. *Samguk yusa* (hereafter SY), vol. 3, "Ado [provided] the Foundation [of Buddhism] in Silla".

5. Chŏng Chung-hwan, "Silla ŭi pulgyo chŏllae wa kŭ hyŏnse sasang" (Introduction of Buddhism in Silla and Its Realistic Nature), *Cho myŏnggi paksa hwagap kinyŏm pulgyo sahak nonch'ong* (Festschrift in Honor of Dr. Cho Myŏnggi), (Seoul, 1965); Lee ki-baek, "Samguk sidae pulgyo chŏllae wa kŭ sahoejŏk sŏnggyŏk" (The Introduction of Buddhism in the Three Kingdom Period and Its Social Repercussions), *Yŏksa hakpo* (Journal of History), vol. 6 (1954).

6. Yoneda Miyoji, *Chōsen jōdai kenchiku no kenkyū* (Study of the Architecture of Ancient Korea), (Osaka, 1944), pp. 139, 159, 203.

7. Ko Yu-sŏp, *Chosŏn t'appa ŭi yŏn'gu* (Study of Korean Pagodas), (Seoul, 1948), pp. 158, 176.

8. SY, vol. 3, "Yŏng'tap Monastery of Koryŏ".

9. *Haedong kosŭngchŏn* (hereafter HK), vol. 1, "T'an-shih"; *Kao-seng chuan* (hereafter KSC), vol. 10, "Biography of T'an-shih".

10. KSC, vol. 8, "Biography of Fa-tu"; Cho Myŏnggi, *Silla pulgyo ŭi inyŏm kwa yŏksa* (Ideas and History of Silla Buddhism), (Seoul, 1962), pp. 68-72; Kim Ing-sŏk, "Koguryŏ sŭngnang kwa samnonhak" (Sŭngnang of Koguryŏ and His Study of the *San-lun*), *Paek sŏnguk paksa songsu kinyŏm pulgyohak nonmunjip* (Festschrift in Honor of Dr. Paek Sŏng-uk), (Seoul, 1959); T'ang Yung-t'ung, "She-shan chih san-lun-tsung-shih lueh-k'ao" (Short Study of the History of the San-lun School on Mt. She), *Shih-hsueh tsa-chih*, vol. 2:5 (1931); Hirai Shunei, "Sanron gakuha no genryū keifu" (The Origin and Lineage of the San-lun School), *Tōhōgaku*, vol. 28 (1964); Richard A. Gard, "The Mādhyamika in Korea", *Journal of Indian and Buddhist Studies*, vol. 7, no. 2 (1959).

11. *Hsu kao-sengchuan* (hereafter HKSC), vol. 14, "Biography of Fa-min", and "Biography of Ling-jui"; Sakamoto Yukio, *Kegon kyōgaku no kenkyū* (Investigations on Avataṃsaka Study), (1964), pp. 189-92.

12. HK, vol. 1, "Uiyŏn"; HKSC, vol. 8, "Biography of Fa-shang".

13. HKSC, vol. 17, "Biography of Chih-yueh".

14. Kim Tong-hwa, "Koguryŏ sidae ŭi pulgyo sasang" (Buddhist Thought in the Koguryŏ period), *Asea yŏn'gu* (Study of Asia), vol. 2, no. 1 (1958), included in the present volume, pp. 79-108.

15. *Ta-t'ang hsi-yu chiu-fa Kao-seng-chuan*, vol. 3.

16. Kim Won-yong, "Koguryŏ kobun pyŏkhwa e issŏsŏŭi pulgyojŏk yoso" (Buddhist Elements Appearing on Koguryŏ Tomb Murals), *Paek sŏn guk* . . . (1959).

17. *Han'guk pulsang sambaek sŏn* (300 Selected Works of Korean Buddhist Sculpture, hereafter HPSS) (Sŏngnam, 1982) Koguryŏ: no. 1.

18. HPSS, Koguryŏ: no. 12.

19. HPSS, Koguryŏ: no. 15.

20. Yi Nŭng-hwa, *Chosŏn pulgyo t'ongsa* (History of Korean Buddhism), (Seoul, 1918), vol. 1, p. 181.

21. *Koryŏsa*, vol. 123.

22. *Samguk sagi* (hereafter SS), vol. 21.

23. Yu Sŏk-u, "Koguryŏ ŭi hŭngmang kwa chonggyo kwan'gye" (Rise and Fall of Koguryŏ and Their Religious Reasons), *Kyŏngbuk taehakkyo nonmunjip* (Journal of Kyŏngbuk University), vols. 1-4 (1956-58).

24. Yi Nŭng-hwa, vol. 1, pp. 21-31.

25. *Sung kao-seng chuan* (hereafter SKSC), vol. 18, "Biography of Hyŏn'gwang of Silla."

26. SY, vol. 5, "Hyehyŏn seeks quietness"; HKSC, vol. 28, "Biography of Hyehyŏn."

27. Kim Tong-hwa, "Paekche sidae ŭi pulgyo sasang" (Buddhist

Thought in Paekche Period), *Asea yŏn'gu*, vol. 5, no. 1 (1962).

28. SY, vol. 2, "King Mu".

29. Yun Chang-sŏp, *Han'guk kŏnch'uksa* (History of Korean Architecture), (Seoul, 1973), pp. 81-86.

30. Yun Mu-byŏng, *Puyŏgun Unsanmyŏn kŭmgongri paekche saji palgul chosa pogo* (Excavation Report of a Monastery Site of Paekche in Kŭmgok-ri, Unsan-myŏn, Puyŏ-gun), (Seoul: National Museum of Korea, 1969).

31. Hwang Su-yŏng, "Sŏsan maae samjonbul e taehayŏ" (On the Rock-cut Buddha Triad Images in Sŏsan), *Chindan hakpo*, vol. 20 (1959).

32. Hwang Su-yŏng, "Ch'ungnam t'aean maae samjon pulsang" (The Rock-cut Buddha Triad Image in T'aean, South Ch'ungch'ŏng Province), *Yŏksa hakpo*, vol. 17 (1962).

33. Chin Hong-sŏp, "Kyeyu myŏng samjon ch'ŏnbul pisang e taehayŏ" (On the Buddha-triad Stele Inscribed in the Year of *Kyeyu*), *Yŏksa hakpo*, vol. 17 (1962); Hwang Su-yŏng, "Ch'ungnam yŏn'gi sŏksang chosa kaeyo" (An Examination of Stone Steles in the Yŏn'gi Region, South Ch'ungch'ŏng Province), *Yesul nonmunjip*, vol. 3 (1964).

34. Hwang Su-yŏng, "Paekche pan'ga sayu sŏksang sogo" (Stone Contemplating Images with One Leg Pendent of Paekche), *Yŏksa hakpo*, vol. 13 (1960).

35. Makita Tairyō, *Rikuchō koitsu kanzeon ōkenki no kenkyū* (Study of Records of Spiritual Responses of Avalokiteśvara of the Six Dynasties Period) (Tokyo, 1970), pp. 58-60.

36. Yi Nŭng-hwa, vol. 1, pp. 37-46.

37. Yi Hong-jik, "Silla sŭnggwanje wa pulgyo chŏngch'aek ŭi munje" (On the Saṅgha System of Silla and Its National Policy Concerning Buddhism), *Paek sŏnguk paksa . . .* (1959).

38. Kim Tong-uk, "Tosolga yŏn'gu" (Study of Tosolga), *Sŏul tahakkyo nonmunjip: inmun sahoe kwahak p'yŏn*, vol. 6, (1957).

39. Kim Yŏng-t'ae, "Silla chinnŭngwang ŭi sinbul kwa kŭ sasang yŏn'gu" (Study of King Chinhŭng's Faith in Buddhism and His

Thought), *Pulgyo hakpo*, vol. 5 (1967).

40. SY, vol. 3, "Mirŭk sŏhwa, Misi-rang".

41. "Shiragi shakai to jōdokyō", *Shichō*, vol. 7, no. 4 (1937).

42. Kim Sang-gi, "Hwarang kwa mirŭk sinang e taehayŏ" (On the *Hwarang* and the Maitreya Cult), *Yi hongjik paksa hoegap kinyŏm han'guk sahak nonch'ong* (Festschrift in Honor of Dr. Yi Hong-jik), (1969).

43. Kim Yŏng-t'ae, "Sŭngryŏ *nangdo* ko" (Study of the Monk *Nangdo*), *Pulgyo hakpo*, vol. 7, (1970).

44. Kim Ch'ŏl-jun, "Silla sangdae sahoe ŭi dual organization" (Dual Organization in Early Silla Society), *Yŏksa hakpo*, vol. 2 (1953); Chŏng Chung-hwan, "Silla chin'gol ko" (Study of *Chin'gol* of Silla), *Yi Hongjik* . . . (1969).

45. SY, vol. 4, "Wŏn'gwang studied in the West (i.e., China)"; HKSC, vol. 13, "Biography of Wŏn'gwang"; Imanishi Ryū, "Shiragi enkō hōshiden" (Biography of Wŏn'gwang of Silla), *Shiragi shi kenkyū* (Study of the History of Silla), (Seoul, 1933); Lee Ki-baek, "Wŏn'gwang kwa kŭ ŭi sasang" (Wŏn'gwang and His Thought), *Silla sidae ŭi kukka pulgyo wa yugyo* (State Buddhism and Confucianism during the Silla Period), (Seoul, 1978).

46. SS, vol. 4, "The thirty-fifth year of King Chinp'yŏng".

47. SY, vol. 4, "Wŏn'gwang . . . "

48. SS, vol. 45, "Biography of Kwisan".

49. His biographies are found in SY, vol. 4 and HKSC, vol. 24.

50. Min Yŏng-gyu, "Silla changsorok changp'yŏn" (List of Buddhist Writings of Silla), *Paek sŏnguk paksa* . . . (1959).

51. SY, vol. 3, "Relics brought twice"; Kim Yŏng-su, "T'ongdosa ŭi kyedan e taehayŏ" (On the *Śīla* Altar in T'ongdo Monastery), *Ilgwang*, vol. 7 (1933); Ahn Kye-hyŏn, "Pulsari sinang kwa han'guk pulgyo" (Buddha's Relic Cult in Korean Buddhism) Pulgyo sasang, vol. 13 (1963); "Kankoku no butsu shari shinkō ni tsuite" (On the Buddha's Relic Cult in Korea), *Chōsen gakuhō*, vol. 45 (1967).

52. SY, vol. 3, "The rock pedestal of Kāśyapa Buddha", "Nine-story pagoda in Hwangnyong monastery", "Relics brought twice".

53. SY, vol. 3, "The rock pedestal of Kāśyapa Buddha", "Nine-story pagoda in Hwangnyong monastery", "Relics brought twice". SY, vol. 3, "Colossal Buddha in Hwangnyong Monastery."

54. SY, vol. 1, "The heaven gives a jade-belt".

55. SY, vol. 3, "Fifty thousand true bodies on Mt. Tai"; Eda Toshio, "Shiragi no Jizō to Godaisan" (Chajang of Silla and Mt. Odae), *Bunka*, vol. 21, no. 5 (1957).

56. SY, vol. 4, "Two Hye-s (Hyesuk and Hyegong) joined in the dusty world".

57. SKSC, vol. 4, "Biography of Wŏnhyo".

58. *ibid.* and SY, vol. 4, "Wŏnhyo, the unbound one".

59. Kim Tong-uk, "Silla chŏngt'o sasang ŭi chŏn'gae wa wŏnwangsaengga" (The Development of Pure Land Thought in Silla and the Wŏnwangsaengga), *Chungang taehakkyo nonmunjip*, vol. 2 (1957); Ahn Kye-hyŏn, "Wŏnhyo ŭi mit'a chŏngt'o wangsaeng sasang" (Wŏnhyo's View of the Rebirth in Amitābha's Pure Land), *Yŏksa hakpo*, vol. 21 (1963).

This is an edited translation of the first half of the original article, "Han'guk pulgyosasang, kodaep'yŏn" (History of Korean Buddhism, Part 1: Ancient Period), *Han'guk munhwasa taegye* VI (Seoul, 1970), pp. 171-220. Some out-dated information, particularly on Buddhist art and archaeology, has been corrected. The second half, on the Unified Silla period, will appear in the next volume of this series.

The Reception of Buddhism in Korea and Its Impact on Indigenous Culture

by Inoue Hideo

Translated by Robert Buswell

Introduction

Korean historical sources, such as the *Samguk sagi*, relate that Buddhism was transmitted to the Korean kingdom of Koguryŏ in the second year of the reign of King Sosurim (372), to Paekche in the first year of King Ch'imnyu (384), and to Silla in the fifteenth year of King Pŏphŭng (528). *Nihon shoki* and other Japanese sources give the transmission of Buddhism to Japan as occurring during the twelfth year of the reign of Emperor Kimmei (552). While doubts have been raised previously concerning these transmission dates,[1] I will leave that problem aside in this article and examine instead the kinds of influences that a multifaceted religion like Buddhism exerted on the Korean kingdoms and Japan during the periods of their transitions from primitive societies to ancient states. Buddhist culture encompasses a wide spectrum of cultural phenomena ranging from such physical aspects as arts, crafts, and religious rites, to the more spiritual sphere of philosophical thought, doctrinal tenets, and religious faith. In this essay, however, I wish to take up only Buddhism's relationship to the use of writing systems in those countries and its effect on indigenous conceptions of spirits; this is representative of its influence on secular and religious culture respectively.

The changing attitude toward both spirits and indigenous religious rites that accompanied the reception of Buddhism in

Korea and Japan has been explored by previous scholars.[2] Drawing upon such studies, I wish to investigate the transformation in the way spirits were viewed by the intellectuals of the three kingdoms of early Korea. Since there are few relevant sources, there is the constant danger of lapsing into arbitrary interpretations if one attempts to resolve this question on the basis of philosophical thought and religious tenets alone. I propose, therefore, to examine changes in the conception of spirits against the backdrop of the general material culture of the peninsula, and specifically in relation to the changes in indigenous religious ritual prompted by Buddhism.

If we propose to explore the impact of Buddhism on northeast-Asian culture, we cannot restrict the period of our examination to that of the traditional dates of transmission. We would prefer instead to use either the entire era of the formation of ancient states in Korea, or the whole of antiquity. By concerning ourselves with such long-term social phenomena, we will be able to make renewed use of Chinese historical materials, which are rather more objective than the partisan accounts found in ancient Korean and Japanese historical materials, upon which previous studies drew exclusively. Chinese historical sources, in accordance with sinitic thought, portray Japan and the Korean states as tribes of eastern barbarians; however, if one keeps that traditional bias in mind and makes allowances for it, I think that they can be used for scholarly purposes. For this reason, I want first to examine pre-T'ang Chinese sources relating to Buddhism in the three kingdoms of Korea, as well as in Japan.

The Reception of Buddhism and the Adoption of a Writing System

Information concerning Korean Buddhism first appears in Chinese historical sources in the "Paekche chuan" (Paekche Annals) in the "Chu-I chuan" (Records of the Various Barbarians) of the *Liang-shu* (Book of the Liang Dynasty). It relates the following.

Chung-ta-t'ung, sixth year (A.D. 534) and Ta-t'ung, seventh year (A.D. 541). [Paekche] sent successive delegations [to Liang], presenting local products. It also solicited commentarial texts on the *Ta pan-nieh-p'an ching* (*Mahāparinirvāṇasūtra*), and appealed for a scholar on the *Mao-shih* (Mao commentary to the Book of Odes), as well as craftsmen, painters, etc. [Kao-tsu (Liang Wu-ti; r. 502-549)] decreed that all the requested items be conferred.[3]

This account is quoted almost in its entirety in the "I-man chuan" (Record of Barbarians and Savages) of the *Nan-shih* (History of the Southern Dynasties), and it also occurs with one or two modifications in the "Liang Wu-ti pen-chi" (Annals of Emperor Wu of Liang) of *Nan-shih*, as well as in the *Samguk sagi*.[4]

A problematic point in the accounts found in these Chinese sources is that, unlike the native Korean materials, references to Buddhism appear first in relation to Paekche, not Koguryŏ. Even such texts as *Samguk sagi* and *Samguk yusa* acknowledge no more than a twelve-year difference between the introductions of Buddhism into Koguryŏ and Paekche. But the essential issue here has nothing to do with the respective order of their transmission dates; rather, it concerns what was sought through accepting this alien religion. Regardless of whether Buddhism was brought to Paekche in 534 or 541, the sophisticated request of its king indicates that there was already some understanding of the religion in that kingdom by the mid-sixth century. What is especially compelling here is not so much the request for scriptural commentaries, as instead the request for artisans who could produce the religious paraphernalia associated with the material culture of Buddhism.

We must also take note of the fact that the interest in things Buddhist was accompanied by a fascination with Confucianism as well, since the requested *Mao-shih* specialist would have been an expert on the Confucian scholarly apparatus to the *Shih-ching* (Book of Odes). It has been a basic assumption of modern scholarship that Confucianism and Buddhism stand opposed to one another as distinct religious and/or scholastic disciplines. But the case of the Korean reception of these new sinitic influences suggests that people recognized few substantive differences between the two teachings during that period. This can be ascertained from the following account of the introduction of Buddhism to Koguryŏ, which is preserved in *Samguk sagi*.

> King Sosurim's reign, second year, summer, sixth month (A.D. 372). The Ch'in king Fu-Chien (r. 357-384) dispatched a diplomatic envoy and the Buddhist monk Shun-tao (d.u.; Kor. Sundo) with Buddhist images and scriptures. The [Koguryŏ] king dispatched an envoy to convey his gratitude and to present local products. T'aehak (royal academy) was established for the education of the sons of the nobility.[5]

The Chinese Royal Academy system was established by Han Wu-ti as an institution for educating officials, under the tutelage of experts in the Five Confucian Classics. Although the reference in this passage is too brief to tell us much about the Korean version of this academy, we may assume that it was largely based on the Chinese model. It is probably not coincidental that the foundation of a Royal Academy appears in an entry concerning the introduction of Buddhism; it seems safe to conclude that both events coincided.

The transmission of Confucianism and Buddhism from Paekche to Japan occurred in a manner similar to their introductions into Paekche and Koguryŏ: that is to say, the 552 introduction of Buddhism appears amid records concerning a series of Five Classics scholars who began to arrive in Japan in the seventh year of Keitai (513). For example, the "Kimmei Annal" of the *Nihon shoki* notes that among the objects brought to Japan from Paekche were a gilded bronze Buddha-image, several streamers and canopies, and a number of scrolls of sūtras.[6] Buddha-images and sūtras may be interpreted as intrinsic aspects of Buddhist faith in East Asia. Considered in that light, we may see a link between this Japanese account of receiving from Korea streamers and canopies—decorative artifacts that must have enhanced the majesty of Buddhist halls and images—and the special request in the "Paekche Annals" of the *Liang-shu* for the artisans and painters who would have manufactured such artifacts. Moreover, a similar attitude is also found in the account of Emperor Kimmei's interrogation of his vassals about the acceptability of Buddhism: "The Buddha-image presented by Seiban (the western barbarians = Paekche) is slanderous in appearance, unlike anything ever seen before. Should this image be worshipped or not?"[7] The instinctive interpretation of this passage is that Emperor Kimmei did not consider whether to adopt Buddhism because of any compelling religious inspiration, but instead because he was enchanted by the glittering form of that gilt icon. Seen in that light, the role played by religious artifacts and the activities of artisans and painters in the reception of Buddhism seems to deserve reevaluation.

One further problem, to which I have alluded previously, is the integration of Confucianism and Buddhism during this early period. In both Japan and Koguryŏ, the introduction and adoption of Confucian culture were closely tied to the transmission of Buddhism. The transmission of Chinese logographs, which may be considered to be the foundation of Confucianism, is recorded as follows in the "Paekche pon'gi" (Paekche Annals) of the *Samguk sagi*, under the entry for King Kŭnch'ogo (r. 346-374), thirtieth year (375; *sic*)—ten years before the date of the transmission of Buddhism, which is said to have occurred in the first year of King Ch'imnyu's reign (384). An ancient record says:

> Since the foundation of the Paekche kingdom, there had never been a means of recording events with written characters. In this year [Paekche] welcomed the scholar Ko Hŭng (Ch. Kao Hsing) and for the first time there were written records. Unfortunately Ko Hŭng does not appear in any other record and nothing is known about his ancestry.[8]

The origins of the otherwise unidentified scholar Ko Hŭng remain a mystery. We only know that he transmitted the Chinese writing system to Paekche; other than that, he is completely unknown. From the fact that his surname was Ko, we may surmise that he was a member of the Koguryŏ royal family. Be that as it may, three years earlier, in the twenty-seventh year of King Kŭnch'ogo's reign (372), Paekche is presumed to have established diplomatic relations with the Eastern Chin dynasty and its king was given the title "General Stabilizing the East, Administrator-Designate of Lo-yang, King of Paekche."[9] We may thus assume that, simultaneous with the opening of relations with Eastern Chin, Confucian scholars were dispatched to Paekche. This seems to indicate in turn that diplomatic exchanges with the Chinese court led inevitably to the importation of sinitic culture into Korea. And since Confucianism and Buddhism were introduced together as parts of Chinese civilization, we may thus conclude that the Korean states felt no need to treat the two separately.

The fact that the northeast Asians did not strictly distinguish between Confucianism and Buddhism can be discerned also in the memorial presented when Paekche brought Buddhism to Japan. In the entry in the "Kimmei Annals," there is a panegyric attributed to the Paekche King Sŏng (r. 523-553) praising the merits accruing from worshipping Buddhism, which includes the following passage:

> This Dharma (of Buddhism) is preeminent among all dharmas (viz. religions); it is difficult to understand, and difficult to access. Even the Duke of Chou and Confucius were unable to know of it. This Dharma can catalyze the production of infinite, unlimited fruitions of merit, and even the achievement of supreme *bodhi*.[10]

Here, both religions seem to be viewed from the same standpoint —as parts of sinitic culture—since both Buddhism and the saints of Confucianism are mentioned in the same passage. The Paekche king may have been exaggerating his claim about the efficacy of Buddhism here, in order to goad the Japanese people, who were unfamiliar with the religion, to embrace it. While such an interpretation cannot be ruled out, on the basis of the account in the "Paekche Annals" of the *Liang-shu* cited earlier, it seems that Paekche intellectuals of the mid-sixth-century did not treat Confucianism and Buddhism as being especially distinct from, or opposed to, one another. As its manner of reception indicates, it is inconceivable that the general social phenomenon that was Japanese Buddhism would have been sharply distinguished from Confucianism, with the possible exceptions of Buddhism's ordained clergy and ecclesiastical rituals. This I would like to confirm in the "Wei-kuo" (Kingdom of Japan) entry in the "Tung-i chuan" of the *Sui-shu* (Book of the Sui Dynasty), which describes fairly objectively the situation in Japan between the latter sixth and early seventh centuries. It narrates as follows the circumstances surrounding the reception of Buddhism.

> Being without written logographs, [the Japanese] made notches in slips of wood or tied knots in code [as mnemonic aids or to mark compacts]. Once they revered the Buddhadharma, Buddhist scriptures were procured from Paekche and for the first time [Japan] had a writing system.[11]

The *Nihon shoki* also records that as early as the reign of Emperor Ojin (r. 270-310) Chinese logographs were transmitted to Japan by the Paekche scholar Wang In and others, who were dispatched from Paekche.[12] While there is no specific implication in these notices that the reception of Buddhism and the use of the Chinese writing system were interconnected, their existence does demand that we examine the possibility of such a relationship. Two examples follow, from the *Nihon shoki* entry for Empress Suiko.

> Tenth year, winter, tenth month (602). The Paekche monk Kwallŭk arrived here [in Japan] and presented

documents on calendrics, astronomy, and geography, and
works dealing with *tun-chia* divination[13] and the magical
arts. At that time, three or four pupils were selected to
study under Kwalluk. The pupils included Tamafuro, the
ancestor of Yago no Fobito, who studied calendrics;
Ōtomonosuguri no Kōsō, who studied astrology and *tun-
chia* divination; and Yamashiro no omi no Hinamitate,
who studied the magical arts. Each of them finished their
training in these arts.[14]
Eighteenth year, spring, third month (610). The Koguryŏ
king [Yŏngyang (r. 590-617)] dispatched the senior monks
Tamjing and Pŏpchŏng. Tamjing not only understood the
Five Classics but was also adept in producing paint, paper
and ink; in addition, he had mastered the art of manufac-
turing stone handmills. It may be that this was the first
time such stone mills were produced [in Japan].[15]

The use of written characters was a necessary precondition
for the reception of Buddhism in northeast Asia, for without it
the religion could not hope to convey the doctrines that
appeared in its prolix scriptures. This is why the copying of
scriptures became an important religious rite in Mahāyāna
Buddhism. This literary expertise of Buddhist monks also gave
them familiarity not simply with Buddhism but also with all
aspects of sinitic culture, including Confucianism, as the
historical sources suggest. Consequently, it was Buddhist
missionary-monks, even more than Confucian scholars, who
transmitted the full range of Chinese civilization to the kingdoms of Korea. But this dissemination did not take place only
within the three kingdoms of Korea; various aspects of this
sinitic culture—including, but not limited to, Buddhism—were
subsequently transmitted to Japan, again primarily by Buddhist
monks.
     With the exception of such examples as Tamjing, who
personally transmitted some of these new arts to Japan, it is
clear that much of this diffusion of culture was carried out
primarily through written instructions. While the sources cited

here describe cultural interchanges occurring between nations, it was actually individual monks, actively engaged in missionary activities among the people, who carried out these exchanges. The early reception of Buddhism was often promoted by the religion's role as an agent of national protection. This role encouraged the northeast Asian kingdoms to sponsor the construction of monasteries and the ordination of monks. But in order to establish Buddhism firmly in these new areas, the monks decided it was necessary to present Buddhism as a device for gaining worldly benefits as well, a view they encouraged through performing therapeutic and apotropanic services on behalf of the people. For example, until the Silla king Pŏphŭng (r. 514-539) finally accepted Buddhism officially, there were two unofficial transmissions of the religion.

In the first record, from the period of King Nulchi (r. 417-458), the monk Mokhoja is said to have come from Koguryŏ to the Silla country of Ilsŏn. At that time the Silla court had just received a sample of incense from Liang China, but knew neither its name nor its use. Searching throughout the length and breadth of the kingdom for a person who could teach them about it, they found Mokhoja, who told them what it was and instructed them in the rite of offering incense before the altar of the Buddha. Mokhoja was also called upon to cure a critically ill princess, which he was able to accomplish through burning incense.[16]

According to the second source, during the third year of King Mich'u's reign (264), the duchess of Sŏngguk was struck by illness, which neither incantations nor medical treatments could cure. Seeking out doctors throughout the entire country, the king finally located Master Ado, who went to the royal palace and cured the woman's illness. The king was greatly relieved and offered him a reward; Ado sought permission to build temples and disseminate Buddhism, which was granted. It is said, however, that after the death of King Mich'u, Buddhism was proscribed due to opposition from the masses.[17]

Regardless of whatever historical value these two stories may have, they do indicate that at the time of the reception of

Buddhism missionaries could not but depend upon the healing arts and other shaman practices as an expedient means of conveying the profundity of their doctrine. In other words, these stories seem to indicate that, in contemporary Silla, there was an indigenous notion that spirits could confer earthly felicity, which Buddhism attempted to usurp for itself. Coincidentally, in both these references, there appears the topos of curing a princess' sickness. This suggests that, in general, people regarded Buddhism as a means of conquering either personal misfortunes like sickness, or social ills as war and famine, the separation of relatives, or domestic quarrels.

A similar situation is seen in the case of Paekche, where the introduction of Buddhism is narrated as follows in the *Samguk yusa.*

The ascension to the throne of the fifteenth monarch, Ch'imnyu, cyclical *kapsin* (384). The Serindian monk Mālānanda arrived from Chin and was welcomed reverently to the palace. The following year, cyclical *ŭryu* (385), a Buddhist monastery was constructed in the new capital of Hansan, and ten men received ordination as monks. This was the beginning of the Buddhadharma in Paekche. Furthermore, at the time of King Asin's coronation, seventeenth year of the Ta-yüan (alt. T'ai-yüan) era, second month (392), a directive was issued: "Seek merit through worshipping the Buddhadharma."[18]

In the same year, virtually the identical proclamation was issued in Koguryŏ as well, some twenty-one years after the introduction of Buddhism to that kingdom.[19] But I do not think that the word "merit" (*pok;* Skt. *puṇya*) in these phrases meant to convey the profound doctrinal sense implicit in such Buddhist technical terms as "field of merit" (*pokchŏn;* Skt. *puṇyakṣetra*); it seems instead to cover more primal religious goals, such as relief from disaster, a secure livelihood, and spiritual peace.

In this wise, Buddhism was seen as nothing more than a

type of indigenous, shamanistic faith during its incipient period in Korea. The special interest shown in the Buddhism, however, was prompted not by its profound philosophy, but instead by its material culture—Buddhist sculptures resplendent with gold, ornamented with such superbly manufactured artifacts as heavenly parasols and garlands, or colorful wall paintings of the Pure Land of Ultimate Bliss. The subsequent transmission of Buddhism from the three Korean kingdoms to Japan also testifies to this same trend, for the eminent doctrinal specialists who introduced the religious beliefs of Buddhism were almost always accompanied by image-makers and painters, who could pass along the artistic culture of Buddhism as well.

This interest in Buddhist culture soon generated a corresponding interest in the sublime doctrines of the religion, which demanded familiarity with its written scriptures. Indeed, there was an especially intimate and unique relationship between Buddhist culture and literacy. There were several stages through which this relationship developed, as can be glimpsed in Korea in stele inscriptions and the use of *han'gŭl*, the indigenous Korean syllabary. Korean inscriptions are first found dating from the beginning of the fifth century in Koguryŏ and the middle of the sixth century in Paekche and Silla. The earliest Korean inscriptions from the Three Kingdoms period were all written in elegant literary Chinese, including the stele of Koguryŏ King Kwanggaet'o, erected in 414, a stone slab found in Paekche King Muryŏng's tomb which records the ritual purchase of the land from the god of earth, inscribed in 523 and 526, and four stelae commemorating the annexation of territory by the Silla king Chinhŭng, erected between 561 and 568.[20] It is only in such inscriptions as the *Ojak-pi* (Embankment-construction Stele), completed ca. 578, and in such Silla stelae as the *Namsan Sinsŏng pi* (Five Stelae of the New Citadel on Mt. Nam), erected in 591, that there is found the first use of phonetic transcriptions of Korean proper nouns; neologistic, composite logographs, in which two Chinese characters were written as one; and the indigenous *idu* (Clerical Readings) transcription system, in which Chinese logographs were used for their phonetic value in transcribing Korean grammatical forms.[21] These inscriptions, which are concerned with local administration, show that the Silla people had developed their own indigenous writing system, with its own unique phraseology, soon after they became literate. In the Koguryŏ inscription, a commemorative inscription to the fortifications of the city of P'yŏngyang, dated ca. 566, simplified native logographs and *idu*-style phraseology also appear.[22] Although this inscription is dated some 150 years later than the earliest Koguryŏ inscription of 414, it shows that there were parallel efforts in Koguryŏ as well to develop an indigenous Korean writing system. In Paekche, there are found no such stelae inscriptions containing composite characters or neologistic Paekche-style logographs; however, the paucity of extant Paekche inscriptions does not permit us to say conclusively that Paekche made no such attempts, as occurred in Silla and Koguryŏ, to develop a native system of writing. In fact it is much more plausible that inscriptions containing such attempts were composed, but are simply lost to us today.

A tremendous shift in the character of Korean inscriptions is noticed between the Three Kingdoms and the Unified Silla periods. During the Three Kingdoms period, the most common type of stelae are royal funerary eulogies and commemorations of territorial annexation, or royal construction projects like city fortifications, mountain citadels, moats, and dykes; Buddhist inscriptions are relatively rare. In contrast, inscriptions dating from the Unified Silla period are overwhelmingly concerned with Buddhism while such secular themes are rare, suggesting that Buddhism was flourishing during that period. Inscriptions related to Buddhism display certain conspicuous characteristics, which we shall survey *infra*.

Buddhist inscriptions from the Unified Silla period include both indigenous Silla logographs as well as *idu*-style phraseology. The oldest Silla inscription associated with Buddhism is the one on a stone stele of Amitābha Buddha triad carved in the cyclical year *kyeyu*, assumed to date from 673, the thirteenth year of the reign of the Silla king Munmu. It uses composite logographs for official titles, as for example where the two logographs for the bureaucratic rank *taesa* are written as one.[23] It is the first example of the tendency for Buddhist inscriptions concerned with Silla popular faith to draw on indigenous terminology and phraseology, while those that honored eminent monks in the elite hierarchy of the religion do not.

While Confucianism was inexorably tied to the aristocratic government and bureaucratic administration, Buddhism was more concerned with propagating its religion among the people; consequently, it required a means of catering to a broad strata of the intelligentsia. This Buddhism was able to do through catalyzing the development of an indigenous writing system, which reflected native phonology and grammar. Buddhist monks were typically more sophisticated than Chinese secular scholars in their understanding of phonetics because of the Buddhists' need to transcribe the polysyllabic technical terminology of their Sanskrit and Middle Indic texts. This left them uniquely prepared to develop transcription systems for the native languages of northern Asia. I also suspect that Silla Buddhists created their own writing system because they felt that Chinese, as a foreign language, was inadequate to express their own native faith. The only possible exception to this characterization of Buddhism would be the doctrinal and scriptural exegetes, who were part of the elite society that had mastered literary Chinese.

This close connection between indigenous writing systems and Buddhism is further illustrated by the fact that, from the latter Koryŏ to early Chosŏn periods (ca. fourteenth to fifteenth centuries), the interlinear punctuation readings called *hyŏnt'o* (lit. "hanging adjutory") were employed most commonly in Buddhist texts. *T'o*, which were used to indicate Korean grammatical particles and auxiliary verbs, derive from either abbreviated forms of Chinese characters or the indigenous composite logographs. Their origin, development, and usage thus resemble those of the Japanese *kana* syllabaries, which share a similar derivation from simplified Chinese logographs. *T'o* even include forms homophonous and homologous to *katakana*, suggesting that there may have been some mutual influence between the two.[24] The reason why *t'o* are so commonly used in Buddhist texts was probably because Chinese alone could not adequately express the faith of the Korean people. This is adumbrated also in the development of the Korean *han'gŭl* alphabet, which was promulgated in 1443 and actively championed by King Sejong of the Chosŏn dynasty. *Han'gŭl* received its most widespread use in the areas of production (viz. agricultural texts) and religion (viz. Buddhist scriptures and commentaries), not in government documents or Confucian literature. Indeed, Buddhist support of the new alphabet helped to sustain it in the face of consistent Confucian neglect, if not outright antagonism.

It is, thus, in Buddhist materials that the earliest, and most sustained use of Korean vernacular writing systems is found. This connection provides further proof that Buddhism evolved in association with autochthonous religion and culture. This same relationship is found in Japan as well. For example, the "Wei-kuo chuan" of the *Sui-shu* records that Japan became literate only after the transmission of Buddhism.[25] The significance of this statement is best understood if it is construed as referring to a certain stage in the use of a writing system, rather than to the very inception of literacy, for obviously, diplomats and others entrusted with official duties would long have been conversant with Chinese. Therefore, rather than taking this reference to mean that Japanese first learned to read and write at the time of the reception of Buddhism, it probably suggests that Japanese from multifarious walks of life were actively learning to use Chinese logographs in order to understand the Buddhist scriptures then being introduced from Paekche—i.e., that the place of a writing system in the field of religious endeavor was expanding rapidly.

There is, however, another interpretation of this *Sui-shu* account, which is much more speculative. Based on the relationship between Buddhism and the written language that we saw developing in both Korea and Japan, we could interpret this reference to literacy among the Japanese not as referring to pristine, classical Chinese, but instead to an indigenous writing system created to record vernacular Japanese, perhaps the *man'yōgana*. But regardless of which the *Sui-shu* actually meant, the introduction of Chinese logographs and the development of an indigenous Japanese writing system occur almost simultaneously. Thus, this account must refer to the diffusion of some sort of writing system among the Japanese intelligentsia, which was prompted by the transmission of Buddhism from Paekche to Japan.

Dragon Faith and the Reception of Buddhism

The next issue I wish to take up is the type of fusion that developed between the received Buddhist faith and autochthonous beliefs in dragon and snake spirits. Following are some historical sources relating to this question.

[King Chinhŭng,] fourteenth year, spring, second month (1-29 March 553). The king ordered that his officers construct a new palace to the east of Wŏlsŏng. A yellow dragon (*hwangnyong*) appeared at the site and, suspicious of it, the king had the palace redesigned as a Buddhist Monastery, which he named "Hwangnyong."[26]

There is obviously a close connection in this story between the appearance of a dragon, an indigenous agricultural deity, and the foundation of the Hwangnyong Monastery. There are some ten stories involving dragons in Korean historical sources, beginning with the legend of the birth of Aryŏng, the queen-consort of the founder of Silla, King Hyŏkkŏse (r. 57 B.C.-A.D. 3), from the left-side of a dragon's ribs.[27] In those legends, dragons frequently appear as theriomorphs of baleful spirits (*aramitama*) rather than as their more common identity as transformations of water-spirits.

The following legend from *Samguk sagi* is a rather unusual tale concerning dragons.

[King Munmu,] twenty-first year, autumn, seventh month, first day (19 August 681). The king died and was given the posthumous name Munmu. Obeying his last request, his assembled vassals entombed him atop a great boulder on the shores of the Eastern Sea. According to popular legend the king metamorphosized into a dragon. That rock is still designated Taewang-sŏk (Great King's Rock).[28]

This same event is narrated in much greater detail in volume two of the *Samguk yusa.*

After ruling the kingdom [of Silla] for twenty-one years, the great king [Munmu] passed away in the second year of the T'ang Yung-lung era, cyclical *sinsa* (681). Following the king's command, he was entombed atop a great boulder on the Eastern Sea. During his lifetime, King Munmu always said to his chaplain, Dharma Master Chiŭi, "After my death, I vow to become a great dragon protecting the kingdom. I wish to worship the Buddhadharma and guard the families of the nation." The chaplain responded, "A dragon is an animal; how can this be appropriate rebirth for you?" Munmu answered, "Since long ago, I have done nothing but disdain worldly glory. If it is my lot to be reborn as an animal, then that will suit me just fine."[29]

The following elaboration of King Munmu's vow appears in an interlinear note in the following entry in the *Samguk yusa,* "Manp'asikchŏk" (Flute to Calm Myriad Waves).

A record in that Monastery (Kamŭn-sa) says, "Because King Munmu wished to suppress the incursions of Japanese pirates, he first began to construct this Monastery. Before its completion, the king died and was reborn as a sea-dragon. His son, Sinmun, assumed the throne and, in the second year of K'ai-yao (682), [the construction of Kamŭn

Monastery] was completed. Under the stairway leading to the Golden Hall opened a cave that faced east. This made it convenient for the dragon to enter the Monastery and move about.

Alternately, it might be that, on the posthumous order of King Munmu, the place where the great king's remains were kept was named Taewang-am (Great King's Boulder) and the monastery was named Kamŭn-sa. Sometime later, the place where the appearance of that dragon was seen was named Igyŏndae (Auspicious Sighting Terrace).[30]

As is clear from these aforementioned examples, dragons functioned as spirits of national protection and were particularly concerned with guarding against the incursion of pirates. It was with this purpose in mind that King Munmu apparently decided to become a dragon spirit guarding Silla. Dragons were considered to have great powers and to move freely between both the terrestrial world of men and the ethereal world of spirits; they were imaginary beasts which were thought to manifest in any number of ways, and in China were regarded as a symbol of royalty. Because the dragons' form resembled that of snakes, however, after entering Korea and Japan they came to be recognized either as great snakes or as spirits who possessed the magical powers of snakes, only many times enhanced. Just as the mythic founder of Silla was called Sarŭng (*Sa* = alt. character for snake), in primitive agricultural societies snakes were worshipped as gods who were indispensable in controlling the waters. It was believed that dragon spirits possessed the power of snakes many times multiplied. For this reason, when dragons appear in that era of legend represented by the *Samguk yusa*, they are to be taken as the harbingers of torrential rains or as bolts of lightning. This dragon spirit was conceived of as a baleful spirit, apparently because it represented the enormous power of a dragon who took the form of a wrathful water divinity. Because dragons thus possessed enormous powers as water divinities, there are many examples of them serving as spirits of the sea; hence in this story of Munmu, the great power possessed by dragons allows him to manifest as a deity of national protection, guarding against marauders. This way of perceiving dragons was a new conception of spirits that developed either in China or northern Asia. Its origins derive from the faith in snakes as a type of water divinity, which is widespread in primitive agricultural societies, especially in the monsoon belt. The legends in the *Samguk yusa*, however, portray dragon spirits not as simple water divinities, but as extraordinarily powerful, even wrathful, water spirits—a somewhat different conception of deity. Once Buddhism was introduced into Silla, the dragons that appear prominently in Buddhist legends came to be imbued with the same qualities as snakes and were introduced into local, snake-worshipping cults. This is how I interpret the appearance of the yellow dragon in the above story about King Chinhŭng. Therefore, in Silla just after the reception of Buddhism, there was a great need to fuse this alien faith with the indigenous worship of yellow dragons as either autochthonous or water divinities; thus, that Monastery was initially named Hwangnyong-sa (Yellow Dragon Monastery), and not long afterwards was renamed the homophonous Hwangnyong-sa (Royal Dragon Monastery).

Buddhism in Silla dates from around 528, some twenty-five years before this event. Although Pŏphŭng, the king at that time, tried to support the foreign religion, the nobility vigorously opposed Buddhism, regarding with suspicion the odd appearance of its monks, their strange clothes, and the heterodoxy of its doctrines. Through the miracle that took place at the martyrdom of the Grand Secretary Ich'adon in 529,[31] the public dissemination of Buddhism was finally allowed. But even after the official acceptance of Buddhism, the Silla nobility governing in various outlying regions probably did not appreciate the changes that the religion fostered in the social hierarchy. Because of this antagonism from the Silla aristocracy, Buddhism perforce needed to assimilate indigenous forms of religious faith if it was to survive in Silla—even more than it had to do in Koguryŏ or Paekche. Thus, Buddhism embraced the snake and dragon cults of native Silla agricultural society.

During the reign of King Chinhŭng, when Buddhism flourished on a grand scale, Silla annexed not only all the neighboring Kaya territories but also the area from the basin of the Han River to the regions along the Japan Sea in present-day South Hamgyŏng province. It thus became necessary to rule regions populated by peoples of different cultural backgrounds. In order for the Silla ruling classes to absorb the culture of these newly acquired areas, they adopted measures that would be accommodating to the people of those regions. It was because of such political exigencies that Buddhist culture was able to make inroads among the Silla aristocracy. In fact, from the early part of the reign of King Chinhŭng (ca. mid-sixth century), Silla Buddhism developed in conjunction with the nobility by actively assimilating indigenous beliefs.

The next major change in social conditions occurred during Silla's peninsular unification drive of the middle seventh century. The vow of King Munmu to be reborn as a dragon adumbrates the role of Mahāyāna Buddhism in protecting the nation. Munmu's attempt to fuse it with the indigenous dragon spirits that represented the baleful aspect of the water divinities helped to inspire a national consensus during the unification wars. Once Silla had vanquished the T'ang army with the help of powerful local clans, a monarchical government was rapidly put in place. The king apparently wished to adopt as the spiritual foundation of this new ruling system this new guardian spirit, which embodied both local cultic beliefs and Buddhism. Thus the inception of the Unified Silla dynasty saw the primitive faith in dragons as local agricultural deities transformed into an integral part of the national *Weltanschauung*.

To lend support to this interpretation, I will cite the following passage from the entry, the "Flute that Calms Myriad Waves," in *Samguk yusa*.

In the following year, cyclical (*imo*), fifth month, first day (11 June 682), a naval official, the *p'ajinch'an* Pak Sukch'ŏng,[32] reported, "There is a small mountain on the Eastern Sea coming over the swells toward Kamŭn

Monastery." The king thought this report strange, and ordered the astronomer Kim Ch'unjil to divine its meaning. Kim reported, "Your saintly, deceased father has now become a sea dragon and is protecting Samhan (Silla). In addition, General Kim Yusin, who has become a son of Indra, the king of the Trayastriṃśa heaven, has now advented in Silla as a great vassal. By combining their virtue, these two saints plan on producing a treasure that will protect the capital. If your majesty would go down to the seashore, priceless treasures are certain to come into your possession."

Elated, the king visited Igyŏndae on the seventh day of that month (18 June), where he saw the mountain. He sent a scout to examine it. The mountain looked like a tortoise's head. Atop it was a bamboo that split into two in the daytime but became one at night. ([Note:] One [version of the story] says that the mountain also divided and recombined in the mornings and evenings, like the bamboo.) The scout returned and informed the king of this. The king went to the Kamŭn Monastery to stay overnight. The next day during the noon hour the bamboos combined into one. Heaven and earth shook and it was stormy and dark for seven days.

By the sixteenth day of that month (27 June) the winds subsided and the waves calmed. The king sailed over the sea and landed on the mountain, where a dragon came to present respectfully a black, jade belt to him. The king accepted it graciously and they sat down together. [The king] then asked [the dragon], "Why is it that this mountain and this bamboo are sometimes split in two and sometimes united as one?" The dragon replied, "It is like clapping: clapping with one hand produces no sound, but if two hands are clapped together the sound will issue forth. In the same way, this bamboo makes sound only when its two parts are brought together. It is an auspicious sign that will allow the sagely king to govern the world by means of its sound. If the king would make a flute from this bamboo and play it, then all the world under heaven will be at peace. At present, the king's deceased father has become a great dragon in the sea, and Kim Yusin furthermore has become a heavenly spirit. These two saints have made these priceless treasures with the same intention in mind and ordered me to present them to you.[33]

The father of King Sinmun, the thirty-first monarch of Silla, was Munmu and his mother, who was herself the daughter of Kim Yusin, was the queen-consort Munmyŏng. King Munmu and Kim Yusin cooperated in unifying the three Kingdoms and defeating the T'ang army. In the temple record of the Kamŭn Monastery excerpted earlier, it is recorded that King Munmu became a dragon in order to guard against incursions by another of their enemies, the Japanese pirates. In this tale Kim Yusin is said to have become a prince in the Thirty-third Heaven (Trayastriṃśa; a class of Indian Buddhist gods), thereby taking on a form more in keeping with the spirit of Buddhism. The story therefore implies that a dragon spirit (part of Silla native faith) and Buddhism cooperated to produce these priceless treasures—treasures that would protect the monarchy and the ruling aristocracy. Thus by the time of the Silla victory in the unification wars, indigenous cults and Buddhism were fully cooperating with one another in the great task of protecting the nation, and served as the bedrock of Silla axiology.

One point I would like to raise here concerns the unique Silla understanding of Buddhism. I am referring specifically to that part of the tale that made Kim Yusin into a prince of the Trayastriṃśa heaven who then advented in Silla. That legend suggests that the Silla people considered the world of the Buddhas and the world of heavenly beings to be virtually interchangeable. Hence when seventh-century Silla people learned of Buddhism, they considered stories about the appearance of Buddhas and bodhisattvas to be identical to their own native tales of racial and cultural progenitors.

In Japan, the reception of Buddhism was not carried to the extreme seen in Korea, where the new religion became an essential factor in the formation of the Silla state. While there are a number of widely divergent theories about the establishment of the Japanese nation, there is a consensus that the vast Japanese archipelago was a homogeneous religious culture before the inception of authoritarian rule. The different levels of culture discovered in Japanese burial tumuli suggest that this religious homogeneity continued from the bronze age onward. Because of this continuity, Japan did not need to adopt Buddhism in order to assimilate the different cultures of newly conquered territories, as had Silla. However, this does not imply that the Japanese embraced Buddhism only as a response to harsh environmental or social conditions. Japanese indigenous faith was polytheistic, and its society displayed much flexibility in matters of religion. It thus seems that Japan accepted Buddhism merely in order to enhance its own religious culture.

The indigenous religions of both Japan and Korea viewed snakes as being either water spirits or their theriomorphs. Silla saw those snakes as being equivalent to Chinese dragons, and dragon worship and legends about the dragon cities flourished. Such legends about the palace of the dragon-king eventually became part of Japanese folklore. However, in real distinction to the vast number of tales concerning dragons that appear in literature describing Silla, Japanese historical collections like the *Nihon shoki* and *Shoku nihonki* contain few records concerning dragon worship.

In *Nihon shoki*, apart from several personal, place, and spirit names that include the logograph for dragon, the appearances of that word are decidedly rare.[34] Something similar to this Korean belief in dragon spirits appears in the "Sindai" (Age of spirits) section of the *Nihon shoki*, in the myth of the emperor's visit to the sea palace. There, it is said that after Toyotama-bime gave birth to a son, Hikonagisa-takeugaya-fukimeezu no Mikoto, she transformed into a dragon.[35] This is the only place where it is said that Toyotama-bime was a dragon. Earlier in the text she is called Yahiro no wani (Eight-*hiro*-long Crocodile.)[36] It thus seems possible that the dragon element of the story is a later accretion.

Next, in the entry for the first year of the White Pheasant year of Emperor Kōtoku (650), second month, fifteenth day (*kinoesaru no hi;* 22 March 650) in the imperial edict promulgated on the occasion of presenting the white pheasant, it is said:

> In the time of Ohosazaki no Mikado (Emperor Nintoku) a dragon-horse appeared in the west. In this wise, auspicious omens have occasionally appeared from the past to the present; there are many examples of such responses to the virtue [of the emperor].[37]

But in the chronicle of Ohosazaki no Mikado (Emperor Nintoku), there is no such record of the appearance of this dragon-horse. It is possible that this myth was extrapolated from a legend about a wood-dodder (*sazaki*) that flew into the birth-chambers at the time Nintoku was born.[38] In any case, dragon-horses were unknown in ancient times during the reign of Nintoku, but probably make their first appearance in Japanese legends during the mid-seventh century at the earliest.

An analogous story of a dragon-horse flying through the sky is found in the following myth from the *Nihon shoki.*

> In the first year [of Emperor Saimei's reign], summer, fifth month, first day (10 June 655), someone appeared in the sky riding a dragon. His facial appearance was like that of a T'ang Chinese and he wore a green bamboo-hat coated with oil. From the peak of Kazuraki Precipice, he flew off to Mt. Ikoma, and at noon he flew off toward the west from the top of Matsu Precipice in Suminoe.[39]

We are not going to question whether this so-called "dragon" may actually have been a kite. We shall simply stop at showing that Japanese in the mid-seventh century were at least somewhat familiar with East Asian folklore about dragons flying through the air. While we might assume that the dragon in the legend of

Toyotama-bime was the theriomorphosis of a water divinity, it is not altogether clear whether, or to what extent, dragon-horses were believed to have associations with water spirits. In *Shoku nihonki* (Supplementary records of Japan) there is only a single mention of dragon spirits. The entry for the fourth year of Emperor Mombu (700), includes an account of the Upadhyāya Tojo's travels travels to T'ang China to meet the Tripitaka Master Hsüan-tsang (fl. ca. 596-664). As Tojo was returning home over the Sea of Japan after receiving instruction, his ship was becalmed for seven days and nights by the Dragon King—or so a diviner told him—who was after a gong that Hsüan-tsang had given him. The ship was able to continue on its way only after the gong was thrown into the water.[40] It is unclear whether that diviner was Chinese, Japanese or Korean; but because Japanese stories relating to the dragon king are rare, we may presume that he was the Korean. Even so, legends from the latter half of the seventh century that contain the word dragon are rare. It seems, therefore, that such legends were neither as prominent as they were in Silla, nor were their relationships with Buddhism as intimate.

Eminent Monks who Advented from Heaven

The acceptance of Buddhism in Silla transformed its court ritual. Official monasteries were constructed and the Buddhist faith spread rapidly from the mid-sixth century onward. However, the Silla interest in Buddhism focused principally on complex doctrinal research, which was undertaken by a few scholar-monks, and the adoration of the material aspects of Buddhist culture, such as images, which was more prevalent among non-elite believers. I have already touched upon the fact that a fairly long period of time was necessary in order to transform the indigenous religious conceptions of the Silla people. In the present section, I will introduce several stories from *Samguk yusa* that illustrate the process by which the traditional conception of spirits was co-opted by the theology of Buddhism.

About 100 *li* (leagues) to the east of Chungnyŏng[41] there is a mountain that imposingly juts high into the sky. In the ninth year of King Chinp'yŏng, cyclical year *kapsin* (587), there was a great boulder that unexpectedly fell from heaven onto the peak of that mountain. It was a cube one *chang* (10 feet) square, and images of the Tathāgatas were carved on its four sides, all of which were protected by red gauze. Hearing of this, the king ordered a trip to pay respects [to the boulder]. He then had a monastery founded next to the boulder and named it Taesŭng-sa (Great Vehicle Monastery). He invited an anonymous bhikṣu, who was a reciter of the *Lotus Sūtra*, to reside at the temple, sprinkling and sweeping [the grounds], worshipping the boulder, and keeping incense burning without interruption. [The mountain] was called Yŏktŏk-san (Also Virtuous Mountain) or Sabul-san (Four Buddhas Mountains). When the bhikṣu died and was buried, lotuses grew from atop the tumulus.

Furthermore, King Kyŏngdŏk (r. 742-765) visited Paengnyul Monastery.[42] He reached the foot of that mountain and heard the sound of Buddha-invocation emanating from inside the earth. He ordered excavation on that spot and uncovered a great boulder. Inscribed on its four sides were the Buddhas of the four directions. For that reason he built a monastery there, which he named Kulbul-sa (Excavated Buddha Monastery).[43]

These two tales are similar to legends concerning the advent on earth of heavenly deities and subterranean spirits, which were part of the indigenous religious beliefs of the Silla and Kaya regions. Korean myth rarely records anything about the activities of celestial deities. It is here that we find a major difference between Korean and Japanese myth; the latter places great emphasis on the need to relate to the spirits (*kami*). The advent of heavenly beings on mountain peaks is a topos that often appears in Korean myth, as for example, in the story of Tan'gun (The Lord of Sandalwood), the founder of the Korean nation. The foundation legends of Silla and Kaya in particular includes numerous myths that involve a figure appearing on a mountain peak.

The fact that the boulder in the story from King Chinp'yŏng's era is wrapped in red gauze is strongly evocative of the foundation-legend of the Karak (Kaya) kingdom located on the southern coast of the Korean peninsula. It relates the following:

> Eighteenth year of Chien-wu (A.D. 42), reign-period of Kuang-wu-ti, the founder of Latter Han, cyclical *imin*, third month, the day of the spring purification rite at the Nak River. In Kuji, to the north of the village, there was a strange voice calling out. Two to three hundred villagers gathered there. The voice sounded human, but its form was hidden and only the voice was heard. It asked, "Is there anybody here?" The nine chieftains replied, "We're here." It asked again, "Where am I?" The chieftains replied, "At Kuji." It said once more, "High Heaven ordered me to come and found a new country here and serve as its ruler. This is why I have advented here. You should excavate the top of this peak and sing as follows while shovelling the earth. 'Turtle! Turtle! Stick your head out! If you don't, we will roast and eat you.' By this dance will you welcome a great king, at which you will jump with joy."
>
> The nine chieftains did as they were told, and everyone sang and danced with delight. After a while they looked up and saw a vermillion rope dangling all by itself from heaven to the ground. Searching for the end of the rope, they found a gold case that was wrapped inside red cloth. Unwrapping it, they discovered six golden eggs, which were round like the sun. Elated, the crowd made one-hundred prostrations before them.[44]

Both this legend and the previous story of the excavation of a Buddha image tell of the advent of a transcendent spirit who orders the people to excavate the sacred ground at a mountain top, and then sing and dance while reciting spells. Some of the same topoi appear in both tales: for example, the advent of the offspring of heavenly deities and the appearance of Buddha images both occur at the top of mountains, and the Buddha image and the gold case are both wrapped in red cloth. It also appears that the ways in which people chose to pay honor to the Buddha were similar to the ways in which they worshipped their own indigenous deities. Thus the Buddhist legends of Sabul-san and Kulbul-san contain many points that are congruent with indigenous myths about celestial and autochthonous deities. This implies that the Korean people responded to Buddhism in two very distinct ways: as far as its material culture was concerned, the alien tradition of Buddhism was regarded as being virtually identical with Confucianism; but as a type of religion, it was treated like any other indigenous faith.

Folk beliefs involving interactions between celestial spirits and human beings are especially conspicuous in dynastic foundation-legends. But such associations appear in many other types of legends, as for example in the story of the Silla general Kim Yusin (595-673).

> At the age fifteen, his lordship [Kim Yusin] became a *hwarang* (Flower Boy). His contemporaries followed him without exception, styling themselves "Solemn Disciples of the Dragon Flower [of Maitreya]."
>
> In the twenty-eighth year of King Chinp'yŏng's Kŏnbok reign-period, cyclical *sinmi* (611), his lordship was seventeen. He saw Koguryŏ, Paekche, and the Malgal [a Tungusic tribe in Manchuria] encroaching on his nation's borders and, enraged, resolved to vanquish the enemy invaders. Alone he entered a stone grotto at Middle Peak,[45] where he engaged in purification rites and swore an oath to Heaven: "These hostile countries are wayward. Like wolves or tigers, they disturb our frontiers till there are virtually no peaceful years. Though I am but a mediocre

vassal without sufficient talent or power, I resolve to pacify this ruinous disorder. I entreat Heaven to watch over me and lend me a hand."

He stayed there for four days when suddenly a gaffer dressed in coarse garments came and said, "This place is filled with venomous insects and ferocious beasts; it is a frightful land. Why have you come here, oh noble youth, to stay all alone?" [Kim] answered, "Where are you from, elder? May I ask your venerable name?" The gaffer said, "I have no residence but stop over wherever conditions take me. My name, then, is Nansŭng (Difficult to Vanquish)." Hearing this, his lordship realized that this was no ordinary man. He bowed twice and approached him, saying, "I am a subject of Silla. I came here because I am deeply disturbed by the appearance of these enemies of my country and I hope for nothing more than to happen upon some solution. I beg the elder to be sympathetic to my earnest sincerity and bestow a stratagem on me." The gaffer was utterly silent. His lordship besought him tirelessly, shedding tears all the while. By the sixth or seventh time the gaffer finally said, "While you are young, you are of a mind to unify the three kingdoms. Is this not courageous!" He then bestowed a secret technique on him, saying, "Be careful not to pass this on indiscriminately. If you abuse it, you will receive retribution in return." Once he was finished speaking, [the gaffer] left and walked on for about two *li* (leagues). Chase him as he did, [Kim] could not find him anywhere. There was just a light atop the mountain, which shown brilliantly like the five colors.

Kŏnbok era, twenty-ninth year (612). The neighboring invaders encroached still further, which only aroused still more his lordship's mettle. Carrying a precious sword, he entered alone into the deep ravine of Mt. Inbak.[46] Burning incense and calling out to Heaven, he prayed as he had done before at Middle Peak. He swore his oath and prayed yet again, "May the Keeper of Heaven let fall a light, dropping its noumenon into this precious sword!" On the night of the third day, the two asterisms of "Barrens" (in Aquarius and Equuleus) and Horn (Spica, et al.) shown their light onto the sword, till it seemed to quiver tremulously.[47]

The *hwarang* mentioned in this story of Kim Yusin were a congregation of village youths, originally deriving from the indigenous religion, that originally was at the core of Silla agricultural society. During the reign of King Chinhŭng, the *hwarang* groups were incorporated into the national aristocracy by forming them into an institution that was designed to instill moral virtue and patriotism in the sons of the nobility. A *hwarang* by virtue of his noble birth, Kim Yusin had natural leadership talents, but he often entered deep into mountain fastnesses and dark ravines, apparently on vision quests for the mountain god. During that time of national crisis, creating in the local populace a sense of national identity and a loyalty to the state was vital if the Silla monarchy was to defend itself from hostile incursions. It was with this aim in mind that the story of Kim Yusin was told. First, the legend sought to enhance the prestige of these village youth-groups by investing them with supernatural power deriving from celestial and subterranean quarters; this elevation of the *hwarang* system made the village youths a tool of national policy, thereby helping to expand political loyalties from a regional to a national level. Second, in seeking the help of local deities like the mountain god in the fight against his country's rivals, the Silla general was in fact attempting to recruit the local populace into the national campaign. Thus this legend illustrates a situation in which both local social structures and indigenous religious beliefs were manipulated to serve the national-protection ideology (*hoguk sasang*) of Silla. The elder who bestowed on Kim Yusin the secret stratagem for protecting the nation was the mountain god, an indigenous local deity, whom this legend dignifies as a celestial spirit. As if in evidence that this elder was the mountain god, a five-colored spectrum of light radiates from atop the mountain. Finally the luminary noumena of the stars descends into the precious sword, investing it with their power as well. The advent of celestial spirits on mountain peaks is a folk belief found throughout Asia and thus should be regarded as part of native Silla religion. Star worship is also observed widely from northern China to Mongolia; this practice was also transmitted to Korea. Lack of space precludes me from exploring the regional variations in these folk beliefs, and I shall be content to treat them simply as part of indigenous Korean religion.[48]

We thus see that folk beliefs accepted that celestial deities, divine noumenon, and even the heavenly asterisms were able to descend to earth. This belief persisted long after Buddhism had been transmitted to Korea, as is evident in the aforementioned tale of a lithic Buddha-image that fell from the skies onto Sabul-san (Four Buddhas Mountain). In addition, there are also Korean legends concerning the advent on earth of bodhisattvas like Mañjuśrī and eminent Buddhist monks, as I shall now introduce. In the *Samguk yusa* entry "Chajang Establishes the Vinaya" the following account of such an appearance is given.

In his declining years, Chajang left the capital and moved to Kangnŭng-kun, where he built the Suda Monastery as his residence. Once he dreamed of a strange monk, whom he had met previously when he stayed at Mt. Wu-t'ai [in China]. The monk came and announced, "I will meet you tomorrow at Taesongjŏng." Startled, Chajang arose and left early for Taesongjŏng. Sensing that he was in the presence of Mañjuśrī Bodhisattva, he asked about the essentials of the Dharma. [Mañjuśrī] said, "Let us meet again at Mt. T'aebaek, where creepers are coiled." He then vanished. Chajang travelled to Mt. T'aebaek in search of him. Seeing a large python coiled under a tree, he said to his attendant, "This is where the creepers are coiled." There he built Sŏngnam-wŏn (Monastery), and waited for the advent of the saint.[49]

Chajang built Sŏngnam-wŏn sometime after 650, the fourth year of Queen Chindŏk's reign. Despite the fact that Buddhism had already flourished for over a century in Silla, it is clear from this story that the appearance of Mañjuśrī Bodhisattva was interpreted as being the advent of a divine spirit. Thus, even during this Golden Age of Buddhism in Silla, there was a persistent tendency to interpret Buddhist faith from the standpoint of indigenous beliefs.

The appearance on earth of a celestial bodhisattva like Mañjuśrī and the advent of a divine spirit from heaven are similar phenomena, and it is hardly surprising that people would have treated the two as identical. But there were times when even monks were assumed to have advented from heaven. Such a story appears in the entry "Wŏnjong (King Pŏphŭng) Promotes the Dharma" in the *Samguk yusa.*

> Five years after the ascension of Great King Chinhŭng, cyclical year *kapcha* (554), Taehŭngnyun Monastery was built. At the beginning of the Ta-ch'ing era (547-549), Shen Hu, an envoy from the Liang, brought a Buddhist *śarī* relic. In the sixth year of the T'ien-shou (alt. T'ien-chia) era (565), the Ch'en envoys, Liu Ssu and the monk Ming-kuan, presented Buddhist scriptures to the throne and both stayed over [in Silla]. Monasteries spread like stars in the sky, and pagodas were aligned like ducks flying in formation. Dharma banners were raised and *brahma* bells hung. Venerable (lit. dragon and elephant) disciples of Śākyamuni served as fields of merit for the world, and the Hīnayāna and Mahāyāna Dharmas became like a compassionate cloud spreading over the capital and the countryside. Elsewhere, bodhisattvas manifested in the world, and eminent monks from the Western Regions advented in the border regions. By these events the Samhan (Three Han: Korea) were unified into a single country and all the four seas united as one family.[50]

This source confirms that the Buddhadharma flourished during King Chinhŭng's reign. The phrase, "bodhisattvas manifested in the world," is an expression that accords with Buddhist religious concepts. However, the phrase, "eminent monks from the Western Regions advented in the border regions" draws directly on indigenous Silla beliefs in the descent of divine spirits to earth.

It is extremely significant that careful analysis of the terminology appearing in such Buddhist works as the *Samguk yusa* allows us to isolate elements that are drawn from indigenous Silla folk religion. In works written by Buddhist monks, it is common for folk legends to be retold in a Buddhist manner. It would have been only natural for the committed, educated monks who wrote these records to interpret the beliefs and practices of the illiterate non-elite in traditional society according to the standards of their adopted religion. Unbiased, sympathetic accounts of folk religion would have been committed to writing only rarely, rendering even more important the accounts preserved in works like the *Samguk yusa*. Hence, regardless of how trivial they might at first seem, all extant accounts of popular faith must be culled in order to reconstruct the indigenous religion of Korea—even if those accounts appear in Buddhist texts.

In the above sections, I have cited various historical materials concerning the native impressions of Buddhism during its early tenure on the peninsula and attempted to analyze their significance. We have seen that in receiving the Buddhist religion, the Korean kingdoms in general, and Silla in particular, interpreted Buddhism as if it were just another type of folk belief. One of the characteristics of this newly received tradition was that it was a multifacted cultural endeavor, involving material, social, and religious aspects. Another of its principal characteristics was that Buddhism was regarded less as a religious creed than a tool for diffusing sinified culture. This is exemplified by two things: first, monks moved freely across international boundaries in their proselytizing activities, thereby spreading the Chinese *Weltanschauung;*

and second, the writing systems popularized by monks were used to unify newly conquered territory.

Interactions Between Buddhist Clergy and Local Spirits

As we have seen in the preceding discussion, even one century after its reception in Silla, Buddhism was still treated as if it were part of the indigenous religion. Monks were considered to be shamans with thaumaturgic skills who were able to subdue demonic spirits through the use of spells. But Buddhism was accompanied by a new, distinctive culture, which gradually attracted the interest of the Silla people. There are several legends that tell of the uneasy relationship that existed between the indigenous spirits and Buddhism during this early period. I will cite as a representative example the story, "The Holy Mother, Transcendent Peach, Joyfully Performs a Buddhist Ceremony," which appears in the *Samguk yusa*.

During the reign of King Chinp'yŏng (r. 579-632), the bhikṣuṇī Chihye, who excelled in her religious practice, resided at Anhŭng Monastery. She planned to repair the Buddha Basilica at Anhŭng Monastery, but was without resources. She dreamed of a female Transcendent of modest demeanor, who was wearing a headdress adorned with pearls and kingfisher's feathers. She appeared before Chihye and consoled her, saying, "I am the divine mother of Mt. Sŏndo (Transcendent Peach Mountain). I sympathize with your desire to repair the Buddha hall, and wish to donate ten *kŭn* (catties) of gold to help with it. Take the gold out from beneath my pedestal and adorn the three principal images [of the hall] with it; paint on the walls fifty-three buddhas along with the six types of holy assemblies, the various celestial deities, and the divine lords of the Five Peaks (the Silla holy mountains). Each spring and autumn, bring together good men and women

and hold a Chŏmch'al (Ch. Chan-ch'a) Dharma service on the behalf of all sentient beings; make it a regular observance."
        Startled, Chihye awakened. Leading her followers, she went and dug a hole under the pedestal. There she found 160 yang (taels) of gold, enough to complete her project. All of this was possible due to the commands of the divine mother.[51]

        The legend of the Holy Mother of Transcendent Peach Mountain, which was part of the foundation-myth of the Silla kingdom, was so famous that it was known even in Sung China.[52] To summarize the legend briefly, the divine mother was a Chinese princess, named Sha-su, who gave birth to a child out of wedlock. Because of her indiscretion, she was set adrift on the ocean and eventually landed on Korean shores. She became the mountain spirit of Transcendent Peach Mountain. It was her child who became the founder of Silla, King Hyŏkkose. Mt. Sŏndo is a tall mountain northwest of Kyŏngju, the capital of Silla. During the Silla period, it was of special importance as the abode of the mountain god who guarded the capital. As the spirit of that mountain, the divine mother was widely revered throughout the land.
        The legend of Chihye, above, relates that this most powerful of indigenous deities assisted in the reconstruction of the main shrine hall. It remains unclear whether the divine mother meant merely to assist Chihye personally in her project, or actually to lend aid to the religion in which the nun believed. But nowhere does the legend imply that the divine mother herself took refuge in Buddhism. In fact, indications are that Buddhism was still not firmly implanted in Silla society since, despite Chihye's obvious devotion to her vocation and the sincerity of her efforts, the people had such little faith in Buddhism that they were unwilling to donate sufficient funds to cover the repair of the shrine. By assisting Chihye in raising the money, the divine mother was indirectly supporting the Buddhist religion as well. This suggests that Buddhism was dependent

on the assistance of indigenous deities during this period. And it is probably not far from the truth to assume that this was typical of the association between indigenous Silla religion and the newly imported tradition of Buddhism during the latter-sixth and early-seventh centuries.

Next I would like to turn to the entry, "Hyet'ong Subdues a Dragon" and will excerpt from it the section that describes the relationship between Buddhism and the indigenous spirits.

A princess of T'ang Emperor Kao-tsung fell ill. He sought the help of the Tripiṭaka Master (Subhākarasiṃha). The Tripiṭaka Master recommended Hyet'ong to serve on his behalf. Hyet'ong received his instructions, and in a separate room placed one *tu* (peck) of white beans in a silver vessel. They transmuted into divine soldiers clad in white armor, who battled in an effort to expel [the dragon] but were finally defeated. Hyet'ong next placed one *tu* of black beans into a golden vessel. They transmuted into divine soldiers clad in black armor. Hyet'ong ordered both troops of soldiers into battle to drive out the dragon. Suddenly the flood-dragon fled from the princess' body and the illness was cured.

The dragon resented being expelled by Hyet'ong and came to Muning Forest in the mother country [of Silla]. There he went on a killing spree, and became increasingly venomous. At that time Chŏng Kong went as an envoy to T'ang, where he met Hyet'ong and told him, "The venomous dragon that the Master drove out has come to Silla where he is wreaking havoc. Quickly go and drive him out." Hyet'ong then accompanied Chŏng back to Silla in the second year of the Lin-te era (665), cyclical *ŭlch'uk*, where he again expelled it. . . .

[In the first year of King Hyoso's reign (692)], his princess suddenly fell ill and Hyet'ong was summoned to treat her. The disease was cured and, ecstatic, the king . . . appointed Hyet'ong National Master. . . .

The dragon then moved to Mt. Kijang and became a

bear spirit.[53]   He became increasingly ferocious, greatly disturbing the local populace. Hyet'ong entered the mountain, admonished the dragon, and gave him the precept against killing.   The spirit's mayhem then came to an end.[54]

It is probably an overstatement to call the bear/dragon of this legend an indigenous Silla spirit, since it came originally from China.   But the dragon's mainland origins suggest that the Buddhist monks who first told this story were the ones who transmitted the Chinese dragon cult to Silla.   There, the monks invested local spirits, like the bear, with the power and prestige of Chinese deities, enriching the indigenous religion of the Silla people in the process.   We thus see that Buddhist monks did not merely disseminate the teachings of their own religion, but were the conduits through which many aspects of Chinese culture entered the Korean peninsula.

It was of course only natural that the principal efforts of the Buddhist missionaries were with the transmission of Buddhist doctrines and rituals to Silla.   However it is inevitable that their Silla contemporaries received these new teachings into their native cultural and religious milieu, thus treating Buddhism as a form of indigenous belief.   If such reinterpretations transpired in even the pristine orthodoxy of Buddhism, then how much more common must it have been if that Buddhism had already been suffused with Chinese folk beliefs even before it was introduced to Silla?   Stories about rivalries between local spirits and Buddhist monks—which is what the legend of Hyet'ong and the dragon portrays—may have been intentionally selected by Silla missionaries, for they would have graphically illustrated the superiority of Buddhism over autochthonous cults.   If this scenario proves correct, then the Silla people who heard this legend would, more often than not, have already noticed the similarities between autochthonous Chinese deities and their own spirits even before they became aware of the superiority of Buddhism.   By the same token, the Silla monks who learned of these legends in China would inevitably have identified these local Chinese deities with those in their own native beliefs. This characterization would have become still more pronounced in the minds of the Silla audience who subsequently heard them tell the legends. It was thus assured that most of the explicitly Chinese features in the legend would have been expurgated by the time it became common lore to the Sillan people.

The interchange between autochthonous beliefs in different regions of Asia is itself an extremely important research topic, which deserves better than the sweeping oversimplifications dictated here by limitations of space. It does not however seem entirely implausible to speculate, as I have above, that the Chinese dragon appearing in the legend of Hyet'ong projects more Silla, rather than T'ang, features. I do not deny of course that the T'ang legends would have exerted important influence over the development of the Silla versions of such tales. One such example is found in the story of Hyet'ong curing the illness of the Chinese princess, which exemplified the efficacy of Buddhism in the healing arts. The fact that the patients in such tales are always princesses and never princes is a uniquely Chinese topos, otherwise unknown in Korea. This story also derives in part from the lineage of Tantric Buddhism; hence, when a baleful spirit possesses a patient, the illness is cured through the thaumaturgic technologies in which that branch of Buddhism specializes. This is the case in the stories of both the T'ang and Silla princesses, illustrating the influence of Chinese legends on Korean literature.

In contrast to the above, the transformation of the dragon into a bear is a distinctly Silla topos, which has no Chinese antecedent. The T'ang dragon is said to have taken over the princess' body, and never showed itself. The dragon subsequently transformed into a bear spirit at Mt. Kijang, where he wreaked havoc throughout the countryside. More precisely, we might say that the dragon entered Mt. Kijang and possessed the bear, who was the mountain god there, and engaged in spiteful acts. The founder of the Koguryŏ kingdom, King Tongmyŏng (r. 37-20 B.C.), was conceived at Bear Spirit

Mountain by a princess of the dragon-king,[55] and a bear who possesses a woman is also said to have been the mother of Tan'gun.[56] Among the folk beliefs of southern Korea, numerous locales include in their place-names the logograph for "bear" (*ung*), as for example Ungjin (Bear Crossing). Bears are also commonly regarded as totemic deities in those regions. We may thus interpret the Hyet'ong legend as describing the assimilation of a T'ang Chinese dragon deity into the local bear cults that abound in southern Korea. It is hard to accept that this bear deity was originally a baleful spirit; rather he seems to have transformed into a demonic force after being possessed by the sinitic dragon. The implication here is that when Tantric Buddhism was introduced to Silla, its missionaries intentionally invested these spirits with wrathful qualities they did not originally possess, so as to impress the people when those spirits were defeated by superior Buddhist technology. The inevitable victory of Buddhism would then reveal the new religion's vast superiority to the local cults.

Finally, let us consider one last aspect of this legend: the docility of the bear spirit after the dragon who had possessed him received the Buddhist precept against killing. Told in the context of religious hagiography, it of course is unnecessary to look for any historical fact in this claim that a dragon received the Buddhist precepts. At the very least, however, the legend includes nothing of the Japanese Buddhist theory of *honji suijaku* (manifestation from the original state), in which Buddhas and bodhisattvas were claimed to have reincarnated as Shinto gods, as a means of reconciling the alien Buddhist pantheon with indigenous Shinto deities. Japanese Buddhists in the eighth century claimed that the Shinto *kami* were suffering from extreme hardship and sought refuge in Buddhism. The mention of the dragon's receiving the precepts may testify to his conversion to Buddhism; however, it would still have been the foreign dragon who converted, not the indigenous bear spirit. Even though the legend does not say so, if the bear were assumed to have converted also, that need not imply Buddhism's superiority to local beliefs; rather, it could still be taken as testimony only to Hyet'ong's thaumaturgic prowess. But since the legend includes no such reference, however, the best interpretation is that it was the dragon alone that converted to Buddhism, and was compelled thereby to end his possession of the bear. The relationship between Buddhism and the local bear spirit is thus extremely tenuous throughout this legend.

The *Samguk yusa* was compiled by the monk Iryŏn (1206-1289), and it is to be expected that the stories he compiles betray a Buddhist bias. This is why indigenous spirits like demons and bears are usually presented as baleful. This representation was not intended to provide a complete picture of these deities; they were simply given the role required by the narrative. It is for this reason that it is dangerous to speculate on the relationship between local beliefs and contemporary Buddhism based solely on such legends. If we compensate for this narrative device, then we cannot construe these legends as advocating the supremacy of Buddhism over the indigenous religion. Neither can we assume that the local deities appearing in these legends were inferior religiously to Buddhism, as was the case with the Japanese *kami*. Rather, indigenous religion and Buddhism were distinct and separate in the Korean case, and did not need to compete with one another. There may be a few elements in these Korean legends that could have paved the way for the evolution of theories in which indigenous spirits were identified with Buddhist deities, as happened in Japan. But whatever such elements are found in Korean legends were limited: first, the shamanesses who acted on behalf of local spirits or performed priestly functions in the indigenous religion were replaced by Buddhist clergy; second, these indigenous deities were ascribed a wrathful aspect they did not originally have.

The legend of the Korean Tantric specialist Milbon (fl. ca. mid-seventh century) contrasts strikingly with the story of Hyet'ong, who is traditionally presumed to have flourished some three to four decades after Milbon.[57] In the legend of Milbon, a Buddhist monk is called in to exorcise a host of demons who were tormenting a young boy, but the demons strike the monk over the head with iron clubs, killing him. The

Tantric master Milbon, who specialized in the art of spells, is summoned and succeeds in driving them away. The legend in essence describes a competition between Milbon's spells and indigenous spirits; it is neither a confrontation between Buddhism and indigenous religion, nor does it advocate that either is superior. The legend instead testifies to the superiority of the thaumaturgic skills learned through Tantric practices, but against the backdrop of the indigenous religion.[58]

In contrast, the legend of Hyet'ong, while generally the same, adds specific Buddhist elements to the tale, such as the dragon's acceptance of the precept against killing. These imply the widening diffusion of Buddhist practices in Silla. Hyet'ong's story is also different from Milbon's in that it does not imply the supremacy of Buddhism over such Silla totemic spirits as the bear; it instead describes Buddhism's subjugation of an indigenous Chinese deity (the dragon), an element that is missing entirely in the legend of Milbon. Because Hyet'ong is presumed to postdate Milbon, the differences in these two stories could suggest that indigenous religious cults and Buddhism eventually reached an accommodation in Silla, which allowed both to coexist with one another.

Summation

Both Korea and Japan were strongly attracted to Chinese culture and made active efforts to introduce it into their countries. The process by which sinitic civilization was received in the kingdoms of Koguryŏ and Paekche was, however, quite different from that seen in Silla and Japan. Koguryŏ had direct contacts with the sources of Chinese political power on the Asian mainland, while Paekche had active international exchanges with China and acted as the principal agent of cultural transmission in East Asia. Because of their less provincial, more cosmopolitan outlooks, Koguryŏ and Paekche accepted Buddhism much earlier than did Silla and Japan: in the latter half of the fourth century for the former kingdoms, the early to mid-sixth century for the latter. But despite the fact that Silla and Japan both embraced Buddhism around the same time, there were considerable variations in the way that religion was received, especially as regards the relationship that developed between Buddhism and indigenous beliefs. While much research has already been done concerning this relationship, most of it has focused on Buddhism, not on indigenous religions, and has shown little concern for the modification in native culture that contact with Buddhism may have engendered. In fact, as this article has attempted to demonstrate, the influence of Buddhism on indigenous northeast Asian societies was pervasive. Buddhism was not just abstract philosophical ideas and religious doctrines. Its vast material culture helped to mature many civilizing influences on Korea and Japan, such as the diffusion of vernacular writing systems, which in turn catalyzed massive changes in the structure of these native societies. Such innovations were often more important that the changes Buddhist dogma fostered in the indigenous *Weltanschauung*. Buddhism's effect on native religion was also generally positive. By introducing local spirit-cults into its own literature, Buddhism was able to disseminate its beliefs throughout these newly sinified territories by investing them with a national identity. In this wise, indigenous religion was extricated from its limited role as local cultic practice, allowing it to exert a wider influence over the entire national culture.

In this essay I have been able to touch upon only a few of the many ways in which Buddhism affected the Koreans and Japanese. I have been forced to ignore many related issues, such as the relationship between the ruler and Buddhism,[59] which would reveal much about the way in which the acceptance of the alien religion changed indigenous culture. We know, for example, that during the early period of Buddhism in Silla many kings took Buddhist names: e.g. King Pŏphŭng (Promoting the Dharma). By contrast, during the same period in Japan, there were no rulers with Buddhist names. How this contrast should be interpreted remains an open issue.

The reception of Buddhism prompted tremendous changes in indigenous Korean culture. We have observed these transformations from the standpoint of Buddhist history, taking up only those aspects that were related to religious belief. While the present article has been merely a preliminary attempt to sketch out the larger issues involved, we have raised the following points. The sheer breadth of Buddhist culture brought about massive alterations in the societies that received it. That such changes occurred does not mean that the indigenous cultures passively allowed themselves to be replaced completely by Buddhist culture. It was much more common that Buddhism instead stimulated enormous internal evolution within the autochthonous cultures themselves, prompting them to expand and grow in new and independent ways. Typically, past research has rigorously separated indigenous, Confucian, and Buddhist culture, and treated their origin and development as being completely distinct from one another. Even in areas where symbiotic influence was obvious, scholars intentionally focused on only one of the traditions, ignoring completely possible complementarities between the three. This essay will hopefully show the fallacy of such a compartmentalized approach.

We have shown that the reception of Buddhism stimulated the acceptance of Confucian culture, including perhaps its most representative feature: its unique writing system. Until Buddhism's arrival, Confucian culture was accepted only by the ruling elite, but spurred by the openness of Buddhism, a wider stratum of society embraced it. As a result, the Koreanization of Confucian culture occurred. Next, we saw that Buddhist monks may have introduced the Chinese belief in dragons to Korea, where it evolved in unique ways through its interaction with indigenous mountain and ursine spirits. As another aspect of the interaction that occurred between Buddhism and indigenous religion, we discussed the Silla propensity to assume that Buddhist images and eminent monks advented from heaven. This is hardly a typical Buddhist view and shows that Buddhism was understood within the framework of indigenous beliefs even one century after its reception in Silla. Finally, the relationship between baleful spirits and Buddhist monks was covered. We tried to show that there was nothing innate that determined which of the two prevailed in direct competitions, but was instead a matter of thaumaturgic prowess. In this particular instance, religion meant little more than thaumaturgy, and had virtually nothing to do with sophisticated doctrines or philosophies. Ultimately, the Koreans of the Three Kingdoms period seem never to have regarded the local spirits as being subordinate to Buddhism, as occurred in Japan. Instead Buddhism and indigenous cults existed in mutual coexistence, enriching in the process not only each other, but the entire religious life of the Korean people.

NOTES

* This is an edited translation of Prof. Inoue Hideo's "Chōsen ni okeru bukkyō juyō to shinkan nen" [The Reception of Buddhism in Korea and the Conception of Spirits] which appeared in *Nihon bunka kenkyūsho kenkyū hōkoku* [Research bulletin of the Japanese Cultural Research Center] 13 (1977), pp. 45-69. I have made the following modifications in the presentation of the article. Where Inoue gives Japanese renderings of passages from East Asian historical collections, I translate instead from the original literary Chinese. Most of Inoue's annotation consists of the passages from primary materials that he discusses in the main body of the article; I cite the precise references to those materials, and, in addition, provide precise references to the passing allusions to additional sources Inoue frequently makes. Finally, I have taken the liberty of giving additional references to the secondary literature where I felt they might aid the interested reader. All of Inoue's own notes are indicated as such in brackets. All references to the Histories are to the *Po-na pen erh-shih-ssu shih* edition (Shanghai, 1930-1937; reprint ed., Taipei, 1965), cited by *chüan* and page number(s). I would like to thank William McCullough for his valuable comments on portions of an earlier draft of this translation.

1. See Suematsu Yasukazu, "Shiragi bukkyō denrai densetsukō" (On transmission-legends concerning the transmission of Buddhism to Silla), in *Shiragi-shi no shomondai* [Issues in Silla History] (Tokyo: Tōyō bunko, 1954), pp. 207-234. [Author's note.] Cf. also the

discussion in the Introduction to the translator's *The Korean Approach to Zen: The Collected Works of Chinul* (Honolulu: University of Hawaii Press), pp. 72-73, n. 11, for discussion of additional evidence raised by Korean scholars that Koreans knew of Buddhism prior to the official dates of introduction. G. Renondeau ("La date de l'introduction du bouddhisme au Japon," *T'oung Pao* 47 [1959], pp. 16-29) proposes the date of 538 for the introduction of Buddhism from Paekche to Japan.

2. Mishina Akihide, "Chōsen ni okeru bukkyō to minzoku shinkō: Bukkyō no juyō keitai" (Buddhism and Folk beliefs in Korea: the Reception of Buddhism), *Bukkyō shigaku* (Buddhist Historical Studies) 4-1 (1954). Kim T'aekkyu, "Silla oyobi Nihon kodai no shinbutsu-shūgō ni tsuite" (The Integration of Spirits and Buddhas in Silla and Japan during Ancient Times), in *Shiragi to Asuka, Hakuhō no bukkyō bunka* (Silla and the Buddhist culture of Asuka and Hakuhō), ed. Tamura Enchō and Hong Sunch'ang (Tokyō: Yoshikawa kōbunkan, 1975). [Author's note.] For an English-language treatment of the Japanese context, see Alicia Matsunaga, *The Buddhist Philosophy of Assimilation* (Tokyo: Sophia University Press, 1969).

3. *Liang-shu* 54, p. 31a-b; see also *Liang-shu* 3, pp. 16b (Chung-ta-t'ung, sixth year), 24a (Ta-t'ung, seventh year).

4. *Nan-shih* 79, p. 4b; *Nan-shih* 7, p. 10b (Ta-t'ung 7); *Samguk sagi*, ed. Shin Sŏk-ho, trans. Kim Chong-gwŏn (Seoul: Sŏnjin munhwasa, 1960), vol. 26, p. 434 (Korean translation), p. 437 (Sino-Korean text) ("Paekche pon'gi", King Sŏng, nineteenth year *Samguk sagi*).

5. *Samguk sagi* 18, p. 303, p. 312 ("Koguryŏ pon'gi," King Sosurim, second year).

6. Sakamoto Tarō, Ienaga Saburō, Inoue Mitsusada, and Ono Susumu, ed., *Nihon shoki, Nihon koten bungaku taikei* (Collection of Ancient Japanese Literature), vol. 68-69 [hereafter I and II] (Tokyo: Iwanami shoten, 1965-1967); *Nihon shoki* II, vol. 19, p. 101 (Emperor Kimmei, 13th year, winter, tenth month).

7. *Nihon shoki* II, vol. 19, p. 103 (Emperor Kimmei, 13th year, winter, tenth month).

8. *Samguk sagi* 24. ("Paekche pon'gi" 2, King Kŭnch'ogo 30,

autumn, seventh month).

9. This according to the account in *Chin-shu* 9, p. 3a6-7. As Jonathan W. Best notes ("Diplomatic and Cultural Contacts between Paekche and China," *Harvard Journal of Asiatic Studies* 42 [1982], p. 453 n. 12), there is no mention in Korean sources of this title being conferred. For this title see Michael C. Rogers, *The Chronicle of Fu Chien: A Case of Exemplar History, Chinese Dynastic Histories Translations*, no. 10 (Berkeley and Los Angeles: University of California Press, 1968), pp. 228-229, n. 258, cited also in Best, *ibid.*

10. *Nihon shoki* II, vol. 19, p. 101 (Kimmei, 13th year, winter, tenth month). For a comprehensive listing of references to Korean Buddhism in Japanese sources, see Kim Yŏng-t'ae, "Ilbon sasŏ e poinŭn Han'guk pulgyo saryo" (Historical sources on Korean Buddhism found in Japanese historical documents), *Han'guk pulgyohak* [Korean Buddhist studies] 4 (1979), pp. 130-152.

11. *Sui-shu* 81, p. 14b3-4.

12. *Nihon shoki* I, vol. 10, p. 371-373 (Emperor Ojin, 15th year, eighth month, and 16th year, spring, second month).

13. For background on this type of calendrical prognostication, which was often used during the T'ang period to divine an individual's fate, see Kristofer Marinus Schipper, *L'Empereur Wou des Han dans la legende Taoiste: Han Wou-ti nei-tchouan*, Publications de l'Ecole francaise d'extreme-orient, vol. 58 (Paris, 1965), pp. 34-38.

14. *Nihon shoki* II, vol. 22, p. 179 (Empress Suiko, 10th year, winter, 10th month).

15. *Nihon shoki* II, vol. 22, p. 195 (Empress Suiko, 18th year, spring, 3rd month).

16. *Samguk yusa* 3, *T.* 2039.49.986a27-b9, citing the "Silla pon'gi" of the *Samguk sagi; Haedong kosŭngchŏn, T.* 2065.50.1017c-1018a, Peter H. Lee, trans., *Lives of Eminent Korean Monks: The Haedong Kosŏng chŏn*, Harvard-Yenching Institute Studies, vol. 25 (Cambridge, Mass.: Harvard University Press, 1969), pp. 50-51.

17. Cf. *Samguk yusa* 3, *T.* 2039.49.986b9-987a8, citing *Silla pon'gi* of the *Samguk sagi; Haedong kosŭng chŏn, T.* 2065.50.1017c-1018c, Peter Lee, trans., *Eminent Korean Monks*, pp. 50-56.

18. *Samguk yusa* 3, *T.* 1039.49.986a22.

19. *Samguk sagi* 18. p. 304, p. 312 (King Kogunggyang, ninth year, third month).

20. For the stele of King Kwanggaet'o, see *Chōsen kinseki sōran* (Collection of Korean Metal and Lithic Inscriptions), vol. 1 (Keijō (Seoul): Chōsen sōtokufu, 1919), pp. 2-6; Katsuragi Sueji, *Chōsen kinsekikō* (Korean Epigraphy) (Keijō: Osaka yagō shoten, 1935), pp. 104-115; Boleslaw Szczesniak, "The Kōtaiō Monument," *Monumenta Nipponica* 7-5 (1951), pp. 242-268, who translates the text of the inscription at pp. 255-268; for a survey of scholarship on the inscription and a different reading, see Takashi Hataka, "An interpretation of the King Kwanggaet'o Inscription," translated by V. Dixon Morris, *Korean Studies* 3 (1979), pp. 1-18. For the stelae of Silla King Chinhǔng, see *Kinseki sōran*, vol. 1, pp. 6-8; Katsuragi, *Kinsekikō*, pp. 115-122.

21. For Silla writing systems see Yi Sung-nyǒng's *Silla sidae ǔi p'yogibǒp ch'egye e kwanhan siron* (An Essay on Silla-period Writing Systems) (Seoul: T'ap ch'ulp'ansa, 1978), which provides also a methodology for reconstructing Silla toponyms and personal names; this is a reprint of his earlier article, "Silla sidae ǔi p'yongibǒp ch'egye e kwanhan siron," which appeared in *Sǒul taehakkyo nonmunjip* 2 (1955), pp. 62-166. An invaluable survey on pre-alphabetic Korean writing systems appears in Gari K. Ledyard, "The Korean Language Reform of 1446: The Origin, Background, and Early History of the Korean Alphabet" (Ph.D diss., University of California, Berkeley, 1966), pp. 21-57.

22. See *Kinseki sōran*, vol. 1, pp. 8-9; Katsuragi, *Kinsekikō*, pp. 122-129.

23. *Taesa* was the twelfth of the seventeen Silla bureaucrat ranks; see John Jamieson, "The *Samguk sagi* and the Unification Wars" (Ph.D. diss., University of California, Berkeley, 1969), p. 319.

24. For possible Korean influences on the development of the Japanese syllabaries, see Yi Sung-nyǒng, *Silla sidae ǔi p'yogibǒp ch'egye e kwanhan siron*, pp. 2-10, 103-106; and see Ledyard, "The Korean Language Reform," p. 380, n. 32. Many of the same logographs used in transcribing Korean toponyms were also employed in the *man'yogana*, which became in turn the basis for the later Japanese

syllabaries as well.

25. *Sui-shu* 81, p. 14b.

26. *Samguk sagi* 4, p. 66, p. 79 (King Chinhŭng, fourteenth year); see also *Samguk yusa* 3, *T.* 2039.49.990a24-26.

27. *Samguk yusa* 1, *T.* 2039.49.965a; see Tae-Hung Ha and Grafton K. Mintz, trans., *Samguk Yusa: Legends and History of the Three Kingdoms of Ancient Korea* (Seoul: Yonsei University Press, 1972), p. 50.

28. *Samguk sagi* 7, p. 136, p. 144 (King Munmu, twenty-first year).

29. *Samguk yusa* 2, *T.* 2039.49.972c1-6; see Ha and Mintz, p. 100.

30. *Samguk yusa* 2, *T.* 2039.49.973a21-23; see Ha and Mintz, p. 103.

31. See *Haedong kosŭng chŏn, T.* 1018c21-1019b; Peter H. Lee, trans., *Eminent Korean Monks*, pp. 58-63.

32. *P'ajinch'an* was the fourth rank of the seventeen Silla bureaucrat ranks, which was occupied only by aristocrats of "true-bone" (*chin'gol*) status; see Jamieson, "*Samguk Sagi*," p. 319.

33. *Samguk yusa* 2, *T.* 2039.49.973a24-b11; Ha and Mintz, pp. 104-105.

34. Inoue cites in the main body of his text the following personal names and toponyms that contain the logograph for dragon (Jpn. *tatsu;* Sino-jpn. *ryō*): Furuichi no kohori no hito fumi no obitokaryō (*Nihon shoki* I, vol. 14, p. 485 [Yŭryaku, month year, seventh month]); Funa no fubitotatsu (*Nihon shoki* II, vol. 22, p. 193 [Suiko, seventeenth year, fourth month]); Noto no omimamutatsu (*Nihon shoki* II, vol. 26, p. 343 [Saimei, sixth year, vol. 27, p. 369 [Tenchi, seventh year, second month]); Tatsuta no kazakami; Hinose tatsuta no kami; Tatsutayama. I have moved this section of the text to the notes to preserve the flow of the narrative.

35. *Nihon shoki* I, vol. 2, p. 167. In the same section (pp. 165-167), Toyotama-bime's husband, Hikohoho-demi no Mikoto, is said to have spent three years in the sea-palace of the dragon king after his marriage to Toyotama-bime.

36. See *Nihon shoki*, vol. 2, pp. 173 and 179; a *hiro* (Ch. *hsün*) was a measure of eight (alt. seven) feet in length.

37. *Nihon shoki* II, vol. 25, p. 315.

38. *Nihon shoki* II, vol. 28, p. 389.

39. *Nihon shoki* II, vol. 26, p. 327.

40. Kuroita Katsumi, ed., *Shoki nihongi* (Supplementary Records of Japan), vol. 1, Kokushi taikei (Outline of National History), vol. 2 (Tokyo: Yoshikawa kōbunkan, 1935), pp. 5-6 (Emperor Mombu, 4th year, 3rd month, 10th day [4 April 700]).

41. Chungnyŏng is located on the border of present-day Yŏngju-kun in North Kyŏngsang Province and Tangyang-kun in North Ch'ungch'ŏng Province. [Author's note.]

42. Located on Mt. Sogŭmgang in North Kyŏngsang Province, near Kyŏngju; it was originally constructed in commemoration of a visit of the Silla King Pŏphŭng to the site in 528. See Yang Sŏng-ji and No Sa-jin, *Sinjŭng tongguk yŏji sŭngnam* (Revised Survey of Korean Geography) (edition reprinted by Tongguk munhwasain, 1958), vol. 21, pp. 19a-20a.

43. *Samguk yusa* 3, *T.* 1039.49.991b21-29; Ha and Mintz, pp. 212-213.

44. *Karak kukki* (Records of the Karak kingdom), in *Samguk yusa* 2, *T.* 1039.49.991b21-c10; Ha and Mintz, pp. 158-159. The eggs eventually hatched into six boys, the eldest of whom was crowned as King Suro, the founder of the Karak kingdom; the other five became rulers of the five neighboring Kaya tribes.

45. Yi Pyŏng-do (trans., *Samguk sagi* [Seoul: Uryu munhwasa, 1977], p. 615) surmises that Middle Peak may be Mt. Hyŏllye (present-day, Mr. Orye in Ch'ŏngdo-kun), the central-most of the three major mountains of Silla.

46. Yi Pyŏng-do (trans., *Samguk sagi*, p. 616) suggests that Mt. Inbak may have been in the vicinity of the Silla capital of Kyŏngju.

47. *Samguk sagi* 42, pp. 634-35, p. 643. In preparing my translation, I have benefitted from John Jamieson's rendering of the entire

biography, which appeared in his "Biography in the *Samguk Sagi* (Paper delivered at the Conference on the Nature and Function of Biography in the Korean Tradition, University of California, Berkeley, 9-11 December, 1983). The translation is, however, my own. See also Frits Vos, "Kim Yusin, Personlichkeit und Mythos: Ein Betrag zur Kenntnis der altkoreanischen Geschichte," *Oriens Extremus* 1 (1954), pp. 29-70, and 2 (1955), pp. 210-236. For the identifications of the Chinese asterisms, see Edward H. Schafer, *Pacing the Void: T'ang Approaches to the Stars* (Berkeley and Los Angeles: University of California Press, 1977), p. 61.

48. For the place of mountains in Asian autochthonous religion, see, among many possible references, H. G. Quaritch Wales, "The Sacred Mountain in the Old Asiatic Religion," *Journal of the Royal Asiatic Society* (1953), pp. 23-30; Michel Soymie, "Le Lo-feou chan: Etude de geographie religieuse," *Bulletin de l'ecole francaise d'extreme-orient* 48-1 (1956), pp. 1-139; Michael Sullivan, "The Magic Mountain," *Asiatic Review* 50 (1955), pp. 300-310; Yi Ki-yŏng (Rhi Ki-yong), "Silla-in ŭi san'ak sungbae" (Worship of Mountain Peaks by the Silla People), in his *Han'guk pulgyo yŏn'gu* (Studies in Korean Buddhism) (Seoul: Han'guk pulgyo yŏn'guwŏn, 1982), pp. 507-509. For star worship, see Ching-lang Hou, "The Chinese belief in Baleful Stars," in *Facets of Taoism: Essays in Chinese Religion*, edited by Holmes Welch and Anna Seidel, pp. 193-228 (New Haven: Yale University Press, 1979); Edward Schafer, *Pacing the Void*, passim.

49. *Samguk yusa* 4, *T.* 2039.49.1005c12-19; Ha and Mintz, p. 303. For python cults in China, see Miyakawa Hisayuki, "Local Cults around Mount Lu at the Time of Sun en's Rebellion," in *Facets of Taoism*, pp. 96-99.

50. *Samguk yusa* 3, *T.* 2039.49.987c20-20; Ha and Mintz, p. 189.

51. *Samguk yusa* 5, *T.* 2039.49.1011c12-22; Ha and Mintz, p. 340-341. For the Chŏmch'al divination rite, see Whalen Lai, "The *Chan-ch'a Ching:* Faith and Magic in Medieval China," in *Buddhist Apocryphal Literature*, edited by Robert Buswell (Berkeley: Berkeley Buddhist Studies Series, forthcoming); Kim Yŏng-t'ae, "Silla ŭi Chŏmch'al pŏphoe wa Chinp'yo ŭi kyobŏp yŏn'gu, *Pulgyohakpo*, Vol. 9, 1972.

52. See *Samguk yusa* 5, *T.* 2039.49.1012a5-13.

53. During the Silla, Kijang prefecture corresponded to the present South Kyŏngsang Province, Tongnae-kun, Kijang-myŏn; Mt. Kijang may have been the major mountain of this prefecture. [Author's note.]

54. *Samguk yusa* 5, *T.* 2039.49.1010c24-1010a2, a15-16, 18-19. Ha and Mintz, pp. 334-336.

55. *Samguk yusa* 1, *T.* 2039.49.963c17-18.

56. *Samguk yusa* 1, *T.* 2039.49.962a4-7.

57. The legend of Milbon relates events that occurred in the mid-seventh century during the reign of the Queen Sŏndŏk, while the story of Hyet'ong takes place at the end of the seventh century during the reigns of the kings Sinmun and Hyoso—a three-to-four decade difference. Since these are legendary accounts, we cannot regard these dates as being historically accurate, but we will tacitly accept them in order to compare the two stories. [This part of the text was moved to the notes.]

58. For the legend of Milbon, see *Samguk yusa*, *T.* 2039.49.1010a-b; Ha and Mintz, pp. 331-333.

59. For the relationship between Buddhism and the state in Korea, and the national-protection ideology of Mahāyāna Buddhism, see Yi Ki-baek (Lee Ki-baek), "Samguk sidae pulgyo chŏllae wa kŭ sahoejŏk sŏnggyŏk" (The Introduction of Buddhism during the Three Kingdoms Period and Its Social Character), *Yŏksa hakpo* (Journal of History) 6 (1954), pp. 128-205, and especially pp. 146ff. For the close relationship between Buddhism and the state in Korea: Kim Tong-hwa, *Pulgyo ŭi hoguk sasang* (The National Protection Ideology of Buddhism) (Seoul: Pulgyo sinmunsa, 1976); Yi Ki-yŏng (Rhi Ki-yong), "*Inwang panya-kyŏng* kwa hoguk pulgyo: kŭ ponjil kwa yŏksajŏk chŏn'gae" (The Sūtra of Benevolent Kings and National Protection Buddhism: Its Sources and Historical Development), in his *Han'guk pulgyo Yŏn'gu*, pp. 163-193; Matsunaga Yukei, "Gokoku shisō no kigen" (The Origin of National Protection Ideology), *Indogaku bukkyōgaku kenkyū* (Journal of Indian and Buddhist Studies) 15-1 (1966), pp. 69-78; Buswell, *Korean Approach*, pp. 1-2, and p. 71, n. 1.

The Buddhist Thought
of the Koguryŏ

by Kim Tong-hwa

Buddhism it is said was first introduced into the Koguryŏ by Sundo in 372; but what kind of Buddhism was it? The answer to this question is not readily apparent. We are told, in various sources, that Sundo brought Buddhist sūtras and images; again, we do not know of what kind they were—even though this information would be invaluable in understanding the earliest phase of Koguryŏ Buddhism. We must, therefore, rely on information provided in later sources. Although his source of information is not given by Kakhun, author of the *Haedong kosŭngchŏn* (1215), he says concerning the introduction by Sundo:

> The master, arriving in a foreign country (Koguryŏ), transmitted the benevolent lamp (Buddhism) of the Western region [as if] hanging the sun of wisdom in the Eastern sky (Koguryŏ). He taught by means of cause and effect, and enticed [people into the religion] by [promising the avoidance of] disaster and [the attaining of] fortune.[1]

This information suggests to us the actual situation pertaining in Koguryŏ at this time. Sundo put his efforts into propagating a teaching of karmic retribution, rather than into the teaching of profound philosophical doctrines; it is apparent, therefore, that a highly developed philosophical tradition had yet to appear in Koguryŏ. Notwithstanding, his influence was profound, and by teaching people he gradually cultivated their faith in Buddhism. However, the people of the Koguryŏ were still philosophically unsophisticated, and did not have a proper understanding of the teachings. Even though Sundo's learning was deep and his understanding was extensive, he was not able to transmit its finer points.

Kakhun also discussed the Buddhism which was introduced by Tamsi:

> Towards the end of the reign of T'ai-yuan of the Eastern Chin, the master Pai-tsu (Tan-shih; Kor. Tamsi) went to Liao-tung (at that time part of Koguryŏ) for the purpose of propogating the Faith; he carried with him a large number of sūtras and *Vinaya* texts. Teaching according to the capacity of people, he instructed them about the Three Vehicles, and he encouraged them to take refuge and observe the precepts. For this reason, the *Liang kao-seng-chuan* refers to this as the first introduction of the Dharma into Koguryŏ. . . . It was 25 years after the first transmission of the sūtras, which were sent to the kingdom by Fu-chien of the Former Ch'in.[2]

In this record the names of the sūtras and *Vinaya*s were not recorded; the account by Kakhun only mentions that they were sūtras and *Vinaya*s. He also said that in teaching to the common people, Tamsi taught by means of the three vehicles (i.e., the *Prajñāpāramitā*) and attempted to improve them morally by having them take refuge and observe the precepts. Here "taking refuge" means to take refuge in the three Jewels, and "observe the precepts" refers to the five precepts. Therefore, the contents of the teachings by Sundo and Tamsi are similar in that they were both relatively simple doctrines, easily understood by their audience. In general, they belong to Hīnayāna Buddhism.

However, the teaching of the three vehicles, which were also included in the teachings of Tamsi, has a different nature from the teaching of Sundo or the other teachings of Tamsi. The Three Vehicles means the vehicles of the śrāvakas, pratyeka-buddhas and bodhisattvas; this is an important Mahāyāna doctrine found in the *Lotus Sūtra*. Of the three, the former two may not be in conflict with the Hīnayānist teachings of Sundo and Tamsi in general. But, the third one, the *Bodhisattvayāna*, is the final achievement of Mahāyāna. Therefore, we can see here that even though the general substance of the teachings in this earliest period were Hīnayāna, some Mahāyāna elements were already present.

Tsung-mi of the T'ang (born in 780) classified the teaching of the Buddha into the five levels according to the profundity of doctrine:

(1.) The teaching of cause and effect for men and gods

(2.) The Hīnayāna

(3.) The Mahāyāna teaching of the characteristic of the dharma

(4.) The Mahāyāna teaching of the destruction of characteristics of the dharmas

(5.) The teaching of manifesting the nature of the One Vehicle[3]

According to Tsung-mi's classification the teaching of Sundo would belong to the first type and that of Tamsi would belong to the second type. But the first and second teachings are largely the same in that they are both the teaching of the Hīnayāna.

These two accounts suggest to us the composition of the Buddhist teachings introduced into Koguryŏ. However, these records should be supported by corroborating evidence, because the sources used by Kakhun are unknown, and because of the fact that he wrote his account 842 years after the introduction of Buddhism into Korea. Another source of information can be found in the Buddhism of the Former Ch'in (of the Six Dynasties) from whence Buddhism was introduced into the Koguryŏ. That is, we should investigate the characteristics of the Buddhism popular in the Ch'in during the reign of Fu-chien; it was at this time that Sundo must have brought the Buddhist teachings popular in that state to Koguryŏ.

In China the first sūtra said to have been translated was a
Hīnayāna text called the *Forty-two Section Sūtra*, produced
by the monks Kāśyapamātanga and Dharmakara. This was
followed by the work of An Shih-kao who made Chinese translations of Hīnayāna sūtras and śāstras. After this initial phase
the translations were for the most part limited to Mahāyāna
texts. Thus, most of the important Mahāyāna materials came
into China after the time of Fo-tu-ch'ung and Tao-an. During
the reign of King Fu Chien of the Ch'in, Mahāyāna thought
in the main was already well known, although it is doubtful that
its profound philosophical teaching and high religious ideals
were properly understood. One reason for believing that there
was a limited comprehension of the more subtle thought of
Mahāyāna is the fact that so few commentaries had been written
by the Chinese. The lack of commentaries which could give
an explanation of the ideas included in the primary scripture
of the Buddhists, leads to the conclusion that even among the
best informed monks, there was not a full understanding of
Mahāyāna. As evidence for this view of the situation, we look
at what the biography of Tao-an says on this point:

> It has already been a long time since the first trans-
> lation of Buddhist texts appeared. But the old translations
> often have mis-translations; therefore some of them had
> to be stored away and were not widely distributed. Hence,
> everytime Tao-an lectured, he only gave general ideas and
> merely went through a text reciting a few lines from the
> beginning, the middle and the end.[4]

Tao-an did this because the common people did not understand the doctrine in any depth and even among monks and
aristocratic laymen, the Hīnayāna practices described in the
early translations were dominant. All of the population, from
king to commoners, generally understood Buddhism in terms
of its magic and precepts of behaviour. This was the situation
in the Ch'in period, at the time when Buddhism came to Koguryŏ. We can then surmise that the texts being brought at

that time were Mahāyāna, but it is difficult to believe that the thought presented in these documents could have been understood by the people of Koguryŏ, any more than it was in Ch'in. The remarks of Kakhun quoted above, even though from a much later time, would appear to have some validity. Koguryŏ Buddhism must have reflected the same basic situation as that of Tao-an's time, that is the presence of Mahāyāna texts while practice was limited to such things as the precepts and magic.

Buddhist Studies in the Later Period

Buddhism existed in Koguryŏ for nearly three centuries before the fall of the dynasty in 668. While we have very few sources for the study of the development of the tradition, there are some records that can be of use to us.

Ninety-two years before the end of the Koguryŏ kingdom, we know of a monk named Uiyŏn, who had entered the monastic life as a child. We have no information about his original family nor his subsequent career as a monk. He was strict in the observance of the rules of the *Vinaya* and possessed profound wisdom and a broad understanding which included Confucian teachings. Because of his learning he was well respected by monks and laity and was active in propagating the Dharma. While his determination was strong, he felt frustrated that he was unable to develop his understanding to its fullest. At that time an official named Wang Ko-dŏk, was devoted to Buddhism and revered the teachings of Mahāyāna and wished to spread it. He learned of a Chinese monk, Fa-shang of the Southern Ch'i, who lived in great virtue in the Ting-kuo Monastery. Wang was at work on a history of the major events in Buddhism and he dispatched Uiyŏn to China to learn more about these matters. He wanted to know for example: (1) how many years had passed since the nirvāṇa of Śākyamuni Buddha (2) how many years had Buddhism existed in India before it came to China (3) who ruled China and in what year of his reign did Buddhism arrive (4) which emperor was first converted to Buddhism and how many years have elapsed since then (5) who were the authors of the *Shih-ti* (*Daśabhumi*), *Ta chih-tu lun, Chih-t'i lun* and the *Ching-kang pan-jo lun*, what were the circumstances of their composition, what magical powers did they possess and how had they been transmitted?[5]

It was in the eighteenth year of King P'yŏngwŏn (576) that the official Wang Ko-dŏk sent Uiyŏn. The record of the questions which were asked indicates the level of understanding of Buddhist thought at the time. One of the surprising aspects of the officials questionings is the lack of knowledge about historical details concerning Buddhism, even though the tradition had been in Koguryŏ for two centuries. This suggests that the tradition of thaumaturgic Buddhism was still dominant at that time.

Fa-shang (495-580) of Yeh was the ordinand and disciple of Hui-kuang (486-537) the founder of the Ti-lun school and was, in turn, the teacher of Ching-Ying Hui-yuan. His reputation regarding his insights and level of practice caused him to be in demand as a teacher and so he gave lectures on the *Daśabhūmi*, *Ch'ih-ti* (*Dharaṇīmdhara?*), *Lankāvatāra, Nirvāṇa*, and wrote the *Ti-lun-shu*. Later, he went to Yeh and became a *t'ong shuai* for the Northern Wei and Ch'i and was responsible for maintaining the monk registry; he also had around fifty *shih-yuan* under him, and had overall responsibility for more than two million monks and nuns. He worked there for more than forty years. During this time he wrote the following works: the *Tseng-i-shu-fa* (40 volumes), the *Ta-cheng-i-chang* (6 volumes), the *Fa-hsing-lun* (2 volumes), and the *Chung-ching-lu* (91 volumes). It was during his stay in Yeh that Uiyŏn went to study under him. We know that Fa-shang was an eminent scholar-monk in the Ti-lun school, which was popularly studied in contemporary Buddhist circles; this must, naturally, also have become the central concern of Uiyŏn's scholarship. The essence of the Ti-lun School is their explanation of the *ālayavijñāna;* their aim was to gain an enlightened understanding of it.

It is important to take note of the fact that Wang wanted to know the origin of the four texts mentioned above in order to understand popular Buddhist thought at the time; even though a large number of Mahāyāna sūtras were known, he mentioned, in particular, some important Mahāyāna śāstras which undoubtedly were of great interest to contemporary scholars in Koguryŏ. The *Shih-ti lun* was the most important text of the Ti-lun school; the *Ta chih-tu lun* was the basic text of the Ssu-lun School and the same time expressed the fundamental thought of the San-lun School; the *Ch'ih-ti lun* is another translation of the *Pu-sa ti* from the *Yogācārabhūmi* and discussed *bodhisattvaśīla*. The *Chin-kang pan-juo lun* is a treatise by Vasubandhu on the *Chin-kang pan-juo ching*. Wang's interest in these texts suggests that the study of Buddhist thought had already turned towards theoretical studies. Unfortunately we have no way to determining what the scholarly works produced in Koguryŏ were like. These records show, however, that in Buddhist circles, although knowledge of the history of Buddhism was still lacking, they were already beginning to turn towards theoretical studies.

Interest in the Study of the San-lun School

When we examine the scholarly activities of Koguryŏ monks in foreign countries, we see that eighty years before the downfall of the kingdom, Koguryŏ monks had already begun to appear in China for study and in Japan for missionary work. The reason Koguryŏ monks traveled to foreign countries may be sought in the Koguryŏ policy of oppressing Buddhism and encouraging Taoism. The *Samguk sagi* tells us that the monk Podŏk moved to Paekche because of this policy. Even though Koguryŏ monks had to leave their country for others in the peninsula, they did not give up their study and many of them became well known for their excellent scholarship and great virtue.

Here we should keep in mind contemporary currents in Chinese Buddhism. In Ch'ang-an, the capital city of China, the monk Kumārajīva (A.D. 344-413) from Kashmir was absorbed in the translation of sūtras and commentaries, supported fully by King Yao-hsing of the Later Ch'in. He not only translated many texts anew correcting the mistakes of others, but also translated many texts never seen before in China. This great project, in which approximately eight hundred monks, including his famous disciples, Seng-chao and Seng-lueh, etc., were engaged, resulted in the translation of 35 works in 244 volumes and included selections from the sūtras, commentaries and *Vinaya.* Some of these translations would become the texts on which a number of Chinese Buddhist schools were founded, such as the T'ien-t'ai, Ching-t'u, San-lun and Ch'eng-shih; hence his works are considered to have a pivotal position in the history of Chinese Buddhism. Of these we should note his translations of the Three Commentaries: the *Ch'ung-kuan lun* by Nāgārjuna, the *Shih-erh-men lun* also by Nāgārjuna and the *Pai lun* by Āryadeva. These Three Commentaries, first translated by Kumārajīva, contain the essence of Nāgārjuna's philosophy. Emptiness (*k'ung*), phenomena (*chia*) and the mean (*chung*), dominant concepts in his thought, became the basis on which the San-lun School was founded. Furthermore, Kumārajīva's translation of the *Three Treatises* stimulated the development of an indigenous Chinese Buddhist philosophy.

Can any relation be established between the study of the San-lun school in China and the development of Koguryŏ Buddhism? Although we do not have any irrefutable evidence that this school was known in Koguryŏ, it seems quite possible that it was. First, we know that at the time of Uiyŏn, Nāgārjuna's *Ta chih-tu lun*, which offers a more positive presentation of his ideas than that of the *Chung-lun* and the *Shih-erh-men lun*, was known in Koguryŏ. Therefore, it is reasonable to assume that the *Three Treatises* of the San-lun school also must have been known. Second, Wŏnhyo of the Silla (617-686) wrote a work called the *Samnon chongyo* (Essential Doctrines of the *Three Treatises*).[6] Therefore, we can be sure that the *Three Treatises* were known in Wŏnhyo's time. Uiyŏn went to China just 41 years prior to Wŏnhyo's birth and very likely knew of these treatises. This is further re-inforced by the fact that the study of the *Three Treatises* by Koguryŏ monks contributed

considerably to the establishment of the San-lun School in China and Japan.
Originally, the study of the San-lun begins from the translation of the *Three Treatises* and their main sūtra, the *Ta-p'in pan-juo ching* translated by Kumārajīva. His basic ideas were from the *Prajñāpāramitā*, as can be seen in the thought of his disciples. He is said to have had 3000 of them, and the best is considered to have been Tao-Sheng. His tradition was handed down to T'an-chi, Tao-lang, Seng-ch'üan, Fa-lang, and Chi-tsang.[7] Some say that the lineage of the study of San-lun should be continued from Kumārajīva through Seng-sung, Fa-tu, Seng-lang (Kor. Sŭngnang), Seng-ch'üan, Fa-lang and Chi-tsang,[8] these seven patriarchs of the San-lun School. In this lineage the fourth one, Sŭngnang was a monk from Koguryŏ. Although the *Kao-seng-chuan* has no separate biography for him;[9] he is briefly mentioned in the biography of Fa-tu:

> Fa-tu had a disciple named Sŭngnang. After his teacher's death, he also became the abbot of the monastery on Mt. [She]. He was originally from Liao-tung (at that time Koguryŏ territory), and was by nature a scholar of extensive learning whose intelligence was profound and broad. He was able to lecture on most of the sūtras and *Vinaya*s, but the *Avataṃsaka* and the *San-lun* were his speciality. The present emperor (Wu of the Liang) deeply appreciated his great virtue and knowledge and has sent many scholars to study on Mt. [She under Sŭngnang].[10]

In the biography of his successor Seng ch'üan we find:

> At the beginning, Seng-chüan of Mt. She studied under Sŭngnang. His speciality was the *Madhyamakaśāstra*.[11]

Another account of Sŭngnang by Chi-tsang says:

> Master Nang of the Koryŏ (Koguryŏ) on Mt. She was

originally from Liao-tung. He went to Northern China and
learned the ideas of Kumārajīva. He went down the southern China and stayed in the Tsao-tang Monastery on Mt.
Chung . . . Later, Emperor Wu of the Liang, who had great
faith in the Three Jewels, hearing that the master had come
[to the South], sent ten monks including Chih-chi to study
under him.[12]

From the records above, it is evident that this monk from
Koguryŏ was the fourth patriarch of the San-lun School of
China. These records also indicate that he succeeded in the
lineage of Fa-tu. A different opinion is found in the work of a
Japanese Sanron (Ch. San-lun) scholar, Anchō (died in 841)
in his *Chūron shugi* (vol. 1):

> The Great master Nang (Sŭngnang) from Liao-tung
> of Koryŏ (Koguryŏ) travelled far to the place of the master
> T'an-ch'ing in Tun-huang and studied the *Three Treatises.*
> At the end of the Ch'i and the beginning of the Liang he
> resided on Mt. She-ling.[13]

In the account of Chi-tsang, Sŭngnang is said to have
studied the teaching of Kumārajīva and therefore it is difficult
to say that Sŭngnang received only the teaching of Fa-tu.
Furthermore, it is likely that Sŭngnang did not at first learn
San-lun in China, but had already studied it in Koguryŏ and,
after arriving in China, had visited the San-lun masters of China
and received their recognition.

It seems clear that Sŭngnang was active during the reign
of the Emperor Wu of the Liang (502-556). Even though the
study of the San-lun was established as a school in China by
Chi-tsang, its seventh patriarch, his views were greatly influenced by Sŭngnang, whose views he accepted as authoritative;
this is clearly reflected in his writings. Chi-tsang revered Sŭngnang as an un-met mentor, respectfully calling him the master
of She-shan (Mt. She) or the master Nang. Although Sŭngnang,
as a foreign monk may not have established the San-lun School

in China, he has been remembered as an authority on San-lun doctrine, who provided a scholarly basis for it and contributed greatly to its development. According to Chan-jan, the sixth patriarch of the T'ien-t'ai School in China during Sŭngnang's time, the *Satyasiddhi* teaching was studied extensively in Chiang-nan (the region south of the Yangtze), and the *Abhidharma* was especially highly regarded in Ho-pei (the region north of the Yellow River). Master Nang from Koguryŏ went to Chiang-nan during the reign of Chien-wu of the Ch'i and criticized the ideas of the *Satyasiddhi* teachers, who were unable to refute his objections. Thanks to Sŭngnang, the San-lun teaching came to be studied throughout China. The Emperor Wu of Liang gave an order to ten monks of the Chih-kuan Monastery to learn the San-lun from Sŭngnang. Of those only Seng-ch'üan achieved proficiency in its doctrine, and under him four scholar monks, Fa-lang, Hui-pu, Chih-pien and Hui-yung came to study. Insight into the situation at that time may be had from accounts where people, describing the popularity of the San-lun teaching, said of their masters:

> [There is:]
> [Fa-]lang of the Hsing-huang [Monastery] who subdued a tiger;
> [Hui-]pu of the Ch'i-hsia [Monastery] who attained understanding;
> [Chih-]pien of the Ch'ang-kan [Monastery] who was enlightened;
> [Hui-]yung of the Ch'an-chung [Monastery] whose writing was excellent.[14]

We can infer from this that Fa-tu, usually regarded as the teacher of Sŭngnang, may not have played as significant role as Sŭngnang in the popularization of the San-lun teaching. In his biography we find that Fa-tu wished to be reborn in the Pure Land, and lectured on the *Wu-liang-shou ching* (Skt. *Sukhāvatīvyūhasūtra*).[15]

So far we have seen Sŭngnang's contribution to the San-
lun tradition in China. The accounts suggest that Sŭngnang had
a profound knowledge of the teachings of the Hua-yen, the
Abhidharma and the *Satyasiddhi*, and was not limited merely
to the teachings of the San-lun. The Emperor Wu of Liang
originally took the *Satyasiddhi* and the *Abhidharma* as his
spiritual guide—both were popular in contemporary South
China. But when Sŭngnang came from the north, the emperor
discarded these Hinayanistic ideas and came to follow the doctrines of the Mahāyāna.[16] This also shows us the depth and
range of Sŭngnang's scholarship.

His philosophy is difficult to determine because his writings
are no longer extant. However, Chi-tsang, when discussing
important issues, often sought their solutions with reference
to Sŭngnang. It is through Chi-tsang's writings we may gain
insight into Sŭngnang's thought.

The Theory of the Two Truths:
Real and Conventional

The theory of the Two Truths, the Real and the Conventional, was first proposed by Nāgārjuna, the founder of the
Mādhyamika (Ch. San-lun) School in India. Nāgārjuna said:

> In the Dharma of the Buddha there are Two Truths:
> One, the Worldly Truth; Two, the Highest Truth. For the
> sake of the Worldly Truth I say there are sentient beings;
> for the sake of the Highest Truth I say there are no sentient
> beings.[17]

The Worldly Truth, here, connotes a phenomenological meaning, and the Highest Truth connotes an ontological one. This
problem is connected to the statement in the "Chapter on the
explanation of the Four Truths" in the *Chung-kuan lun:* "The
dharmas produced from causes and conditions, I say they are
identical with emptiness; their designations are merely provisional labels". Here Emptiness can be said to be the true state

of Reality, and that to which provisional labels are applied can be said to be phenomenon. Even though one may think that the Mādhyamika School held only to the theory of emptiness, this does not express the full extent of their doctrine. Observed from the standpoint of the Ultimate Truth, every phenomenal dharma, both material and mental, is merely empty, for, it is produced by causes and conditions, and thus devoid of self nature; moreover, what is devoid of own nature is, by definition, empty. However, from the standpoint of phenomenality it does not appear to be empty, but existent. Even though it seems to be existent, it is not really existent, but only provisionally existent. Therefore, the phenomenal aspect of phenomena is called the Worldly Truth, while its ontological aspect is understood as the Highest Truth.

As time went by the interpretation of these Two Truths, the Conventional and Real, became more diverse and complicated. Chi-tsang says:

> Since the time of She-ling (Sŭngnang and Seng-ch'üan) and Hsing-huang (Fa-lang) all have understood that the Two Truths were formulated for the sake of teaching. Therefore, the *Erh-ti-chang*, (Commentary on the Two Truths) by the Master on the Mountain (Seng-ch'üan) says: "The Two Truths simply express the excellent (wonderful) teaching of the Middle Path and are the ultimate explanations which exhaust words. Although the Dharma (*tao*) is neither existent nor non-existent, [we] use [the words] existent and non-existent to explain the Dharma. Although the [Fundamental] principle (*li*) is neither unitary nor dual, [we] use [the words] unitary and dual to explain Principle. Therefore, [we] know that the Two Truths were formulated for the sake of teaching."[18]

Comprehensively speaking, the reason for mentioning the Two Truths, the Real and Conventional, is that it is essential for exressing the truth perfectly. In the discussion of the truth, some say that it is existent, and some say that it is nonexistent.

Others say that it is unitary, while still others say that it is dual. However, they do not conceive the whole complete truth, but merely point out one aspect of it. Then, what is completeness or wholeness of the Truth? It is in sublating or inclusively integrating relative distinctions such as existent and non-existent, or unitary and dual. This was expressed above by Chi-tsang: "[The Two Truths] simply express the excellent teaching of the Middle Path and are the ultimate explanations which exhaust words." Therefore, the Conventional Worldly Truth and the Highest Truth are teachings used for instructing ordinary people in the principles of the Middle Path.

There is also a distinction made between three kinds of Two Truths:

Question: The existent and non-existent can [be said to] be the teaching of the Two Truths. It is also said that the existent and non-existent are non-dual. How can this also be the teaching of the Two Truths?

Answer: For this very reason the tradition of Shanmen and the teaching of Hsing-huang (Fa-lang) referred to three kinds of Two Truths. The first kind states that existence is the Worldly Truth and non-existence is the Real Truth. The second kind states that both the existent and non-existent are the Worldly Truth, and says that the neither existent nor non-existent, which is non-dual, is the Real Truth. The question that you ask merely refers to our group's second type, [namely that] the two (existent and non-existent) are the Worldly Truth, and the absence of the two are the Real Truth. I will now tell you the meaning of the third type of Two Truths. These Two Truths [are as follows:] the [description of phenomena as] existent and non-existent is dualism; the [description of phenomena as] neither existent nor non-existent is non-dualism. Both dualism and non-dualism are included in the Worldly Truth; the Real Truth is neither dualism nor non-dualism. The Two Truths can be divided into these three kinds.

Teaching the Dharma must rely on the Two Truths. All explanations do not go beyond these three types [of Two Truths].[19]

In this passage, the Shan in Shan-men indicates Mt. Sheling and the tradition of Sŭngnang. This teaching of the three kinds of Two Truths should properly be accepted as a view first proposed by Sŭngnang and developed in his lineage. In the above passage, the first and second explanations are said to be common views of the Two Truths, but the third explanation may be said to be the ultimate teaching of Sŭngnang and his followers for showing the subtle and profound meaning of the Middle Path.

Again, there is another view which maintains two kinds of Two Truths, the so-called Doctrinally Transmitted Truth (*chiao-ti*) and the Consensual Truth (*yu-ti*). This is said to be peculiar to the tradition of Shan-men. Again Chi-tsang says:

Moreover, now, with respect to the Two Truths there are two understandings. The first is, in accordance [with the capacity] of sentient beings, to say that there are Two Truths; this is the Doctrinally Transmitted Truth. The second is the Two Truths consensually held by sentient beings; this is the Consensual Truth. On the other hand, the Two Truths, Transmitted and Consensual, were not known by other lineages; only the tradition of Shan-men has this understanding.[20]

Originally, the Two Truths were taught by the Buddha for opening the deluded eyes of ordinary people on [the nature of] existence. In this sense they are called the Two Truths of the Transmitted Truth (Chiao-ti). On the other hand, if this is viewed from the side of those ordinary people, they hold the view that either existence is Empty or that it is existent, and there exist Two Truths. In this sense, they are known as the Two Truths of the Consensual Truth (yu-ti).

The Teaching of the *Treatise on the Three Doctrines*

According to the Chi-tsang, Chou-yung, a recluse during the Ch'i, received Sŭngnang's teaching on the Three Doctrines, which the latter forumlated during his stay in Kuan-nai (Present-day Shensi province), and wrote a work titled the *San-tsung lun* (Treatise on the Three Doctrines). These three doctrines are 1) the Non-emptiness of the provisional designation (*Pu-k'ung-chia-ming*), 2) the Emptiness of the provisional designation (*K'ung-chia-ming*), and 3) The provisional designation of Emptiness (*Chia-ming-k'ung*).

Non-emptiness of the provisional designation: A sūtra says that form is emptiness; that is, form has no real nature; [form] is said to be emptiness and the provisional designation is not emptiness. As emptiness indicates no real nature, we call it emptiness; this is *paramārthasatya*. As the provisional designation is not empty, [we call] it *samvṛttisatya*. Later people have likened this to "a chestnut whose meat has been eaten by a rat [leaving only the shell]." . . . [21]

Emptiness of the provisional designation: Every dharma is produced by the various causes and conditions; hence when we consider it from the view point of existence, this is called *samvṛttisatya*. Even though one analyses the cause and conditions into and seeks for [the Ultimate Reality of it], nothing can be found; this is called *paramārthasatya*. Later people have likened this to "a floating weed".[22] When it emerges from the water [and can be seen] it is *samvṛttisatya* and when it is submerged in the water [and cannot be seen], it is *paramārthasatya*.

The third, Emptiness is [also] the provisional name: This was meant by Chou-yung. His main idea is that the provisional name is like emptiness. The origin of his "emptiness as the provisional name" came from Seng-chao's theory of non-absolute emptiness. This theory states:

"Although there is being, it is non-being; although there is non-being, it is being." "Although there is being, it is non-being" means that it is not being. "Although there is non-being, it is being" means that it is not non-being. In this case it is not that there is no phenomena. If a phenomena is not a real thing, then what is a [real] thing? Sengchao has said: "Because a phenomena is not a real thing, it is a false (provisional) thing; because it is provisional, it is empty." Sŭngnang picked up this idea [when he was in] Kuan-nei and transmitted it to Chou-yung. Chou [then] wrote the *Treatise on the Three Doctrines* based on [Sengchao's theory]. . . . The "originally non-being" argument of Tao-an, the "identity with form" argument of Chih-tao-lin, the "emptiness of (provisional) designations" argument of Chou-yung, and the "non-absolute emptiness" argument of Seng-chao have their origins in one source, but their expressions are different.[23]

Chi-tsang also informs us that the purport of the *Treatise on the Three Doctrines* is that for the Two Truths, the Middle Path is its essence:

> The teacher of the master Seng-ch'üan (Sŭngnang) . . . lived in the Ts'ao-tang Monastery on Mt. Chung. There Sŭngnang met a recluse, Chou-yung. Chou-yung studied with Sŭngnang and later wrote the *Treatise on the Three Doctrines* to explain the Two Truths, which has the Middle path as its foundation.[24]

There is an opinion that considering the period of the two people, it is doubtful that Chou-yung studied under Sŭngnang.[25] However, the relationship between Sŭngnang and Chou-yung was already well known before the time of Chi-tsang and Chi-tsang believed the doctrine found in the treatise on the Three Doctrines to have originated with Sŭngnang.

Why were such sophisticated discussions being made concerning the teaching of the Two Truths in the San-lun? Chi-tsang argues that the aims of the *Chung-kuan-lun* (*Madyamakaśāstra*), the *Shih-erh-men-lun,* the *Pai-lun,* i.e., the *Three Treatises* (*San-lun*) was to explain the meaning of the Two Truths:

> The *Chung-lun* takes the Two Truths as its foundation (principle). The reason the Two Truths are used as its foundation is because the Two Truths are the basis of the Buddha's Dharma. The Tathāgata in his own practices, and when teaching others, always depends on the Two Truths. . . . Next we will clarify the teaching of the *Pai-lun:* The *Pai-lun* destroys evil and explains the Two Truths. . . . Next we will clarify the *Shih-erh-men-lun:* This treatise also destroys internal confusion and explains the Two Truths; it also takes the Two Truths as its foundation.[26]

Hence we can see that the problem of the Two Truths was discussed in various ways even before the establishment of the San-lun School.

Chi-tsang said that fourteen different masters had dealt with this problem up to his time.[27] Within the San-lun School, there are two main streams. The view of the San-lun School since Kumārajīva and prior to Sŭngnang is called the Old San-lun; the view started by Sŭngnang and established by Chi-tsang is called the New San-lun. The old San-lun had the same view of the Two Truths as the Satyasiddhi School. The doctrine of the Two Truths had already been discussed in earlier Hīnayāna texts.[28] The Old San-lun thought that these Two Truths were concerned with some objective principle. Therefore, they viewed the original (ontological) aspect of the world as *paramārthasatya* and the phenomenal aspect as *samvṛttisatya.*

However, the New San-lun viewed the primary meaning of the Two Truths to be merely pedigogical; as Nāgārjuna said in the *Madhyamakaśāstra:*

> All the Buddhas rely on the Two Truths in order to preach the Dharma to sentient beings. The first is the truth based on conventional [knowledge]; the second is the Ultimate Truth.[29]

Such an idea was repeatedly mentioned as we see in the following citations:[30]

A. Recently, there are two interpretations of the Two Truths. The first is teaching the Two Truths according to the [capacities] of sentient beings; this is the Docrinally Transmitted Truth. The second is teaching of the Two Truths among sentient beings; therefore it is Consensual Truth.

B. Question: Why did She-ling (Sŭngnang) and Hsing-huang (Fa-lang) maintain that the doctrine of the Buddha is one of the Two Truths? Answer: This has a profound meaning. The reason for this is to teach according to the doctrine of the Satyasiddhi School which holds principle as a truth.

C. The so-called Two Truths are merely pedagogical, and not ontological.

D. Our opponent takes principle as Truth. Here we take doctrine as Truth. Our opponent takes the Two Truths as a natural principle; here we clarify that there is but one Real Truth; [it is only for] expediency that we say there are two. Just like there is only One Vehicle, but for expediency we say that there are three.[31]

The view of the Three Kinds of Two Truths and the *Treatise on the Three Doctrines* by Chou-yung are both phases in the development of views on the Two Truths. Especially, the view held by the *Treatise on the Three Doctrines* which corresponds to emptiness, the third among the Three Kinds of Two Truths. The Two Truths do not ultimately contradict each other, and the formulation of these Two Truths aims to show a single truth, not two; this is the Middle Path. The following citations also convey the same connotations:

A. She-ling and Hsing-huang both saw the Middle Path to be the essence of the Two Truths.

B. The reason for explaining the Middle Path as the essence

of the Two Truths is that the Two Truths were formulated to explicate the principle which is non-dual. It is as if, even though the finger points out the moon, the intention is not to show the finger, but in pointing to the moon. The teaching of the Two Truths is the same. The Two Truths show that there are not two, and its aim is not in the two, but in having one attain 'not two.' Therefore, the Two Truths are not two.[32]

As we have seen so far, the issues in the *Treatise on the Two Truths*, which is the basis for the study of the San-lun, were raised by Sŭngnang and developed in his lineage, the school of Mt. She-ling, through Seng-ch'üan and Fa-lang, and finally being handed down to Chi-tsang.

In the literary sources we find many other Koguryŏ monks who attained eminence in the study of the San-lun. The master Sil, a contemporary of Chi-tsang, has no separate biography, and therefore it is difficult to find detailed information about him. However, according to the account included in the biography of Hui-yung in the *Hsü kao-seng-chuan* (Vol. 14), a Chinese monk, Hui-chih, "learned the San-lun from the master Sil from Koguryŏ. He gathered in profound ideas and his scholarship was good."[33] The scholarship of the master Sil does not seem to have been limited to the San-lun. According to the biography of Fa-min, found in the same source (Vol. 15): "[Fa-]min . . . when twenty-three years of age listened to Master Sil expound upon the sūtras and śāstras of the Mahāyāna."[34]

There is another San-lun scholar monk from Koguryŏ known as Master In. According to the biography of Ling-jui, as Master In came from Koguryŏ to Shu (modern Szechuan) and lectured on the San-lun, Ling-jui became his disciple and practiced the Mahāyāna.[35] The records of these two monks are significant in that they, as foreign monks, made considerable contributions to Buddhist studies in China. The fact that there is no mention of their teachers in China indicates that their scholarship was already well developed by the time they left Koguryŏ.

The literary evidence which we have seen so far indicates

that the relationship between China and Korea in Buddhism
was not always one-sided; Korea also made many contributions
to the development of Buddhist studies in China.
Let us now turn to the issue of the activities of Koguryŏ
monks in Japanese Buddhism. Even though there remains no
record about them in Korean sources, they are recorded in
Japanese sources.[36] There should be no doubt as to the truth
of such literary evidence, because, as is well known, ancient
Japan received enormous influence from Koguryŏ and the other
Korean kingdoms with respect to various aspects of culture
including Buddhist culture.
Hyegwan was the founder of the Sanron School of Japan.
Honchō kōsōden (Vol. 1) says:

> Hyegwan, from Koguryŏ, went to the Sui and learned
> the doctrines of the San-lun from Master Chi-tsang. In the
> 13th year of Suiko (605) he came to Japan and stayed in
> Gankŏ Monastery in accordance with imperial command.
> He enthusiasticly lectured on the doctrine of śūnyata . . .
> After widely propagating this teaching, he died in his
> nineties. He is the founder of the Sanron (Chi. San-lun)
> school in our country.

Furthermore, he is regarded as the founder of the sectarian
tradition of Buddhism in Japan. However, when Hyegwan first
arrived, the situation in Japan did not allow him to teach on the
San-lun; this has been likened to the case of "having an un-
revealed pearl in his pocket". It was the same with another San-
lun master from Paekche, Kwallŭk, who came to Japan three
years before Hyegwan (602) and was not able to propagate the
San-lun teaching. It was more than forty years afterwards, in
646, that Hyegwan became the first to lecture on the San-lun
in the palace following an imperial command; since that time
the way was opened for the wide propagation of San-lun. He
had many good Japanese disciples, among whom there are
Fukuryō, Jizō, Dōchō, Ryōun, Emyō, Jōan, Eren, Chien. There
were probably very few people in Buddhist circles at that time

in Japan who did not receive his influence, considering his position. Todŭng was another monk from Koguryŏ who was active in San-lun in Japan. According to the *Honchō kōsōden* (vol. 72):

> Todŭng, even though his life is now unknown in detail, went to T'ang from Koguryŏ at the end of the Suiko reign (628) and learned the San-lun from Chi-tsang. He came to Japan with a Japanese emissary to T'ang and stayed in the Gankō Monastery. He specialized in teaching the doctrine of emptiness.

It is regrettable that the writings of these monks are no longer extant and, therefore, detailed information about their scholarship can no longer be obtained.

There were also many other Koguryŏ monks active in Japan, teaching and doing missionary work, who were not known especially as San-lun monks, but, considering the popularity of San-lun around that time, may have also been concerned with it. According to his biography in the *Honchō kōsōden* (Vol. 67):

> Hyep'yŏn, a Korean monk, liked our customs and crossed the sea to Japan. At that time, the understanding of the Buddha's Dharma was crude and naive, and the Three Jewels were not revered as "a precious gem concealed in stone". In the ninth month of the thirteenth year of the reign of Emperor Bindatsu (584), an emissary from Paekche, Nongnyang, came bringing with him a Maitreya statue. Soga no umako built a temple near the residence of Ishikawa and enshrined the stone statue within the temple. However, at that time there was no one who could perform a ritual burning of incense. Therefore, they had people from Liang, Ssuma Ta and others, search for a monk in every direction. They happened to find Hyep'yŏn in Banshō and came back with him. Soga welcomed him and let him stay in the temple as his teacher.

As we can see in this record, Hyep'yŏn was a teacher of Soga, a great believer of Buddhism in the early period. Even though his later activities are not known, the fact that he became the teacher of Soga proves his extraordinary scholarly attainments and personality. Hyep'yŏn ordained three Japanese women, Eshin, Zenshin, and Zenrō, and this was the beginning of the Japanese bhiksuṇī community.

Another Koguryŏ monk, Hyeja, went to Japan in the third year of the reign of Emperor Suiko and became a teacher of Prince Shōtoku together with a monk from Paekche, Hyech'ong, who arrivd in Japan in the same year. These two monks were regarded as the "light of the Three Jewels" for their extensive propagation of Buddhism. As is well known, Prince Shōtoku greatly contributed to the establishment of Japan as a Buddhist country since its introduction onward. In fact, it was Hyeja and Hyech'ong who guided Prince Shōtoku into becoming a devoted Buddhist ruler. They do not seem to have educated the Prince only in purely theoretical philosophy, i.e., the *Three Treatises*. They taught the Prince the teaching of the Mahāyāna, which is broad and free, and can be flexible depending on conditions. That this is so is revealed in the fact that the Prince later wrote commentaries on the *Lotus Sūtra*, the *Vimalakīrtinirdeśasūtra*, and the *Śrīmālādevīsūtra*. This suggests their profound understanding of Buddhism.

The Study of the Sarvāstivāda

The Sarvāstivāda is a representative school of Hīnayāna Buddhism, and their arguments have been used as a theoretical basis for various Buddhist doctrines in China. An important text of this school, the *A-pi-t'an wu-fa-hsing* (T.1557) was translated by An-shih-kao (c. 148-170), and the *Pi-po-sha lun* (T.1547) was translated by Seng-chia-p'o-ch'eng (?Samghavartin) from Gandhāra in 383. Another monk from Gandhāra, Seng-chia-t'i-p'o (Gotama Samghadheva), translated the *A-p'i-t'an pa-chien-tu lun* (*Abhidharmajñānaprasthānaśāstra*, T.1543) in 383 and the *A-p'i-t'an hsin-lun* (T.1550) in 391. These treatises, representing the doctrines of the Sarvāstivāda, generally contain theoretical discourses about cosmology and moral philosophy.

In China, by the time of King Fu-sheng of the Former Ch'in, the doctrine of this school had become popular as a form of theoretical Buddhism. Therefore, it is probable that their doctrine was introduced in Koguryŏ. However, it is a bit questionable whether the theoretical arguments of this school, which are close to natural philosophy or realism, were understood properly. Even though it is not known when it was introduced into Koguryŏ, it probably was not understood at the time of its introduction.

In Korean sources there is no actual evidence that this doctrine was known. A Chinese source, however, informs us about a Koguryŏ Sarvāstivādin monk. According to the *Hsü kao-seng-chuan*, an eminent Chinese monk, T'an-ch'ien, originally from Ch'i, came to Chin-ling (present-day Nan-ching) to escape the persecution understaken by the Emperor Wu of the Northern Chou. At the beginning of the reign Kai-huang of the Sui (581) he lectured, in the state of Hsi-liang, on the *Mahāyāna-saṃgraha* and, in Yang-tu, on the doctrines of *vijñaptimātra*. He had depth in both meditation and wisdom and became the teacher of the emperor. This biography is continued by the following remark:

> There was a Koguryŏ monk named Chihwang. He was well versed in the teachings of the Sarvāstivāda. His name was well known, and his position was "as great as the moat of the Dharma Castle". When they first met each other, they became good friends and when again they met they ascended into the profound.[37]

Here we can see that Chihwang had such a lofty personality and scholarship as to become a good friend with a contemporary eminent master, T'an-ch'ien, at their first meeting. That Chihwang was already a scholar in the Sarvāstivāda in Koguryŏ, may be suggested that his biography is not clearly told here.

If such a scholar was a monk trained in China, there must have been a separate biography. Since at that time his stay in China was not long enough to provide detailed information about his career, he may have been recorded merely in the biography of a Chinese monk.

The Study of the *Nirvāṇa Sūtra*

Even though information about the study of the *Nirvāṇa Sūtra* in Koguryŏ is not clearly known, we know from the *Samguk yusa* that the famous monk Podŏk, who moved to Paekche in 650 because of the Koguryŏ's policy of oppressing Buddhism and encouraging Taoism, was a master on the *Nirvāṇa Sūtra*.

Podŏk, who was named Chibŏp, was originally from the prefect of Yonggang in Koguryŏ; the details of his life can be seen below in this biography. He dwelt in the castle of P'yŏngyang. At that time an old monk living on a mountain came and asked him to lecture on the sūtras. Podŏk refused once politely, but was unable to avoid giving the lectures requested of him. Therefore, having arrived at the monastery on that mountain, he lectured on the forty volumes of the *Nirvāṇa Sūtra*.[38]

The forty-volume edition of the *Nirvāṇa Sūtra* was the version translated by T'an-wu-ch'en of the Northern Liang (T.374). Also, the National Teacher Taegak, Uich'ŏn, of Koryŏ eulogized Podŏk in his poem:

The broad and equal teaching of the *Nirvāṇa* [*Sūtra*],
Was transmitted by my teacher (Podŏk).
While the two saints (Wŏnhyo and Uisang) were learning through the sūtras,
The master walked alone.
Following conditions he traveled at will both north and south,
On the road he was neither welcomed nor followed.

It's a pity that after fleeing,
The old country of Tongmyŏng (the founder of Koguryŏ)
faced danger.[39]

From this poem we can see again that he was well-versed in the
Nirvāṇa Sūtra. The remark that even two important Silla
masters, Wŏnhyo and Uisang, learned the doctrine of the
Nirvāṇa Sūtra from him shows his high scholarly position. It
is said that he had eleven senior disciples, Musang, Chŏkmyŏl,
Uiyung, Chisu, Ilsŭng, Suŏng, Sadae, Kaewŏn, Myŏngdŏk,
Kaesim and Pomyŏng, and that each of them founded a monastery and was active in the propagation of the Dharma.[40] From
this we can estimate his influence upon the contemporary Buddhist scene.

The Study of the T'ien-t'ai

The study of the *Lotus Sūtra* or the study of the T'ien-t'ai
established by Chih-i of the Sui must have also been known
in Koguryŏ considering the close cultural relationship between
Koguryŏ and the Sui. Even though we do not have any specific
record of activity in Koguryŏ, again, it is known that a Koguryŏ
monk studied directly under Chih-i and received recognition
from him.

On Mt. T'ai (T'ien-t'ai) there is a monk P'ayak who
came during the Ch'en. Staying in Chin-ling, he listened
to lectures and deeply understood their meaning. Around
the time when the Sui conquered (annexed) the Ch'en, he
wandered about, learning and practicing as he went. At
the age of sixteen, he went up Mt. T'ien-t'ai, and showing
utmost respect, asked Chih-i to teach him meditation. His
intelligence and ability were high, and soon he received
recognition.[41]

In the part following the citation above, Chih-i, seeing the
capability of P'ayak, advises him to go to Hua-ting, the highest

peak of Mt. T'ien-t'ai, where he himself had practised the *dhutas* in the past, and there to practice meditation residing alone in a calm spot. Following the advice of his teacher, P'ayak went up the mountain in 598 and practiced meditation without sleeping. Sixteen years after this, he came down from the mountain and arrived at the Kuo-ching Monastery, where he died at the age of fifty. At that time many monks and lay people came to pay him homage and all developed the aspiration to study the Dharma. As we can see here, P'ayak was a T'ien-t'ai monk who concentrated more on the practice of *Śamatha-vipaśyanā* meditation, than on theoretical study.

Conclusion

The earliest form of Buddhism introduced into the Koguryŏ was that which taught karmic retribution and the following of precepts and taking refuge in the Three Jewels; it was not philosophically sophisticated. However, by the time of Tamsi, certain Mahāyānistic features, such as the teaching of the Three Vehicles had already appeared, though Mahāyāna thought was not well understood. Even two hundred years after its introduction, in the time of Wang Kodŏk, some important historical details were still unknown, and Wang sent an emissary to Yeh with the purpose of learning these details. However, Wang's interest in certain texts, such as the *Shih-ti, Ta chih-tu lun*, etc., shows that interest in, and understanding of, Buddhist philosophy was already high. By this time also Koguryŏ monks had already begun to go abroad: to China for study and to Japan for missionary work. Part of the reason for this may have been Koguryŏ's policy of encouraging Taoism and oppressing Buddhism. One of these monks, Sŭngnang, who became the fourth patriarch in the lineage of Fa-tu, the San-lun master, played a significant role in the propagation of that school, and according to the author, Sŭngnang marks the dividing point between the Old and the New San-lun.

The Koguryŏ contribution to Japanese Buddhism, as we have seen in this article, is also large. Hyegwan, the founder

of the Sanron in Japan, is also regarded as the founder of the
sectarian tradition of Buddhism in Japan; Hyepyŏn, the teacher
of Soga, also established the Japanese bhikṣunī community;
Hyeja, a Koguryŏ monk, was one of Prince Shōtoku's two
Korean teachers. The foundation for Japanese Buddhism was
laid, in part, by Koguryŏ monks.

[Editor's note]

The Korean title of this artice is "Koguryŏ sidae ŭi pulgyo
sasang"; it originally appeared in *Asea Yŏn'gu* 5-2 (June, 1959),
pp. 1-44. In the present rendering, the translator has decided
to remove certain redundant sections of the original text. The
original, moreover, lacked a conclusion; a short concluding
summary has been added to the end of the translation by the
editor.

NOTES

1. *Taishō* (hereafter T.) 2065, vol. 50, p. 1016a.

2. T. 2065, vol. 50, pp. 1016a-1017b.

3. *Yuan-jen lun*, (T. 1886, vol. 45, p. 708c.)

4. *Kao-seng chuan*, vol. 5, (T. 2059, vol. 50, p. 352a.)

5. *Hsü kao-seng chuan*, vol. 8 (T. 2060, vol. 50, p. 485a). In this
record, the name of the monk dispatched to China was not mentioned.
However, it was Uiyŏn according to *Haedong Kosǔng chŏn* (T. 2065,
vol. 50, p. 1016 a,b).

6. Uich'ŏn, *Sinp'yŏn chejong kyojang ch'ongnok.*

7. Gyonen, *Naiden jinrosho*, compiled in *Dai nihon Bukkyō
zensho*, vol. 3.

8. Sakaino Tetsu, *Shina Bukkyō shi kowa* (Tokyo, 29), vol. 2,
pp. 38ff.

9. The reason may be that the author of the *Kao-seng chuan*, Hui-

chiao, and Sŭngnang were contemporaries. When Hui-chiao wrote his work, Sŭngnang was still alive. Therefore, he was not included.

10. T. 2059, vol. 50, p. 380c.

11. T. 2060, vol. 50, p. 477c.

12. *Ta-ch'eng hsüan-lun*, vol. 1, (T. 1853, vol. 45, p. 19b).

13. T. 2255, vol. 65.

14. Chan-jan, *Fa-hua-ching hsüan-i shih-ch'ien*, vol. 19, (T. 1717).

15. *Kao-seng chuan*, (T. 2059, vol. 50, p. 380c).

16. Anchō, *Chūron shugi*, vol. 2.

17. *Ta-chih tu-lun*, vol. 38; *Chung-kuan-lun*, vol. 4.

18. *Erh-ti i*, vol. 1, (T. 1854, vol. 45, p. 86b).

19. *Op. cit.*, vol. 1, (T. 1854 vol. 45, p. 90a, b).

20. *Ibid*, vol. 2, (T. vol. 45, p. 103b).

21. "With respect to the phrase 'a chestnut whose meat has been eaten by a rat [leaving only the shell] . . .' the sūtra explains that the nature of *rūpa* is empty. This means that *rūpa* has no definite nature. This does not mean, however, that *rūpa* is non-being. It is like the case of a chestnut whose flesh has been eaten by a rat; the nutshell and its shape still remain as it was. But inside the chestnut there is nothing. Therefore, the chestnut is empty." (*Erh-ti i*, vol. 1).

22. This is like a weed placed in water; if one picks it up and exposes it [on the surface], that is *samvṛttisatya*. If one puts it into water with one's hands and submerges, this is *paramārthasatya*. (*Ta-ch'eng hsüan-lun*, vol. 1)

23. Chi-tsang, *Chung-kuan-lun shu*, vol. 2, (T. 1824, vol. 42, p. 29a, b).

24. *Erh-ti i*, vol. 3, (T. 1854, vol. 45, p. 108b).

25. Sakaino, vol. 2, p. 110.

26. *San-lun hsüan-i* (T. 1852, vol. 45, pp. 11a-12a).

27. *Erh-ti i*, vol. 3 (T. 1854, vol. 45, p. 107c).

28. For example, *Tseng-i a-han ching*, vol. 3, "A-hsiu-lun-p'in"; *Ta-pi-po-sha lun*, vol. 77; *Cheng-shih lun*, vol. 10, "Li-chia-ming p'in; *Chu-she lun* 22.

29. *Chung-kuan-lun*, vol. 4.

30. The author does not give the sources for these citations except for D. They all seem to have come from the treatises of Chi-tsang.

31. *Ta-ch'eng hsüan-lun*, vol. 1.

32. See note 30.

33. T. 2060, vol. 50, p. 537c.

34. *Op. cit.*, p. 538c.

35. *Op. cit.*, p. 539c.

36. The sources are *Nihōn shōki, Honchō kōsōten*, etc.

37. T. 2060, vol. 50, p. 572a.

38. *Samguk yusa*, vol. 3.

39. Ch'oe Cha, *Pohanjip;* Korean trans. by Yi fang-bo in *P'ahanjip, Yogong p'aesol* (Seoul: Taeyang Sojok, 1972), pp. 323-34. Ch'oe Cha adds a note to this poem that Wŏnhyo and Uisang received the teaching of the *Nirvāṇa* and *Vimalakīrti Sūtra*s from Podŏk.

40. *Samguk yusa*, vol. 3.

41. *Hsü kao-seng chuan* (T. 2060, vol. 50).

Serindia and Paekche Culture[1]

by Kodama Daien

Translated by Kyoko Tokuno

Introduction

Before I begin my discussion of Serindia and Paekche culture, there are a few points I must clarify. First, I use "Serindia" as a synonym for the Chinese designation of the area, the "Western regions" (Hsi-yü), which included both India and Central Asia.[2] Second, since my specialty is the thought and history of the Buddhist religion, Paekche culture for me means specifically the Buddhist culture of Paekche. Third, this study is based primarily on documentary evidence, not archeological remains.

The study of Paekche has been approached from various angles, and many noteworthy studies have been published recently.[3] However, there are still many areas remaining to investigate, one of them being the relationship between Paekche and Serindia. According to traditional accounts, it is said that the Serindian monk Mālānanda (Kor. Maranant'a) was the first to transmit Buddhism to Paekche. We also have an account concerning the monk Kyŏmik, who visited India and returned with the original texts of the *Vinaya*.[4] Although the historicity of these accounts is still open to question, they at the very least suggest that Serindia and Paekche had some sort of contact with one another. However, actual investigation of these contacts unfortunately is extremely difficult. Even when documentary evidence is extant, as it is for Mālānanda and Kyŏmik, the contents of these records are usually too terse to be used alone as reliable source material. It is probably due to such problems with the extant sources that there has been no full scale research done on these two individuals, despite their obvious importance in the development of Paekche Buddhism. However, if we allow the inadequacy of the sources to discourage our examination of these two figures, we will never develop any appreciation of the role they played in the formation of Paekche culture. Hence, I believe it worthwhile to review the records on these monks preserved in the *Samguk sagi*, the *Samguk yusa* and the *Haedong kosŭngchŏn*. After excerpting all the materials relating to Mālānanda and Kyŏmik in these collections, I shall discuss what they indicate about the state of Paekche Buddhism during this early period. Finally, I will speculate on what indirect evidence these records provide concerning the relationship between Paekche and Serindia, which is otherwise unascertainable from the extant sources.

Records Concerning Mālānanda

1.) King Ch'imnyu was the first son of King Kŭn'gusu. His mother was called the matron Ani. He ascended to the throne, succeeding his father. [In 384], in the autumn, during the seventh month, he dispatched an envoy to the [Eastern] Chin, carrying tribute to the court. In the ninth month, the Serindian monk Mālānanda arrived from Chin, and King Ch'imnyu welcomed him to the palace and paid reverence to him. This was the inception of the Buddha's Dharma [in Paekche]. In the following year during the spring, in the second month, [the king] erected a Buddhist monastery in Hansan. Ten people were ordained as monks. During the winter, in the eleventh month, the king died (*Samguk sagi* 24).[5]

2.) The *Paekche pon'gi* says: The fifteenth (*Sŭngjŏn* says fourteenth, but this is an error) King Ch'imnyu ascended to the throne, cyclical year *kapsin* [384] (in ninth year of the T'ai-yüan reign period of Emperor Hsiao-wu of the Eastern Chin). A Serindian monk, Mālānanda arrived from Chin, and was welcomed into the palace, where he was paid reverence. During the following year, cyclical year *ŭlyu*, [the king] erected a Buddhist monastery in Hansanju, near the new capital, and ten monks were ordained. This was the beginning of the Buddha's Dharma in Paekche. Furthermore, King Asin ascended to the throne during the seventeenth year of the T'ai-yüan reign period in the second month [392]. He promulgated [an edict which called on all] to venerate Buddha's Dharma as a means of attaining felicity. The name Mālānanda is translated as *haktong* (Student). (For a detailed account of his supernatural ability, see *Sŭngjŏn, Samguk yusa* 3.)[6]

3.) Sŏk Mālānanda was from Serindia. He was capable of communicating with the supernatural, and there was no fathoming the precise degree of his religious development. He travelled to all places, not confining himself to one corner [of the world]. According to ancient records, he originally came to China from India or Gandhāra. After that, he took the talented as his disciples and by means of incense, which he used to attest the presence of spirits, he attracted companions. He faced dangers undaunted and endured whatever hardships came his way. As long as there were opportune conditions he sought them out, regardless of the distance. He came to this country from the Chin in the ninth month of the ninth year after the enthronement of the fourteenth king of Paekche, Ch'imnyu (384). The king went to greet him on the outskirts of the capital, invited him and his entourage to the palace, deferred to him and worshipped him, and listened respectfully to his sermon. With the court's favor encouraging them, the people were converted. Buddhism thereafter spread widely, was esteemed by both king and subject. The speed of its propagation was as rapid as the transmission of royal orders by stages and couriers. During the second year (385), in the spring, a monastery was erected in Hansan and ten monks were ordained in Mālānanda's honor. Buddhism flourished in Paekche as it had done in Koguryŏ (*Haedong kosŭng chŏn* 1).[7]

Records Concerning Kyŏmik

The *Mirŭk pulgwangsa sajŏk* says: During the fourth year

of King Sŏng of Paekche (526)[8] the monk Kyŏmik sought the *Vinaya* with earnest zeal. He crossed the ocean and arrived in central India, where he stayed at the Great *Vinaya* monastery of Ch'ang-ch'ieh-na (Sangana-mahāvinaya-vihara?). He studied Sanskrit there for five years, and mastered it thoroughly. He pursued deeply the study of *Vinaya*, and adorned himself with the essence of the precepts. He returned accompanied by the Tripiṭaka Master Paedadta (Vedatta) and brought back the *Abhidharma* and five recensions of the *Vinaya*. The Paekche king welcomed his return with canopy adorned with feathers, drums and trumpets, and installed him in the Hŭngnyun Monastery. He summoned twenty-eight learned domestic scholars [from throughout the country] who, together with Dharma Master Kyŏmik, translated the *Vinaya* in seventy-two volumes. Thus he became the founder of the *Vinaya* school in Paekche. Furthermore, the two Dharma Masters Tamuk and Hyein wrote a commentary [to the *Vinaya*] in thirty-six volumes, and presented it to the king. The king wrote prefaces to the *Abhidharma* and the new *Vinaya*, and stored them at the T'aeyo Hall. [The king] desired to have it copied and distributed immediately, but he died before this plan could be carried out.[9]

Let us analyze the content of these records. The accounts related to Mālānanda are all concerned with the first transmission of Buddhism to Paekche. Following are the common elements appearing in them.

1.) King Ch'imnyu is enthroned in 384.

2.) The Serindian monk Mālānanda arrives from Eastern Chin.

3.) King Ch'imnyu welcomes him to the palace and honors him.

4.) The king builds a Buddhist temple in the following year in Hansan.

5.) Ten people are ordained as monks.

Next, the record involving Kyŏmik gives a synopsis of the foundation of the Paekche *Vinaya* school. This account is recorded in *Mirŭk pulgwangsa sajŏk*—the only document that gives this information. I have searched in vain for this text in collections of inscriptions and in all other sources available to me. I was finally unable to locate it anywhere except as cited in Yi Nŭnghwa's *Chosŏn pulgyo t'ongsa*. For this reason, the value of this record remains limited until its authenticity has been proven. Nonetheless, since this is the only source available, we have no choice but to rely on its account, but not without reservation. Unfortunately, also, the *Vinaya* translated by Kyŏmik, along with its Paekche commentary are no longer extant.[10]

We may now proceed to extract the elements common to all the accounts on these two figures. We find roughly three points on which there is rough agreement: First, Mālānanda and Kyŏmik are both directly connected with India. Second, both can be assumed to have taken the sea route: The *Mirŭk pulgwangsa sajŏk* clearly records that this was so in Kyŏmik's case, and there is common scholarly consensus that the same is true for Mālānanda as he arrived in Paekche from the Eastern Chin.[11] Third, both have deep associations with *Vinaya*— Mālānanda as a preceptor, Kyŏmik as a translator. Those three elements are not only shared by Mālānanda and Kyŏmik, but are also common to Paekche Buddhism as a whole. We thus see the vital role that open sea routes played in the importation of Buddhism to Paekche, and the prominent place occupied by the *Vinaya* school within the Paekche Buddhist tradition.

Mālānanda and his Milieu

We now focus on three issues raised in the above accounts concerning Mālānanda. First, what was the contemporary situation in China and Serindia when Mālānanda arrived from the Eastern Chin? Second, what sea routes were in use at that time? Third, how sophisticated was the knowledge of *Vinaya* in East Asia during that period?

The Contemporary Situation

Mālānanda lived during the era of the five barbarian dynasties and sixteen states of northern China (304-439 A.D.), and the Eastern Chin dynasty in southern China (317-420).[12] The year Mālānanda arrived in Paekche (384) was the year after the legendary battle of the Fei River (383), which undoubtedly made possible the preservation of the South as the bastion of Han Chinese culture during the occupation of the North by successive non-Chinese dynasties.[13] In that battle, it is traditionally believed, King Fu Chien (338-385; r. 357-385) of the Former Ch'in dynasty was defeated, catalyzing a dramatic series of changes in the political landscape of northern China, and engendering an air of instability in southern China as well.

In northern China, as soon as Fu Chien was defeated in the Fei River battle, the brothers Mu-jung Hung and Mu-jung Ch'ung revolted against him and in 384 established the dynasties of Western Yen and Latter Yen, respectively.[14] T'ao Ch'ang, whom Fu Chien sent to subdue Mu-jung Hung, was also defeated. Fearing retribution from Fu Chien for his loss, T'ao did not return but instead established his own in dynasty in 384: the Latter Ch'in. Lü Kuang, who was the commander of Fu Chien's expeditionary forces in Central Asia, having heard about the death of Fu Chien, established his own independent kingdom in 386: the Latter Liang. In southern China, the year 384, when Mālānanda arrived in Paekche, falls in the middle of the reign-period of Emperor Hsiao-wu (362-396; r. 373-396) of Eastern Chin; this was also the year before the Eastern Chin general Hsieh-an (320-385) defeated Fu Chien.[15] With the death of Hsieh-an in the following year (385), a change occurs in the political situation of the Eastern Chin, to which we must now pay close attention. This change occurs in the person of Emperor Hsiao-wu, the first committed adherent of Buddhism among the emperors of the Eastern Chin, who was renowned for building Buddhist temples on the palace grounds, and worshipping senior monks. With the death of Hsieh-an, however, the emperor entered upon a life of debauchery. The governing of the country was left in the hands of a minister, Ssu-ma Tao-tzu.

The power of the Eastern Chin gradually declined from that time onwards, but Su-ma's autocratic style of government sowed dissension among the people. Thus the years around 384, when Mālānanda arrived in Paekche, were an extremely volatile period in China.

What was the relationship between China and Serindia during this period? Fu Chien's activities in the region are particularly noteworthy in this regard. Fu Chien ascended the throne of the Former Ch'in in 357. After consolidating his power in the Ch'ang-an area, Fu Chien defeated Former Yen (349-370) in 370, as well as the Former Liang (301-376) and the Tai (315-376) in 376, unifying all of Northern China; he began his campaign against the south by occupying the Eastern Chin territory of Hsiang-yang in 379. He also brought under his control the trade route leading to Central Asia, and in 382 ordered Lü Kuang to undertake an expedition into that region. The years that elapsed between the unification of northern China (376) and the battle of the Fei River (383) were thus the height of his power.[16]

Especially noteworthy is the fact that the kingdom of the Former Liang, which was previously a territory of the Eastern Chin, came under Fu Chien's control in 376. Since trade routes between Serindia and China passed through the Former Liang territory, this change in political control allowed Central Asian caravans to travel all the way to Ch'ang-an, the capital of the Former Ch'in dynasty. In this manner, direct connections were established between Ch'ang-an in the central Chinese plain, and the Central Asian petty-kingdoms.

Ch'ang-an was the major cosmopolitan center in Asia during that period, where good-will ambassadors from countries in both eastern and western Asia gathered. Some traditional accounts state that Fu Chien's previously-mentioned expedition to Central Asia was carried out at the behest of the kings of Ch'e-shih Ch'ien-pu and Shan-shan—two kingdoms of the Taklamakhan basin—who visited Ch'ang-an in 381. But according to the *Chin-shu* and other sources,[17] in addition to those two kings, there were sixty other rulers from both eastern and western Asia who sent envoys to Ch'ang-an in the same year.

As the *Chin-shu* relates:

> The kings of Shan-shan and Ch'e-shih Ch'ien-pu
> (Turfan) came to the court. Ta-wan (Ferghana) presented
> a blood-sweating horse. Su-shen presented arrows made
> of the *hu* tree. India presented fireproof cloth. K'ang-chu
> (Samarkand), Yü-ti'en (Khotan), and Hai-tung (Korea),
> sixty-two kings in all, sent envoys who presented their local
> products (*Chin-shu chuan* 113, Fu Chien Tsai-chi 2).

All of these sources attest to the broad power wielded by Fu
Chien throughout Asia and to the prosperity of Ch'ang-an
during this period. But Fu Chien's activities had important
implications for Buddhist history as well.

First, Fu Chien's defeat of the Former Yen initiated the
transmission of Buddhism to the Korean peninsula.[18] Furthermore, according to the *Chin-shu* we know that among the sixty-
odd kings who sent envoys and tribute to Ch'ang-an were rulers
from various Korean kingdoms.[19] This account thus suggests
that there were indirect connections between Korea and Serindia
via Ch'ang-an. Therefore, we can consider the possibility that
Buddhism was also transmitted to Korea along the same route
through which it entered China. Furthermore, Fu Chien captured the eminent Chinese cleric Tao-an at the time of the
conquest of the Eastern Chin territory of Hsiang-yang.[20] Tao-an
was famous throughout all of China as the most prominent
figure in contemporary Buddhist circles, and commanded respect and devotion from all strata of society. Fu Chien was
enormously pleased at having captured Tao-an, and under
Fu Chien's protection, Tao-an spent the last six years of his
life at Ch'ang-an, passing away in the same year as Fu Chien.

As was said earlier, Ch'ang-an and Serindia were directly
connected at this time over the trade routes that connected the
two regions. The arrival in China of Buddhist monks, who
often accompanied the caravans of merchants who travelled
the silk roads, became more frequent. Kashmir monks from
northwest India were especially prominent during that early

period. These monks brought along the *Tripiṭaka* of the Sarvāstivādin School, the main school of Kashmir Buddhism, in which Tao-an showed keen interest.

The final activities of Tao-an in Ch'ang-an were to assist the translation efforts of such foreign monks as T'an-mo-pi (Dharmapriya), Fo-t'u lo-li, Seng-ch'ieh-pa-ch'eng (Saṃghabhadra), Seng-ch'ieh t'i-p'o (Saṃghadeva), T'an-mo-nan-t'i (Dharmanandin), Chiu-mo-lo-fu-t'i (Kumārabuddhi), as well as the Chinese translator Chu Fo-nien of Liang-chou.[21] Tao-an was personally involved in the study of the *prajñāpāramitā* literature, and with supervising the translations of *Āgama*, *Vinaya*, and *Abhidharma* materials that were newly transmitted to China.

The Central Asian expedition of Lü Kuang was also a pretext for bringing the renowned translator Kumārajīva from Kucha to Ch'ang-an.[22] In 384, Kucha fell to Lü Kuang and Kumārajīva was taken taken hostage. While Lü Kuang was at Liang-chou on his way back to Former Ch'in territory, he heard the news of Fu Chien's death, and established the kingdom of the Latter Liang rather than return to the political upheaval then going on at home. Thus Kumārajīva was also forced to stay in Liang-chou. In the same year (384), T'ao Ch'ang (330-393; r. 384-393) revolted against Fu Chien, conquering Ch'ang-an in 386, after which he ascended the throne of a new dynasty, which he called the Latter Ch'in. Ch'ang-an prospered for the next thirty-two years as the capital of the Latter Ch'in. T'ao Hsing (366-416; r. 394-416) succeeded T'ao Ch'ang, and after defeating the Latter Liang in 401, welcomed Kumārajīva to Ch'ang-an.

Thus far we have explored the contemporary circumstances in China and Serindia during the period around 384 A.D., when Mālānanda visited Paekche; this was right after the war of the Fei River, which was thenceforth regarded as a turning point in the history of China. While it would be interesting to explore whether there may have been some connection between the pilgrimage of Mālānanda and the political situation in China, there is a complete dearth of material on that issue.[23]

We now know that, thanks to Fu Chien, Ch'ang-an and

the various Serindian kingdoms came to be in direct communication with each other. We also saw that there were indirect connections between Serindia and the Korean peninsula by way of Ch'ang-an. Since there were frequent visits of Serindian monks to Ch'ang-an, it seems that foreign monks like Mālānanda would have had easy access to the rest of China and thence to the Korean peninsula.

The Sea Route to Paekche

As was mentioned earlier, Mālānanda is assumed to have travelled from China to Paekche by sea. Although there is no indisputable literary evidence to indicate as such, this seems plausible given Paekche's constant battles with Koguryŏ. Hence, it is quite doubtful that the overland route to China through Koguryŏ territory would have been open. We should also remember that there was a sea route already established by this time over which tribute was sent from Paekche to the Eastern Chin. We have detailed studies by a number of scholars on the development and history of these sea routes connecting the Korean peninsula with China.[24] Based on these studies we may offer the following speculations about the possible sea route taken by Mālānanda.

According to Naitō, there were four major sea routes between the Korean peninsula and the mainland.[25] The first route went from the Shantung peninsula (Teng-chou), transversing the coast of Po-hai, until it finally reached Korean shores. The second left from Shan-tung over the Yellow Sea directly to the Korean coast. The third left from either Yang-chou or Ming-chou near the Yangtze River delta, crossing the Yellow River, and reaching the southern shores of the peninsula (near Hŭksan Island). Fourth, there was a longer route from southern China via the Shantung peninsula, which reached the coast of the Liao-tung peninsula in what was then Koguryŏ territory. The first and second routes may be called northern routes, the third the southern route, while the fourth combined the northern and southern routes. These routes can be summarized as follows:

A. Northern Chinese sea routes

1. The Liao-tung coastal route: From Teng-chou on the Shantung peninsula; this route would first traverse Po-hai, —the Yalu River delta, the Taedong River delta, Ongjin, and finally arrive at Namyang Bay.

2. The Yellow Sea route: From Teng-chou, this route would first cross the Yellow Sea, Ongjin, and finally end at the capital [of Paekche].

B. The Southern Chinese sea routes

1. The Route skirting the northern Chinese coastline: From the Yangtze River delta, this route went first the Ch'eng-shan on the Shantung peninsula, then to coast of the Liao-tung peninsula, and finally to the mouth of the Yalu River.

2. The Yellow Sea route: From Ming-chou or Yang-chou on the Yangtze River delta, or Teng-chou in Shangtung, this route went directly over the Yellow Sea to the vicinity of Hŭksan Island, and from there to various seaports on the Korean peninsula.

The oldest description of these sea routes is found in accounts of the Korean expeditions of Emperor Wu of the Former Han, which appear in the *Ch'ao-hsien Chuan* [Ch'ao-hsien annals] of the *Shih-chi*. This attests to the antiquity of these maritime routes.

Our present concern is specifically with contacts between Paekche and China. Naitō speculates that its tense relationships with its northern neighbor of Koguryŏ would have demanded that Paekche primarily use the northern route crossing directly over the Yellow Sea [route A.1], especially in the period before 475, when it moved its capital south. However, during the early to middle period of the East Chin dynasty, Paekche was more powerful than Koguryŏ, and both northern routes were employed (routes A.1 and A.2). In travelling to the southern dynasties, Paekche in most cases took the northern route, and toward the end of its reign, it came to use the southern routes over the East China Sea as well.[26] We thus see that the southern routes were much less commonly used than the northern. The question here is which route Mālānanda may have used on his journey to Paekche? Judging from the political situation of Eastern Chin, one of the two northern routes is most plausible, as Naitō has suggested,[27] although we may never know which one of the two was actually used.

Vinaya and the Paekche Tradition

The year after Mālānanda arrived in Paekche, it is said that King Ch'imnyu erected a Buddhist monastery in Hansan and had ten monks ordained. We, unfortunately, do not know the details about the role played by Mālānanda on this occasion. But if this account is accurate, this ordination would have been the inception of the Buddhist saṅgha in Paekche. I have doubts however, whether this saṅgha was a Buddhist "saṅgha" in the strict sense of that term. The orthodoxy of the precepts they would have received is questionable, given that Mālānanda came from China where no complete *Vinayapiṭaka* was as yet in circulation anywhere. Fu Chien's own chaplain, Tao-an, was one of those who lamented the lack of a full *Vinaya* recension.[28] Only after Tao-an's death was the translation of the first complete *Vinaya*, the *Shih-sung lu*, finished (409 A.D.). Given this state of affairs, it is hard to imagine that the observance of *Vinaya* practices could have been any more sophisticated in Paekche.

In order to investigate this question further, we need to examine the history of *Vinaya* translations in China. On this topic also, there is detailed research by earlier scholars,[29] which I shall be content to summarize.

The history of the *Vinaya* tradition in China is usually said to have begun with the translation of *Vinaya* texts by the foreign monks T'an-k'o-chia-lo (Dharmakāla) and T'an-ti (Dharmastaya?), who visited China during its Three Kingdoms period. According to the *Kao-seng chuan*, T'an-k'o-chia-lo was a native of central India, and arrived in Lo-yang during the Chia-p'ing reign-period of the Wei dynasty (249-253). There he translated the *Seng-mi-ti-hsin* (*Saṃmatīyahṛdaya?*; unfortunately, no longer extant) at the request of Chinese adherents, and established the monastic ritual (*saṅghakarma*) used in a monks' ordination. It is said, "The Chinese *Vinaya* begins with this event."[30] Soon afterwards, during the Cheng-yuan reign-period (254-255), the Śramana T'an-ti, a *Vinaya* specialist from Parthia, arrived in Lo-yang and translated the *T'an-wu-teh-chieh-mo*. Modern scholarly studies have, however, demonstrated that the *T'an-wu-teh-chieh-mo* actually postdates the 412 translation of the *Ssu-fen lü*, the definitive *Vinaya* text for the Chinese tradition.[31] At any rate, it is the traditional consensus that the history of *Vinaya* in China begins with the translations made by these two figures.

Subsequent to their time, however, there were no transmissions of complete Hīnayāna *Vinaya* collections until the translation of the *Shih-sung lü* at the beginning of the fifth century. In the Chinese Tripiṭaka there are several translations of *Vinaya* texts, including the *Fo-shuo han-chieh tsui-pao ch'ing-chung ching* (T. 1477.24.944d), *T'an-wu-teh lü-pu tsa chieh-mo* (T. 1432.22.1041a), *Chieh-mo* (T. 1433.22.1051b). None of these, however, precedes the translation of the *Shih-sung lu*. Two texts, including *Pi-ch'iu-ni chieh ching* and *Chieh ching*, are attributed to Dharmarakṣa of the Western Chin period; though Hirakawa says that these two were not complete *Vinaya*s but just the *Pratimokṣa* section, which listed the monk's precepts.[32]

During the Eastern Chin period, two texts, *Shih-sung pi-ch'iu chieh-pen* (T. 1436.23.470) and *Pi-ch'iu-ni ta-chieh* (T. 1437.23.479), were translated around 379 A.D. under Tao-an, who was then in Ch'ang-an in the twilight of his career; the preface to the former is still extant.[33] Further, in 383, Chu Fo-nien translated the *Pi-na-yeh* [*Vinaya*] in 10 *chüan* (T. 1464.24.851). Even this was only a partial *Vinaya* collection. Even so, Tao-an wrote a preface to it, expressing his joy at having finally obtained the *Vinaya*.[34] The fact that Tao-an was delighted even with this incomplete *Vinaya* text shows that familiarity with that stratum of literature was extremely tenuous at that time. Hirakawa has shown that among the numerous extant Chinese *Vinaya* translations, two can be definitively considered to be earlier than the *Shih-sung lu*.[35] One is Chu Fo-nien's *Vinaya* in 10 *chüan*; the other is an anonymous translation of a *Chieh-ching* [*Vinayasūtra*], in one *chüan*, which was recovered at Tun-huang and reprinted in Yabuki's *Meisha yoin*. The latter is dated to ca. 265-360, and is speculated to be older than the former. In any case, the above discussion shows that the transmission and translation of Hīnayāna *Vinaya* texts in China prior to the translation of the *Shih-sung lu* was eratic and incomplete.

The translation of the first complete *Vinaya* recension, the *Shih-sung lu*, took place in Ch'ang-an at the beginning of the fifth century (404-409). This was an epoch-making event in the history of the Chinese *Vinaya* tradition. Following this, the *Ssu-fen lu* was also translated in Ch'ang-an (410-412), and the Mahāsaṅghika *Vinaya* and *Wu-fen lu* were translated in Chien-t'ang in 416-418 and 422-423 respectively. Thus, in a period of only some twenty years, the translations of all the full *Vinaya* collections were completed. These events vividly illustrate how Chinese Buddhism was zealously intent on obtaining a complete recension of the *Vinaya*. The dearth of such materials in China even prompted Fa-hsien's famous pilgrimage to India in search of these elusive texts.

I have summarized in the preceding paragraphs the history of the Chinese *Vinaya* school up to the translation of the complete *Vinaya* recensions. Even during this early period, at least partial observance of the *Vinaya* injunctions was probably possible, since translations of some of the principal portions of the *Vinaya*—including the *Pratimokṣa, Saṅghakarma*, and the historical sections (*Suttavibhaṅga*)—were already available.[36] However, if the ordination-procedure sections of the full *Vinaya*s were missing, then strict adherence to the letter of the formal ordination rite would not have been possible, suggesting that the ordination performed by Mālananda in Paekche may have been, in some ways deficient. Given this state of affairs, we may be sure that the understanding and practice of *Vinaya* in Paekche would have been no better than that in China.

Kyŏmik's Milieu

Our discussion concerning Kyŏmik will focus on three points: 1.) The conditions in India at the time of Kyŏmik's pilgrimage. 2.) The Sea routes between China and India in use at that time. 3.) The identity of five separate recensions of the *Vinaya*, which were believed to have been then extant in India.

1.) There are two records that bear on the contemporary situation present in Serindia and India around the time that Kyŏmik returned to Korea, ca. 526. The first is the *Pei-Wei seng Hui-sheng shih hsi-yu-chi* (Record of the Travels of the Northern Wei Monk Hui-sheng in the Western Religions),[37] which is a travelogue about the monks Hui-sheng and Sung-yun, who journeyed to Central Asia and northwest India in 518 on Shih-tsung's orders, and returned to China some four years later with 170 Buddhist scriptures. The record reveals the contemporary situation in those regions of Asia, especially as regards the situation of the Ephthalites [alt. Hephthalites; White Huns]. Hui-sheng and Sung-yun travelled overland, however, and they did not journey any farther than the northwest of India; hence their travelogue provides no evidence that is directly relevant to our concern with Kyŏmik and his sea journey to central India.

The second record is the account of the Indian travels of Hao-ch'ien, which is recorded in *chüan* two of the *Chi Shen-chou san-pao kan-t'ung lu* (Collected Record of Miracles Concerning the Three Jewels in China), and in *chüan* fourteen of the *Fa-yüan chu-lin* (Dharma Garden and Pearl Grove).[38] Hao-ch'ien and seventy-nine of his men were dispatched to India by Emperor Wu of the Liang, who hoped that they would find a Buddhist image he had seen in a dream. The force arrived in

Śrāvastī, where they requested that the king of that land give them the Buddhist image they described. They carried the red sandal-wood image back to China after a sea journey of several 10,000 *li*, arriving in Yang-tu in 511 after much hardship. This record should be helpful, for they returned home via sea and sojourned in central India, as had Kyŏmik. Unfortunately, the information included in the account is rather sketchy. All we are told about central India is that the name of the state they visited was Śrāvastī; the record tells us nothing about the political, economic, religious, or cultural conditions then prevalent in that region. It will take another hundred years, after the pilgrimages of Hsüan-tsang (travelled 629-645) and I-ching (travelled 671-695), until there finally appears detailed documentary information about central India. Unfortunately, the accounts of these two monks are too late to be relevant to Kyŏmik's visit, and there are no other sources which we may learn anything about the contemporary situation in India.

Kyŏmik's journey occured during the reign-period of Emperor Wu of Liang (502-549), when the southern Chinese dynasties reached the pinnacle of their development. In northern China, this was the final period of the Northern Wei dynasty (386-534). The Northern Wei controlled areas where Buddhism prospered, such as Ch'ang-an and Liang-chou, and thus was frequently visited by Serindian monks. It is said that in its capital of Lo-yang the monks P'u-t'i-liu-chih (Bodhiruci), Lo-na-mo-t'i (Ratnamati), Fo-t'o-shan-to (Buddhaśanta), Pan-jo-liu-chih (Gautama Prajñāruci) were all actively engaged in translation work.[19] In southern China also the number of foreign monks increased, especially in Chien-t'ang. But the situation was different from northern China, as foreign monks arriving in the Eastern Chin, as well as Chinese leaving on pilgrimages to India, primarily used the sea route connecting India and the Chinese coastline. This, of course, is not to say that southern China was cut off from the mainstream of the Buddhist transmission coming from Serindia to Ch'ang-an via the Central Asian silk routes. However, for the first time Buddhism was reaching southern China directly from India and Southeast Asia over the burgeoning maritime routes. The fact that Kyŏmik travelled by sea on his own journey to India reflects this trend.

2.) Let us now examine the sea routes that Kyŏmik may have taken. There are several possible ways to ascertain these. My method has been to extract references from accounts found in catalogs or from biographical records of foreign monks and Chinese pilgrims who have likely taken the sea route to India during the time between the Eastern Chin and Nan-pei ch'ao period. The results are as follows.

Eastern Chin period:

T'an-mo-yeh-she (Dharmayaśas) (ca. 407), from Kashmir: (route) Kashmir—Chien-t'ang—Ch'ang-an—Chiang-ling—Central Asia—?[40]

Fo-t'o-pa-t'o-lo (Buddhabhadra) (359-429), from Northern India: (route) Kuśinagara—Kashmir—Liu-kuo (six kingdoms of Turfan)—Chiao-chih—Ch'ing-chou—Ch'ang-an—Lu-shan—Ching-chou—Chien-t'ang[41]

Fa-hsien (ca. 340-420), from P'ing-yang Wu-yang: (route) Ch'ang-an—Kāśi—Magadha (Pāṭaliputra)—Mo-li-ti kuo—Ceylon—Java—Ch'ing-chou—Chien-yeh—Ching-chou[42]

Liu-Sung period:

T'an-mo-chieh (Dharmodgata) (ca. 420), from Yu-chou: (route) Ho-nan—Kao-ch'ang (Turfan)—Kucha—Kashmir—Yüeh-chih[43]

Fo-t'o-shih (Buddhajīva) (ca. 423), from Kashmir: (route) Kashmir—Yang-chou—Chien-yeh—?[44]

Ch'iu-na-pao-mo (Guṇavarman) (367-431), from Kashmir: (route) Kashmir—Ceylon—Java—Kuang-chou—Chien-t'ang[45]

Seng-ch'ieh-pa-mo (Saṅghavarman), (ca. 433), from India: "He left Lui-sha and arrived at the capital . . . He returned to his country on board a ship belonging to Serindian merchants."[46]

Chih-yen (ca. 427), from Hsi Liang-chou: (route) Serindia (Chang-yeh, Wu-i)—Kashmir—Liu-kuo—Chiao-chih—Ch'ing-chou—Ch'ang-an—Kashmir[47]

Ch'iu-na-pa-t'o-lo (Guṇabhadra) (394-468), from Middle India: (route) Ceylon—Kuang-chou—Chien-t'ang—Ching-chou[48]

Seng-ch'ieh-pa-t'o-lo (Saṅghabhadra) (ca. 492), from a foreign kingdom: (route) Kuang-chou—On the tenth year of the Yung-ming reign period (492) . . . fifth month, he returned South.[49]

San-chia-pa-mi (date unknown), Ceylon: from Ceylon—[50]

Man-t'o-lo-hsien (Mandrasena) (ca. 503), from Fu-nan: (route) Fu-nan—Yang-tu[51]

Seng-ch'ieh-p'o-lo (Saṅghabhadra) (459-524), from Fu-nan: (route) Fu-nan—Yang-tu[52]

Ch'en-ti (Paramārtha), from West India: (route) Yu-ch'an-ni—Chinese Southern sea (Kuang-chou?)—Chien-t'ang—Fu-ch'un—Yü-chang—Shih-hsing—Nan-t'ang—Yü-chang—Lin-ch'uan—Chin-an—Liang-an—Kuang-chou[53]

Ch'en period:

Subhūti (dates unknown), from Fu-nan: (route) Funan—[54]

Summarizing the above accounts, the following tabulation of places visited and the birthplaces of the monks may be given.

Place names: Kuang-chou (6); Ceylon (4); Fu-nan (3); Ch'ing-chou (3); Java (2); Chiao-chih (2); Yang-chou (1).

Birthplaces: India (4); Kashmir (3); Fu-nan (3), China (3); Ceylon (1); Unknown (1).

According to our sources, there were five monks who utilized both land and sea routes: Dharmayaśas, Buddhabhadra, Fa-hsien, Dharmodgata, and Chih-yen. An analysis of the above data yields the following points. Based on the frequency of the appearance of place names, we can point out that the major sea route of the time was from Kuang-chou, to Chiao-chih, Fu-nan, Java, and Ceylon. This route coincides with an important trade route between China and India.[55] This suggests that the majority of religious travellers journeyed on the commercial ships frequenting this route.

Concerning the monk's birthplaces, we note that there are many who are from Kashmir in northwest India. Geographically, Kashmir is far removed from the maritime routes; it is instead one of the principal points on the silk route that went through Central Asia to China. I have not examined in detail possible routes connecting Kashmir with the west Indian coast or central India with the eastern coastline. It is noteworthy, however, that many Chinese pilgrims used both land and sea routes. This fact has suggested to some scholars that "the Chinese and Indian cultural spheres were connected by both the overland silk roads as well as the maritime routes, which together comprised a great trade route encircling Asia."[56]

We can safely surmise that the sea route taken to India by Kyŏmik was along the main maritime route between South Asia and East Asia that went via Southeast Asia. The Chinese portion of that route extended further northward to the coastal areas of the Shan-tung peninsula, such as Ch'ing-chou; this is attested to by accounts extant concerning the route taken by the pilgrims Buddhabhadra, Chih-yen, and Fa-hsien. This route would thus have linked up with the sea route between the Chinese mainland and the Korean peninsula, discussed earlier in our treatment of Mālānanda. We can assume therefore that Kyŏmik skillfully used these sea routes to complete successfully his long journey to India.

The sea route between China and India, which passed through Southeast Asia, has a fairly long history.[57] The earliest documentary evidence appears in the geographical record of the *Ch'ien Han shu*.[58] According to that record, during the reign-period of Emperor Wu of the Former Han dynasty (140-87 B.C.), a sea route went from Kuang-tung province, to the northeastern coastal area of Indo-China, and finally to Huang-chih on the east coast of India. In the "Hsi-yü chuan" [Record of the Western Regions] of the *Hou Han shu*, there is a famous account that says that Marcus Aurelius Antoninus (r. 161-180 A.D.), the emperor of Rome, dispatched an envoy, who arrived in China via Jih-nan (Vietnam) in the ninth year of the reign of emperor Huan (166 A.D.). The envoy took this maritime route to China, where he presented the throne with ivory, rhinoceros horns and tortoise shells. From the above account we know that this maritime route would have been one of the important routes connecting the Orient and the Occident.

During the Chinese Three Kingdoms period, Sun Ch'üan from the state of Wu gained control over the southern territory of Han. Sometime between 225 and 230, Lü T'ai, who was the prefect of Chia-chou and Kuang-chou, sent Chu Ying and T'ang T'ai as goodwill ambassadors to Fu-nan and Lin-i (Champa).[59] As a result of this, Chinese knowledge about Southeast Asia greatly increased.

After Chin had abandoned political control of northern China, becoming the Eastern Chin dynasty, it nearly monopolized Chinese maritime trade. During the Nan-pei ch'ao period, sea traffic continued to expand. Fu-nan deserves special attention in this regard.

Contact between China and Fu-nan began with the two goodwill ambassadors sent by Lü T'ai in 225-230. Lü T'ai subsequently sent envoys four times during the Chin period, three times during the Southern Sung period, and nine times during the Liang period.[60] It seems that Buddhist transmissions were also frequent during the Liang period, judging from the fact that the two monks Seng-ch'ieh-p'o-lo (Saṅghabhara) and Man-t'o-lo-hsien (Mandrasena) visited China, as mentioned previously, and engaged in translation activities at a translation bureau called Fu-nan kuan.[61]

The kingdom of Fu-nan historically was heavily influenced

by India, which had, from early on, colonized South Asia.[62] The associations between those two regions were so ubiquitous that Indian-Chinese relations pale by comparison. The Fu-nan ruler was appointed by Indian kings, and the political system, language, and art of Fu-nan were all based on Indian models. Fu-nan was, however, influenced not only by India, but also by cultures of countries west of India, including Kuṣṇa and Persia.

The year 526, when Kyŏmik is said to have returned to Korea, fell during the Liang dynasty in southern China. This was a time when China had frequent contacts with the kingdom of Fu-nan in Southeast Asia. Since the active use of maritime transportation by the Chinese began during the T'ang period, the sea transportation of the Nan-pei ch'ao period is seen in a naissant form. The route taken by Kyŏmik should have closely followed contemporary trade routes, and probably involved all the major routes connecting Korea with China, China with Southeast Asia, and China with India. His activities, therefore, should be understood as an extension of the cultural communications and trade relationships between East and West.

3.) On his return, Kyŏmik is said to have brought back Sanskrit manuscripts of the Abhidharma as well as the five recensions of the *Vinaya* (*Wu-pu lü*). What were these five recensions? The existence of five separate versions of the *Vinaya* was accepted in contemporary China, and all were assumed to be still extant in India. The search for as yet untransmitted *Vinaya* texts was the reason for many Chinese pilgrimages to Serindia, and apparently prompted Kyŏmik's journey as well. In this secton, we shall explore the introduction and translation of the various *Vinaya* recnsions.[63] Our major primary sources are as follows.

(1.) The *Ta-chi ching* 22, T. 397.13.159a-b (*Mahāsaṃnipāta-sūtra*)

(2.) The *She-li-fu wen ching*, T.1465.24.900c (*Śāriputra-paripṛcchāsūtra*)

(3.) The *Ta pi-ch'iu san-ch'ien wei-i ching*, T. 1470.24.925c-926a.

(4.) The *Ch'u san-tsang chi-chi* 3, T. 2145.55.19c (Hereafter CSTCC)

(5.) The *Fan-i ming-i chi* 4, T. 2131.54.1113a-b

(6.) The *San-lun hsüan-i* 2, T. 1852.45.10a

(7.) The *Hsi-yü chi* 3, T. 2087.51.882b

(8.) The *Mo-ho seng-ch'i-lü ssu-chi*, T. 1425.22.548a-b (Mahā-saṅghikavinaya)

Seng-yu, the author of the *CSTCC*, relates in his sections, "Record of newly collected, orthodox *Vinaya* texts" and "Excerpts from the *Vibhāṣa*," that there were five separate recensions of the *Vinaya*, and clearly recounts the historical circumstances under which these came to be established. Since, as Hirakawa has already pointed out, this account comes from the *Vibhāṣa*, the exegesis of the Abhidharma made by the Sarvāstivāda School,[64] this must have been the tradition transmitted in that school. The events surrounding its compilation are outlined by Seng-yu as follows:

> After the parinirvāṇa of the Buddha, during the rain's retreat at Rājagṛha, Mahākāśyapa summoned arhats and ordered Upāli to recite the *Vinaya*. He recited eighty-thousand items in a series of eighty recitations. [The *Vinaya* thus recited was transmitted] first to Mahākāśyapa, second to Ānanda, third to Madhiyāntika, fourth to Śāṇvāsa, and fifth to Upagupta, for 110 more years without alteration. After the first one hundred and ten extra years, King Aśoka emerged in this world. First he had evil views, bringing destruction to Buddhadharma, and burning scriptures. As a result, monks were dispersed, and [the teachings transmitted in] eighty recitations were annihilated. Later [King Aśoka] met a monk, and started life anew with faith [in the Buddhadharma], and expiated all past sins through repentance. He was endowed with magical power, and became the

Iron Cakravartin and ruled as the king of the world. Being
capable of commanding spirits, he took apart the eight
original stūpas and erected eighty-four thousand stūpas in
one day and night. The Buddhadharma was restored to
prosperity. He requested arhats to recite sūtras and the
Vinaya. There were at that time five great arhats, each of
whom led a group of disciples and disseminated the Dharma.
But their interpretation [of the Dharma] differed. Some
adhered to an open [interpretation], while others followed
the rules strictly. As they were all transmitted and studied,
they eventually split into five recensions, which the sixteen
great kingdoms [of India] employed concurrently according
to their needs. [Adherents of the five recensions] vied with
each other in maintaining their practice, and all attained
realization of the way. Unless they themselves had profound
understanding of the sacred way, how could this have
happened? Later five schools based on the different
recensions [of the *Vinaya*] arose in rivalry with each other.[65]

The rain's retreat led by Mahākāśyapa probably refers
to the First Council, which is also alleged to have taken place
in Rājagṛha. The fact that five variant recensions of the *Vinaya*
were produced during the Aśokan period in India is a different
legend from the one that tells of the Second Council under the
same King Aśoka, as a result of which the first schism took
place within the Buddhist religion between the Sthaviravāda
and Mahāsaṅghika. The schism was allegedly caused by the
lax interpretation of the *Vinaya* on the part of the Mahāsaṅghika. Both the schism and the variant recensions were
caused by a common element: differing interpretations of the
Vinaya.
This legend limits the *Vinaya* recensions to five, by refusing
to admit those of other schools. The five are the *Ssu-fen lu* of
the Dharmaguptaka school; *Shih-sung lu* of the Sarvāstivāda;
Wu-fen lu of the Mahiṃśāsaka; and the *Vinaya* of the Kāśyapīya;
and the Mahāsaṅghika *Vinaya* of the Mahāsaṅghika school.
Of these, the *Vinaya* of the Kāśyapīya school is no longer

extant. (However, a *Prātimokṣa* of this school is still extant, in the one-*chüan* translated as the *Chieh-t'o-chieh ching*, by Gautama Prajñāruci.)[66]

Both Seng-yu and other Chinese monks of his time seem to have accepted that five distinct recensions of the *Vinaya* were extant in India. For example, Seng-yu, in the section of "Hsin-chi lü lai han-ti ssu-pu hsü lu" [Preface to the four *Vinaya*s newly arrived at China] of his *CSTCC*, recounted the history of four *Vinaya* recensions—omitting only the Kāśyapīya. He noted that an earlier teacher, Hsien-cheng, had gone to Serindia in search of the *Vinaya* of the Kāśyapīya School, which had not yet been transmitted in China, but was unable to locate it. As he says:

> This particular *Vinaya* [of the Kāśyapīya School] has not been transmitted to the land of Liang. In older times, the former master Hsien-cheng went far into the Western Regions vowing to seek out the text. Although his superb mind was inspired by numinous signs, the Tsang-ling Ranges were treacherously steep, and he could not accomplish [his goal] of bringing out this text. Thus we know that this *Vinaya* as yet has no affinities with the Buddhist Order of Liang.[67]

In Seng-fang's *I-ching yüan-ch'i* [History of scriptural translation], which prefaces the *Chieh-t'o chieh-ching*, the previously mentioned *Prātimokṣa* translation, it is said that many had searched for a text of the complete Kāśyapīya *Vinaya*, but none had yet been located; they lamented over the missing one of the five.[68] It was for that reason that the Chinese were particularly pleased at obtaining a copy of the *Prātimokṣa* of that school. Since this *Prātimokṣa* was translated in 543, there was obviously still an ongoing effort to locate a complete copy of the missing *Vinaya*.

Thus far we have confirmed through documentary evidence that four complete and one partial recension of the *Vinaya* were known in China during Kyŏmik's time. The question here however is whether Kyŏmik was in any way connected with these recensions. The *Mirŭk pulgwangsa sajŏk* reference to "five recensions of the *Vinaya*" suggests that the same materials had already been transmitted to Paekche. If this were the case, it seems that Kyŏmik too believed that all five complete recensions of the *Vinaya* were extant in India, and decided to undertake the arduous journey to India in order to locate a copy of the missing Kāśyapīya *Vinaya*. This goal he shared in common with several other Chinese pilgrims of his time. The text of *Mirŭk pulgwangsa sajŏk*, however, could also be interpreted as meaning "Kyŏmik achieved his goal and returned with this great success," i.e. that he succeeded in obtaining all five *Vinaya* recensions. An even more radical interpretation of this passage might yield the sense that Kyŏmik was fortunate to have been able to obtain all those texts, which fellow pilgrims who risked their lives on their travels had been unable to locate.

The above speculation cannot be proven unless the history of the transmission of *Vinaya* texts to Paekche is understood as clearly as it is for China. For this we need documentary evidence, which is completely lacking. We do know that the translation of the four complete *Vinaya* collections was completed by 423, nearly one hundred years before Kyŏmik's time. But we have no records as to whether any of these collections were transmitted to Paekche by the sixth century. At this stage of our investigation, therefore, we can only say that Kyŏmik must have something to do with the transmission of the five recensions of the *Vinaya* to Paekche, though precisely what his role was remains a mystery.

NOTES

1. The original article is "Chūō ajia to kudara bunka," *Mahan paekche munhwa* (Mahan Paekche Culture) 7 (1984), pp. 85-105.

Abbreviations:

CSTCC: *Ch'u san-tsang chi-chi*
KSC: *Kao-seng chuan*
HKSC: *Hsü kao-seng chuan*

KYSCL: *K'ai-yüan shih-chiao lu*
LTSPC: *Li-tai san-pao chi*
TCKTC: *Ta Chou k'an-ting chung-ching mu-lu*
The original article in Japanese is marred by an inordinate number of misprints, which the translator has corrected in preparing the translation. Sanskrit personal and place names have been supplied, where available. Additional notes have been supplied in square brackets.

2. Although there are many names referring to the area under consideration, including Serindia, Central Asia, Western Regions, Inner Asia, and the Silk Road, I have chosen Serindia in accordance to the editorial policy of the present work. For the definition of Serindia, see Fukada Kyūya, Introduction to the *Chūō ajia tankenshi* [History of the Exploration of Serindia], special volume of the *Seiiki tanken kikō zenshū* (Tokyo: Kōsuisha, 1971).

3. Following is a list of the major studies consulted in the present essay:

1.) Reprint of earlier studies:

Imanishi Ryū. *Kudarashi kenkyū* (A Study of the History of Paekche). Tokyo: Kokusho kankōkai, 1970.

Karube Jion. *Kudara iseki no kenkyū* (A Study of the Historical Monuments of Paekche). Tokyo: Yoshikawa kobundō, 1971.

Tsuda Sōkichi. *Tsuda Sōkichi zenshū* (Collected Essays of Tsuda Sōkichi), vols. 11 & 12. Tokyo: Iwanami shoten, 1964.

Shiratori Kurakichi. *Shiratori Kurakichi zenshū* (Collected Essays of Shiratori Kurakichi), vols. 3 & 5. Tokyo: Iwanami shoten, 1970.

Ikeuchi Hiroshi. *Mansenshi kenkyū* (Studies in the History of Manchuria and Korea), Jōsei hen 2. Kyoto: Sokokusha 1951; repr. Yoshikawa kōbundō, 1960.

Mishina Akihide. *Mishina Akihide ronbunshū* (Collected Essays of Mishina Akihide), vols. 3, 4, 5. Tokyo: Heibonsha, 1971-73.

Suematsu Yasukazu, *Seikyū shisō* (Miscellaneous Essays on Korean History), Tokyo: Kasai shuppansha, 1965, 1966.

2.) Recent studies:

Sakamoto Yoshitane. *Kudarashi no kenkyū* (Studies in the History of Paekche). 2 vols. Tokyo: Hanawa shobō, 1978.

———. *Kodai higashi ajia no nihon to chosen* (Japan

and Korea in Ancient East Asia). Tokyo: Yoshikawa kōbundō, 1978.

Ōkawa Kiyoshi, ed. *Kudara no kōko gaku* (Archeology of Paekche). Tokyo: Yūzankaku, 1972.

Kudarashi kenkyūkai, ed. *Kudarashi no kenkyū* (A Study of the History of Paekche). Tokyo: Kokusho kankōkai, 1979.

Tamura Enchō and Hwang Suyŏng, eds. *Kudara bunka to Asuka bunka* (Cultures of Paekche and Asuka). Tokyo: Yoshikawa kobundō, 1978.

3.) Art:

Mainichi shinbunsha. *Bukkyō geijutsu* (Buddhist Art) 83 (Special volume on the Korean Buddhist art), 1972.

4.) Articles:

Tamura Enchō. "Kudara bukkyōshi josetsu" (Preliminary Investigation of the History of Buddhism in Paekche) in Tamura and Hwang, eds., *Kudara bunka to Asuka bunka*, pp. 305-357.

Saitō Tadashi. "Fuyogun shuri haijiseki ni mirareru garan haichi to sono genryū" (The Layout of Monastery in the Puyŏ Kunsu-ri Temple Ruins and its Origin) in Tamura and Hwang, ed., *Kudara bunka to Asuka bunka*, pp. 83-105.

Kitano Kōhei. "Kudara jidai jiinshi no bunpu to ricchi" (Distribution and Location of Monastic Remains from the Paekche Period), Tamura and Huang, ed., *Kudara bunka to suka bunka*, pp. 107-180.

Chin Hong-sŏp. "Kudara jiin no garan seido" (Monastic Structures of Paekche), in Kudarashi kenkyukai ed., *Kudarashi no kenkyū*, pp. 325-360.

Hong Yun-sik. "Chūgoku hokuchō to kudara no bukkyō" (Buddhism during the Nan-Pei Ch'ao Period in China and Paekche), *Bukkyōshi kenkyū* 18 (1983).

5.) Japanese translations:

Inoue Hideo. *Higashi ajia minzokushi* (History of the Peoples in East Asia), 2 vols. Tōyō bunko series, nos. 264 & 283. Tokyo: Heibonsha, 1974 & 1976.

4. The sources of the traditional accounts concerning these figures include *Samguk sagi, Samguk yusa, Haedong kosŭng chŏn*, and *Mirŭk pulgwangsa sajŏk*. Relevant passages will be discussed below. [Note that the name of the Serindian monk could be reconstructed as Kumāranandin; see Peter Lee, *Lives of Eminent Korean Monks: The Haedong Kosung chon*, Harvard-Yenching Institute Studies 25 (Cambridge: Harvard University Press, 1969), p. 26, n. 64.]

5. Japanese translations of the *Samguk sagi:* Kim Sa-yŏp, *Sangoku shiki*, 2 vols. (Tokyo: Rokkō shuppan, 1980, 1981); Inoue Hideo, *Sangoku shiki*, vols. 1 & 2, Tōyō bunko series, nos., 372 & 425 (Tokyo: Heibonsha, 1980 & 1984). The latter is still in progress.

6. Japanese translation of the *Samguk yusa:* Tsuboi Kumezō & Kusaka Hiroshi, *Genbun wayaku taishō sangoku iji* (Chōsen ken-kyūkai, 1915; Mishina Akihide, *Sangoku iji kōshō* vols. 1 & 2 (Tokyo: Asahi shinbunsha, 1976; Hayashi Hideki, *Sangoku iji* 2 vols., Tokyo: Sanichi shobō, 1975, 1976. [English trans.: Ha Tae-hung & Grafton K. Mintz, *Samguk Yusa:* Legends and History of the Three Kingdoms of Ancient Korea (Seoul: Yŏnsei University, 1972).]

7. T. 2065.50.1017b. [The English translation is quoted, with some slight amendments, from Peter Lee, *Lives of Eminent Korean Monks*, pp. 45-46.]

8. [As regards the date, the text says that seventh year of the King Sŏng (529); however the cyclical year given corresponds to 526. An interlinear comment inserted in the text accepts the latter as correct.]

9. Yi Nŭnghwa, *Chosŏn pulgyo t'ongsa* [A General History of Korean Buddhism] (3 vols. 1918; reprint ed., Seoul: Poryon'gak, 1979), p. 103.

10. Tongguk taehakkyo pulgyo munhwa yŏn'guso, *Kankoku bussho kaidai jiten* (Annotated Bibliography of Korean Buddhist Books) (Tokyo: Kokusho kankōkai, 1982), pp. 4-5.

11. Naitō Shumpo, "Chōsen shinakan no kōro oyobi sono suii ni tsuite" (Sea Routes between Korea and Chin and Their Changes), in *Naitō hakushi sōju kinen shigaku ronsō* (Tokyo: Kōbundō, 1930), p. 333; Satomichi Norio, "Chōsen hantō no bukkyō" (Buddhism in the Korean Peninsula) in *Chūgoku bukkyōshi:* Chūgokuhen IV,

Higashi ajia shochiiki no bukkyō (Tokyo: Kōseisha, 1976), p. 20 ff.

12. The discussion in the following sections are primarily based on Tsukamoto Zenryū, *Chūgoku bukkyō tsūshi* (Comprehensive History of Chinese Buddhism) (Tokyo: Suzuki gakujutsu zaidan, 1968) and Kamata Shigeo, *Chūgoku bukkyōshi* [History of Chinese Buddhism], vols. 1 & 2 (Tokyo: Tokyō daigaku shuppankai, 1982, 1983).

13. [Kodama accepts the historicity of this event; I have changed the translation to the conditional tense, to reflect Michael Rogers' interpretation of this battle as historiographical legerdemain; see Michael C. Rogers, *The Chronicle of Fu Chien:* A Case of Exemplar History, Chinese Dynastic Histories Translations, no. 10 (Berkeley and Los Angeles: University of California Press, 1968), especially p. 64-69.]

14. Tsukamoto, *Chūgoku bukkyō tsūshi*, p. 420ff; Kamata, *Chūgoku bukkyōshi* vol. 2, p. 252ff.

15. Kamata, *Chūgoku bukkyōshi*, vol. 2, p. 19ff.

16. *Chin-shu chuan* 113-114, Fu Chien Tsai-chi; *Shi-liu ch'un-ch'iu chan* 36-38, Fu Chien Chuan; Tsukamoto, *Chūgoku bukkyō tsūshi*, p. 542ff; Kamata, *Chūgoku bukkyōshi* vol. 2, p. 238ff.

17. The *Shih-liu kuo ch'un-ch'iu chuan* 37, "Ch'ien-Ch'in Lu" reads as follows:

Seventeenth year of the Chien-yüan reign period [381], spring, second month. The kings of Shan-shan and Ch'e-shih all came to the court. They had an audience with [Fu] Chien in the Front Basilica of T'ai-chi. Ta-wan (Ferghana) presented a blood-sweating horse, Su-shen presented arrows made of *hu* tree, India [presented] fireproof cloth, Ch'iang-i-mo presented sheep,* the kingdom of Silla presented beautiful women. This kingdom is located east of Paekche; many of its people have beautiful hair of over one foot in length. K'eng-chü (Samarkand), Yü-t'ien (Khotan) and the kingdoms of Hai-tung (Korea), some sixty-two kings in all sent envoys and presented their respective local products (*Shih-liu kuo ch'un-ch'iu* 37, Ch'ien Ch'in lu 5).

[* "Sheep here is literally *yang liu-chueh erh-k'ou ssu-chueh pa- k'ou* (sheep of six horns and two mouths, and four horns and eight mouths), a problematic passage which I have tentatively taken as a reference to sheep. However, *liu-chüeh* and *ssu-chüeh* could be a reference to

Hsiung-nu kings as well, in which case I have yet to determine the precise reference of *erh-k'ou* and *pa-k'ou*. The author cites the Chinese passage, but provides no glosses.]

18. Koguryŏ was under the control of Former Yen. When Former Yen was defeated by Fu Chien in 370, Mu-jung P'ing, a member of the royal family of Yen, fled to Koguryŏ. But the King Kogugwŏn captured him and sent him back to Fu Chien. Fu Chien then sent the monk Hsün-tao together with a Buddha image and scriptures to King Sosurim of Koguryŏ. This is the traditional inception of Buddhism in Korea. See Tamura Enchō, *Kodai chōsen bukkyō to nihon bukkyō* (Tokyo: Yoshikawa kōbundō, 1980), pp. 6-7.

19. According to the *Shih-liu ch'un-ch'iu*, Silla also sent tribute. This apparently refers to the Silla king, Naemul.

20. Tsukamoto, *Chūgoku bukkyō tsūshi*, p. 475ff; Kamata *Chūgoku bukkyōshi* vol., 1, 357ff.

21. CSTCC 8, T. 2145.55.52b, preface to the *Mahāprajñā-pāramitā;* ibid. 9, 64c, preface to *Su a-han mu-ch'ao;* ibid. 11, 80a-c, preface to *Pi-ch'iu ta-chieh*, KSC 1, T. 2059.50.328b-329a.

22. For Kumārajīva, see Ōchō Enichi and Suwa Yoshizumi, *Rajū* (Kumārajīva), *Chūgoku no jinbutsu series.* (Tokyo: Daizō shuppan, 1982.) Kamata, *Chūgoku bukkyōshi*, p. 207ff. Tsukamoto Zenryū, "Kumarajū ron" (Essay on Kumārajīva) (1) & (2), in *Yūki kyōju shoju kinen bukkyō shisōshi ronshū* (Tokyo: Daizō shuppan, 1964), 359-378, and in *Hikata hakushi koki kinen ronbunshū* (Fukuoka: Hikata hakushi koki kinenkai, 1964), pp. 353-370. Ōchō Enrichi, "Kumarajū no honyaku" (The Translations of Kumārajīva), *Ōtani gakuhō* 37:4 (1958), pp. 1-25. T'ang Yung-t'ung, *Han-Wei liang-Chin Nan-pei ch'ao fo-chiao shih* (History of Buddhism during the Han, Wei, Western and Eastern Chin, and Nan-Pei Ch'ao Periods) (Ch'ang-sha: Commercial Press, 1938), p. 278-340.

23. Although not directly concerned with the political situation in China, Tamura Enchō has suggested that the transmission of Buddhism to Paekche was the "bestowment" of Eastern Chin. That is, Paekche entered the sanctioning system (*ts'e-feng ti-chih*) of Eastern Chin in 372, and hence the introduction of Buddhism in 384 was not so much a choice of the King Ch'imnyu or nobilities than a mere acceptance of the inevitable. See his *Kodai chōsen bukkyō*

to nihon bukkyō, p. 10.

24. Naitō Shumpo, "Chōsen shina kan no kōro," pp. 275-380.

Ch'oe Kŭmuk, "Kudara no chūgoku kankei ni kansuru shokō: (A Note on the Ties between Paekche and China), *Kudarashi kenkyū* (Tokyo: Kokusho kankōkai, 1979), p. 214ff. Tamura Enchō, *Kodai Chōsen bukkyō to Nihon bukkyō*, p. 16ff.

25. Naitō, "Chōsen shina kan no kōro," p. 278ff. Note that Ch'oe Kŭmuk recognizes only three routes. See his "Kudara no chūgoku ni kansuru shokō," p. 214ff.

26. "Chosen shina kan no kōro," pp. 332-335.

27. "Chosen shina kan no kōro," p. 333.

28. CSTCC 11, T. 2145.55.80a.

29. Ōchō Enichi, "Koritsu denrai izen no chūgoku ni okeru kairitsu" (*Vinaya* in China before the Transmission of the Complete *Vinaya*s), in his *Chūgoku bukkyō no kenkyū* vol. 1 (Kyoto: Hozōkan, 1958), pp. 11-189. Hirakawa Akira, "Kanyaku ritten honyaku no kenkyū" (A Study of the Chinese Translations of the *Vinaya*), in his *Ritsuzō no kenkyū* (Tokyo: Sankibō busshorin, 1960), pp. 115-289.

30. KSC 1, T. 2059.50.324c-325a.

31. Hirakawa Akira, *Ritsuzō no kenkyū*, p. 202ff.

32. *Ritsuzō no kenkyū*, pp. 189-220.

33. CSTCC 11, T. 2145.55.80a-c.

34. T. 1464.24.851a.

35. *Ritsuzō no kenkyū*, pp. 155-169.

36. Of the *Vinaya* texts translated before the *Shih-sung lu, Pi-nai-yeh* by Chu Fo-nien is also called *Chien yin-yüan ching*, which, as Hirakawa pointed out, describes the history concerning the establishment of each of the 250 precepts, and corresponds to the *Sutta-vibhaṅga* of the complete *Vinaya*. Since a complete *Vinaya* consists of *Bhikkhuvibhaṅga* and *Bhikkhunīvibhaṅga, Khanadhaka*, and *Parivāra*, the *Pi-na-yeh* is an incomplete *Vinaya*.

37. Nagasawa Kazutoshi has translated these as *Hōkenden Sōun kōki* (Biography of Fa-hsien and the Travelogue of Sung-yün), Tōyō

bunka series 194 (Tokyo: Heibonsha, 1971). Uchida Ginpū, "Gogi Sōun shaku Eshō seiiki gukyōki kōnin josetsu" (Historical Investigation of the *Hsi-yü ch'iu-ching chi* by Sung-yün and Shih Hui-sheng of Eastern Wei, a Preliminary Study), in *Tsukamoto hakushi shōju kinen bukkyō* shigaku ronshū, pp. 113-124. Funaki Katsuma, "Hokugi no seiiki kōtsu ni kansuru shomondai" (Issues Concerning the Routes through Serindia during the Northern Wei Period), *Nishi nihon shigaku* 4 (1950). [See also, Nagasawa Kazutoshi, "Iwayuru *Sōun kōki* ni tsuite" (On the So-called *Travelogue of Sung-yün*), in his *Shiruku rōdoshi kenkyū* (Tokyo: Kokusho kankōkai, 1979), pp. 459-480.]

38. *Chi Shen-chou san-pao kan-t'ung lu* 2, T. 2106.52.419b; *Fayuan chu-lin* 14, T. 2122.53.389a; *Kuan Hüng-ming chi* 15, T. 2103.52.202b. Concerning the above sources of Hao-ch'ien, I am indebted to Professor Nakayama Shōkō.

39. On Bodhiruci, see HKSC 1, T. 2060.50.428a; KYSCL 6, T. 2153.55.541b. On Guṇamati, see KHSC 7, 482b-c; KYSCL 6, 540b. On Buddhaśānta, see HKSC 21, 607b-c; KYSCL 6, 542b. On Gautama Prajñāruci, see HKSC 1, 428a; KYSCL 6, 542c-543a.

40. KSC 1, T. 2059.50.329b. [The chart is arranged by name, birthplace, and route taken.]

41. KSC 2, T. 2059.50.334b-c; CSTCC 14, T. 2145.55.103b-104a.

42. CSTCC 15, T. 2145.55.111b; KSC 3, T. 2059.50.337b.

43. CSTCC 15, T. 2145.55.113c; KSC 3, T. 2059.50.338b.

44. CSTCC 2, 3, T. 2145.55.12b, 21a; KSC 3, T. 2059.50.339a.

45. CSTCC 14, T. 2145.55.104a; KSC 3, T. 2059.50.339a.

46. KSC 3, T. 2059.50.342b-c.

47. CSTCC 15, T. 2145.55.112b; KSC 3, T. 2059.50.339a.

48. CSTCC 14, T. 2145.55.105b; KSC 3, T. 2059.50.344a.

49. CSTCC 11, T. 2145.55.82a; LTSPC 11, T. 2034.49.95b-c; KYSCL 6, T. 2154.55.535c.

50. KYSCL 5, T. 2154.55.532c; TCKTC 10, T. 2153.55.433a.

51. LTSPC 11, T. 2034.49.98b; HKSC 1, T. 2060.426a; KYSCL 6,

T. 2154.55.537b.

52. LTSPC 11, 98b-c; HKSC 1, 426a; KYSCL 6, 537c.

53. HKSC 1, T. 2060.50.429c.

54. KYSCL 7, T. 2154.55.547a-b.

55. Major studies on trade routes include: Mikami Tsugio, "Kodai ni okeru kōeki to bunka kōryū" (Trading and Cultural Exchange in Ancient Times), in *Kodaishi kōza* 13 (Tokyo: Gakuseisha, 1966); Fujita Toyohachi, *Tōzai kōshōshi no kenkyū* (A Study of the History of Contacts between East and West), Nankai hen (Tokyo: Oka shoin, 1932); Ishida Mikinosuke, *Nankai ni kansuru shina shiryō* (Chinese Sources on the South Seas) (Tokyo: Seikatsusha, 1945); Matsuda Toshio, Hanboku to nankai: *Ajiashi ni okeru sabaku to kaiyō* (Northern China and the South Seas: Desert and Ocean in Asian History) (Tokyo: Shikai shobō, 1942).

56. Ōchō & Suwa, *Rajū*, p. 134.

57. In addition to the sources mentioned in note 54, see also Sir Charles Eliot: *Hinduism and Buddhism*, vol. 4 (London, 1921), pp. 11-187.

58. Fujita Toyohachi, "Zenkan ni okeru seinan kaijō kōtsū no kiroku" (Record of the Routes on the South-Western Sea during the Former Han Period), in his *Tōzai kōshōshi no kenkyū*, pp. 95-135.

59. The "Fu-nan chuan" in the *Nan-ch'i shu* and *Liang-shu*. Sugimoto Naojirō, "Indonesia kodai shakai no shiteki seikaku: tokuni funan no baai" (Historical characteristics of the ancient societies of Indo-China, with special reference to Fu-nan), in *Tōnan ajiashi kenkyū* 1 (Tokyo: Nihon gakujutsu shinkōkai, 1956), pp. 308-526. Yamamoto Tatsurō, "Indoshina no kenkoku setsuwa" (Foundation Legends of Indo-China), in *Tōzai kōshō shiron* vol. 1 (Tokyo: Toyama shobō, 1939), pp. 261-314. Yamamoto, "Kodai nankai kōtsū to funan no bunka" (Routes through the Ancient South Seas and the Culture of Fu-nan), in *Kodaishi kōza* 13 (Tokyo: Gakuseisha, 1966), pp. 124-144.

60. Yamamoto, "Kodai no nankai kōtsū," pp. 131-132.

61. Biography of Seng-ch'ieh-po-lo, HKSC 1, T. 2060.50.426a.

62. Yamamoto, "Kodai no nankai kōtsū," p. 133.

63. For the study of the transmission of the five recensions of the *Vinaya*, see Hirakawa, *Ritsuzō no kenkyū*, pp. 138-141, 145-146. Miyamoto Shōson, *Daijō to shōjō* (Mahāyāna and Hīnayāna), Bukkyō no konpon mondai vol. 3 (Tokyo: Yagumo shoten, 1944), 278-279, 492-496.

64. *Ritsuzō no kenkyū*, p. 139.

65. CSTCC 3, T. 2145.55.19c.

66. T. 1460.24.659a.

67. T. 2145.55.21b.

68. T. 1460.24.659a.

The Transmission of Paekche Buddhism to Japan [1]

by Kamata Shigeo

Translated by Kyoko Tokuno

The official date of the transmission of Paekche Buddhism to Japan varies in different sources. The *Nihon shoki*, for example, gives the date as 552, while the *Gankōji garan engi narabini ryūki shizaichō* (History of the Gankōji monastery and Ledger of Property and Income) and the *Jōgū Shōtoku hōō teisetsu* (Biography of Prince Shōtoku, King of the Dharma) claim that the transmission occurred in 538; the latter date is the one most commonly accepted by modern scholars. All these documents agree that Paekche Buddhism came to Japan during the reign of King Sŏng (523-553), who sent Buddhist monks, images and scriptures to the royal court in Japan. While this is the official account, it is plausible that the first transmission of Buddhism to Japan occurred earlier. The lack of any corroborating literary evidence, however, prevents us from determining with any precision this earlier date. The purpose of this article is to reexamine the traditional dates as well as the characteristics of that early Buddhism, by referring to the history of the Buddhist transmission in the rest of East Asia.

The Route and Date of the Introduction of Buddhism to China

Previously it was believed that the route of the transmission of Buddhism to China started in northwestern India and proceeded through Central Asia to Ch'ang-an and Lo-yang in the central Chinese plain. From these centers it then spread throughout central and southern China. There were a number of routes through Central Asia, most notably the "silk routes" along the northern or southern edges of the Taklamakan desert as well as those that traversed the northern area of the T'ien-shan Mountains; it is generally accepted that the first transmission must have come from these major trade routes. The official account of the first transmission into China, sets the date at 2 B.C. However, it would be more realistic to assume that Buddhism was introduced to China sometime between the first century B.C. and the beginning of the Common Era.

Recent publications by Chinese archaeologists contain information which is important for determining the transmission route. For example, the discovery of reliefs with images of the Buddhas at Mount K'ung-wang, which is located in the suburbs of the city of Lien-yün-kang in the southern part of the Shang-tung peninsula just north of An-hui Province, dated to the Latter Han period (25-220) raises many questions about the spread of early Buddhism. Another discovery dating to the same period is a Buddhist image on the wall of a tomb at Ho-lin-ke-erh in Inner Mongolia. Mount K'ung-wang is located in an area near the East China Sea, and Ho-lin-ke-erh is near the great bend of the Yellow River. These archaeological discoveries, as I will show below, demand that we reconsider the route of the Buddhist transmission to East Asia—including the Korean kingdoms of Koguryŏ and Paekche—and by extension Japan.

The Transmission Path of Buddhism: A Reconsideration

The recent work of Chinese archaeologists has yielded important discoveries that will assist in the reconstruction of Buddhist history. It is striking that these discoveries, though ranging over a wide area, have all been found outside the central plain of China, the main cultural area for the Han Chinese.[2] It has been traditionally thought that Buddhism was introduced into China by two different routes: the first was overland, which went from India into Central Asia, entering China by way of Tun-huang, Yu-men, and Lan-chou and reaching the Chinese capitals of Ch'ang-an and Lo-yang. The second was the direct route from Central Asia to Lo-yang. From Lo-yang, Buddhism spread throughout the Wei River basin and down to the northern shore of the Yangtze River. The existence of these two routes has been backed up by literary evidence that mentions the Buddhist faith of Ch'u-wang-ying and the wide ranging scope of his religious activities.[3] The *Hsi-ching-fu* (Rhapsody of the Western Capital) also describes a foreign monk who visited Lo-yang during the Latter Han period and Buddhist sources report translations being made of Buddhist texts.[4]

When we look at the archaeological evidence mentioned above, we see that there was an early spread of Buddhism into such areas as Inner Mongolia, Shantung and its periphery, and Szechwan. How can we explain these differing records of the transmission of Buddhism? One way to interpret this evidence is to assume that Buddhism was transmitted to the central plain and the two capitals, in just the way described in the literary sources. From these centers, it then spread to the outlying regions of Shantung, Szechwan and Inner Mongolia, where we find Buddhist images in tombs. A second response, which takes no note of the literary evidence, would be that the transmission routes were direct from Central Asia to Szechwan and Inner Mongolia. A third possibility which could account for the Mount K'ung-wang images, is that the transmission routes were not limited to those that passed through Central Asia; rather, Buddhism was also brought via the sea route through Southeast Asia, and thus Buddhist images were left along the coast line.

There are problems with all of these speculations. If we consider the situation whereby the early transmission came by sea, the introduction of Buddhist sculpture to East Asia at this date would seem imporbable, given the late dating of extant Indian Buddhist images. It is also necessary to explain how the transportation difficulties of the sea route during the Latter Han period were overcome. This leaves us with the more reasonable alternative that Buddhism was first transmitted to the central plains during the Latter Han, from whence it was disseminated throughout the peripheral regions.

We are still left, however, with the question of whether Buddhism was transmitted to the remote regions of East Asia during the Latter Han. This scenario is based entirely on archaeological evidence; there are no literary sources that mention these collateral transmissions. This lack of supporting evidence for the early arrival of Buddhism in these areas, raises the question of whether the artifacts discovered there can correctly be dated to this period. While Chinese scholars have dated some of them to the latter half of the second century A.D., I believe that they should be given a later date, perhaps the end of the Latter Han, the Three Kingdoms period, or even to the Early Chin (ca. early 3rd-early 4th centuries). This would be the logical dating if the first transmission route, via Central Asia directly to the central plain of China and thence to outlying regions, were accepted.

If one were to acknowledge the possibility of an alternate route, this dating would not be an issue. It is, for example, possible to reach the Inner Mongolian Autonomous Region by way of Lan-chou and Yin-ch'uan, or via the northern route that skirts the Pa-t'an-chi-lin Desert using camels for transportation. Given that Ho-lin-ke-erh of Inner Mongolia and the city of Ta-t'ung of Shansi are not far from each other, it would have been possible to bypass the central Chinese plain. This possible northern route would have gone from Inner Mongolia to Ta-t'ung, Chang-chia-k'o, Ch'eng-teh and Chin-chou and then to the northern Korean kingdom of Koguryŏ.

By reconsidering the routes of transmission in this manner, we may conjecture that the transmission to Korea occurred earlier than is indicated in the official records, that is 372 for Koguryŏ and 384 for Paekche. If we are able to push forward the date of the transmission of Buddhism to the Korean peninsula, then we can also do the same for Japan, placing the arrival of Buddhism as early as the 5th century. While these earlier dates are but speculation at this point, future discoveries of artifacts from these regions may give us the verification we need.

The presence of Buddhist images at Mount K'ung-wang provides us with the possibility of an alternate route for the contact with Korea. Going east from Lien-yun-hang across the Yellow Sea, one reaches the Paekche region in the southwest part of the country. At Mount Tan, there is a Paekche cliff image of Maitreya, which is considered to be quite ancient. There was also a huge four-faced stone Buddha discovered in 1983 at Mount Ye in the South Ch'ung-chung Province. The fact that such images are found along the route from the Shangtung area gives us further evidence that the date of the transmission of Buddhism to Korea need not be determined solely on the basis of literary evidence.

The Character of Paekche Buddhism

Paekche was bordered by Koguryŏ in the north and Silla in the east. Because all of the overland routes to China and Japan were blocked by its neighboring states, Paekche with its capital at Hansŏng was forced to develop sea routes. Thus, it is probable that Buddhism came to Paekche by sea rather than land.

With regard to the arrival of Buddhism in Paekche, the twenty-fourth volume of the *Samguk sagi* relates:

Ch'imnyu was the first son of the founding king, Kŭn'gusu. His mother was the matron, Ani. He ascended to the throne succeeding his father. In the autumn, seventh month, he dispatched an envoy to Chin, carrying tribute to the court. In the ninth month, the foreign monk, Maranant'a, arrived from (Eastern) Chin. The king welcomed him and paid reverence to him in the palace. This was the inception of the Buddhadharma.

The third volume of the *Samguk yusa* and the first one of the *Haedong kosŭng-chŏn* give approximately the same account. Thus, the transmission of Buddhism to Paekche was assumed to have been carried out by a Serindian monk and it entered

Paekche by way of the Eastern Chin dynasty. In the second month of the following year (385), a Buddhist monastery was constructed in the capital, Hansŏng, and ten monks were ordained (SS 24). Eight years later, in the second month of the first year of King Asin's reign (392), an edict was issued saying, "Worship the Buddhadharma and seek for merit." In this way the king exhorted his subjects to accept Buddhism. Judging from these early records, Paekche Buddhism was a court-centered religion which was accepted and supported primarily because it was perceived to be of value in averting disasters and gaining success in worldly matters. The same attitudes toward Buddhism were also found in Koguryŏ.

From this time until the fourth year of King Sŏng (526), there are no extant literary records concerning Buddhism. During this period, Paekche was engaged in successive wars with Koguryŏ and Silla. The invasions from the northern kingdom increased dramatically after the Koguryŏ capital was moved south to P'yŏngyang during the first year of the rule of King Piyu (427). In the ninth month of the twenty-first year of King Kaero (148), the Koguryŏ King Changsu secretly sent a monk named Torim to Paekche with the hope of weakening the kingdom by encouraging the power of Buddhism (SS.25). Torim urged King Kaero to restore the citadel, construct a new palace and repair the royal tomb. These projects were undertaken on such a grand scale that the resources of the nation were completely exhausted. In order to raise funds for these projects the King was forced to raise taxes which, being a hardship on the population, brought about internal dissension. Koguryŏ taking advantage of this instability in Paekche undertook a military campaign that resulted in the fall of the Paekche capital of Hansŏng and the assassination of the king. The new king of Paekche Munju quickly moved his capital to Ungjin (present Kongju) to avoid the Koguryŏ invasions. This story from the ancient records gives us insight into the role of Buddhism at court.

Buddhism, however, continued to develop in Paekche despite its problems with the neighboring states. The monk

Kyŏmik returned from a pilgrimage to India in 526, bringing with him the Indian master Paedalta (Vedatta?), who carried with him a *Vinaya* of one of the five schools (*Obuyul*). With the introduction of these rules of conduct for monks, a school based on the *Vinaya* emerged within the ranks of the monastic community in Paekche. Tamuk and Hyein wrote a commentary of thirty-six rolls on this Indian text. In an attempt to strengthen Buddhism, gifts were sent to the court of Emperor Wu of Liang in 541, with a request for a copy of the *Mahāparinirvāṇasūtra*, as well as teachers, artisans and painters. By this time the Paekche capital had again moved, this time to Sabi (Puyŏ) and the name of the kingdom had been changed to "Southern Puyŏ" in 538 (SS 26).

In the first year of King Pŏp (599), an edict was issued which prohibited the killing of any living creatures anywhere within the realm, this included the freeing of all falcons used for hunting and the destruction of all implements used for hunting or fishing. Wanghŭng Monastery was constructed in the first month of the following year (600), and the event was celebrated by ordaining thirty monks. During the summer dry season, the King visited Ch'irak Monastery to pray for rain (SS 27). This event has also been recorded in the third volume of the *Samguk yusa* where another account of the prohibition of killing is given. From these records, we can see that the *Vinaya* precepts were widely observed in Paekche. The scale of Buddhist activity in the Paekche kingdom greatly exceeded that of Koguryŏ. Enormous monastic complexes were constructed, as can be seen from the legend regarding the building of the Mirŭk (Maitreya) Monastery in Iksan as well as the construction of the Wanghŭng Monastery in 634. (There is a possibility that the two were in fact the same). Professor Cho Myŏng-gi has noted some of the domestic problems that resulted from the fact that Paekche invested so much of its national resources in the construction of monasteries:

> Because Paekche Buddhism had the *Vinaya* at its core, the people's way of thinking was affected by the outward

trappings of the tradition, so that Paekche squandered the nation's wealth on the construction of ostentatious monasteries.[5]

It was Paekche among the three Korean kingdoms that first initiated cultural communications with Japan and consequently contributed so much to the development of the culture there. But we must remember that the religious influences from Paekche were overshadowed by the material culture which was being introduced from the Korean peninsula to the aristocracy of Japan. For example, even in Paekche, when the royal family visited a Buddhist monastery it was primarily a pleasure trip rather than a religious pilgrimage. Thus, it is probable that the splendid lifestyle of the court may have been the cause of financial distress rather than their support of Buddhism. In any case, the nation became vulnerable to incursions from its rivals and in 660, the combined forces of Silla and their Chinese T'ang supporters, conquered Paekche. With the fall of Paekche, many Buddhist monks fled to Japan where they gave an impetus to the developing Buddhist movement there.

Transmission of Paekche Buddhism to Japan

Early Japanese Buddhism was transmitted from both Korea and the Chinese mainland. Therefore, we can only understand developments in Japan by understanding the position that Buddhism held in both these nations. As stated above, because of the close ties between the Paekche and Japanese courts, it was the Buddhism of Paekche that was first transmitted to Japan; only later was there contact with the Buddhists of Koguryǒ. The Buddhism that was revered by the Soga clan was primarily that of Paekche.[6] It was probably not until the seventh century that the Buddhist tradition of Silla entered Japan during the reign of Suiko (593-628). During the same century, Buddhism from China entered with the return of monks who had been sent during the Sui dynasty.

Buddhism was transmitted from Paekche in 552, during

the tenth month of the thirteenth year of Emperor Kimmei. At that time King Sŏng of Paekche sent an envoy to Japan. This envoy carried with him a bronze image of Śākyamuni Buddha, as well as pennants, canopies, sūtras and śāstras. He also brought a proclamation from King Sŏng which told of the merit which would accrue to the court from the display and veneration of these objects (*NS* 19). According to the *Jōgū shōtoku hōō teisetsu*, however, the date of transmission was earlier (538). Although it is not clear which of these dates is correct, the latter one seems more likely for the following reason. In 624, the thirty-second year of the Suiko, the Paekche monk Kwallŭk made a statement as follows:

> It has not been even one hundred years since our king, having hear that the Japanese emperor was wise, sent Buddhist images and scriptures to Japan. (*NS* 22).

If we were to accept the 538 date, it would mean that a period of eighty-six years would have elapsed from the time of Suiko until Kwallŭk's statement.[7] In addition to this information, it should be noted that in 523 Paekche gave official recognition to Japan. With this evidence, the date of 538 for the transmission of Buddhism seems plausible.

There was, moreover, interaction between Japan and Paekche before the above mentioned Buddhist gifts were sent. For example the *Nihon shoki* relates that, in 283, "The Paekche king sent a seamstress named Chinmojin. She was the founder of tailoring in Japan." (NS 10). In the following year, Ajikki, who was an expert in both the Confucian classics and Buddhist scriptures arrived in Japan. He is perhaps best remembered because he brought along two very impressive horses. On his recommendation, the scholar Wang In arrived in Japan in 285. He became a tutor to the crown prince and introduced the *Lunyü* (Confucian Analects) and the *Ch'ien-tsu wen* (Thousand-Character Classic) to the court. These cultural contributions from Korea continued into the sixth century; in 513 Tanyangi, a master of the Five Classics arrived from Paekche followed in 516 by the Confucian scholar Han'goanmu. The flow of monks from Korea to Japan continued even after the introduction of Buddhism. In the fifteenth year of Emperor Kimmei (554), ten monks led by Tamhye came to Japan. Prior to the arrival of this group, we have a record that Tosim and seven other monks were already in residence there. Tamhye was housed in a newly constructed monastery and it was said, perhaps erroneously, that he was the first monk to reside in Japan. While we do not know with any certainty the type of Buddhism taught by these two masters, it is possible that they were students of the Mādhyamika and Tattvasiddhi schools. There are various theories about the number of monks who arrived from Paekche during this period. The records assert that not only Buddhist monks travelled to Japan but there were also specialists in the *I-Ching* (Book of Changes), and the classics and medicine. Judging from this account of the variety of specialists who served as the cultural guides, it can be assumed that some sort of educational institutions were established in Japan, where Confucian scholars, Buddhist monks and other adepts lived and taught. These Paekche scholars and monks served a tour of duty in Japan and then returned home.

This contact between Paekche and Japan increased, and in 577 in the sixth year of Emperor Bidatsu, Paekche sent a delegation of Buddhist scholars, teachers and meditation masters to Owakeno ōkimi-dera in Naniwa (present Osaka). The degree of veneration shown to these Buddhists is exemplified by Prince Shōtoku's regard for Illa, who came in 583. The prince considered him to be a divine person and revered him as an incarnation of the bodhisattva Avalokiteśvara. Illa lived on Mount Ken'o in Sesstu (present Osaka and Hyōgo) where he was assassinated by a Silla enemy.[8] These Paekche monks, who were held in high regard, were true pioneers in the process of transplanting the seed of the Buddhadharma to Japan.

The sixth century was an active one for Buddhist missionary activity. In the second year of Emperor Yōmei (587), the

Paekche monk P'ungguk was invited to teach the Dharma by the younger brother of the Emperor, Prince Anahobe. In order to give help to the ailing emperor, Kuratsukuri no Tasuna built Sakata Monastery and commissioned a Korean monk to construct a six foot high image of the Buddha. The emperor's health continued to fail, however, and he died on the ninth day of the fourth month of that year. Fortunately, Prince Shōtoku and his supporters were able to defeat the group that called for the ouster of this alien religion. The culmination of this growing power of Buddhism in Japan came with the building of Shitennō Monastery and the invitation to the Paekche monk P'ungguk to conduct the ritual ceremony commemorating the completion of the building. Afterwards, he was installed as the first abbot of the monastery.

The first year of Emperor Sushun (588), saw the arrival of the monk Hyech'ong who presented sacred relics of the Buddha to the throne. Hyech'ong was accompanied by architects, T'aeryang Mal'tae and Mun'ga Koja[9] as well as by the painter Paekka and an anonymous tile expert. Besides these architects, carpenters, metal workers and other artisans, Hyech'ong had a group monks travelling with him, Yŏngjo, Yŏngwi, Hyejung, Hyesuk, Toŏm, and Yŏnggae. These artisans and monks were associated with the building and completion of Hōkō Monastery and Hyech'ong became a resident in that site.

At the beginning of the seventh century, the tenth year of Empress Suiko (602), the Paekche Mādhyamika scholar Kwallŭk arrived. He brought with him documents on calendrics, astronomy, geometry, divination and numerology—an indication of the breadth of interest among scholar monks. With the blessing of the emperor, he lived at Gankō Monastery and gathered around him a select group of thirty-four students. Among them were Yagonofubito no Oyatamafuru who studied calendrics, Ōtomo no Sugirikōsō focusing on astonomy, divination and numerology, and Yamashiro no Omihitate who was trained in numerology. There was not universal support for this mixture of traditions, for we are told that Prince Shōtoku commented on the matter:

When I was residing at Mount Kō, Kwallŭk was my disciple. He was fond of astronomy and geography, and I admonished him concerning his involvement with such sciences and particularly his confusing them with the True Vehicle. Even so our karmic affinity was not exhasted, he still followed me" (*Honchō Kōsōden* 1).[10]

The support which Kwallŭk had in the court was shown in the thirty-second year of Empress Suiko (624), when he was appointed to the office of "Bishop".[11] At the same time a Koguryŏ monk Tŏkchŏk was made the "Overseer of the saṅgha". This was the inception of the Buddhist ecclesiastical hierarchy in Japan.

Eleven Paekche monks, including Hyemi and Tohŭm, while on their way to the Wu court in China under imperial order, were shipwrecked in a severe storm and drifted into the Ashikita Bay of Higo (present Kumamoto in Kyūshū). The local prefect reported this event to the military headquarters at Dazaifu along with the request from the monks to be granted asylum. This was granted and the eleven were received at Gankō Monastery on the fifth month of the seventeenth year of Empress Suiko (609).

Later in the century, (688, the second year of Emperor Jitō), there was a drought that affected the entire nation. The emperor ordered Tojang[12], who had arrived in Japan during the Hakuhō reign period (673-685), to perform a rain-making ritual. It is said that he was successful, for as soon as he began to chant, the rain started to fall. Tojang was a scholar of the Tattvasiddhi sect, and he compiled a commentary to the *Tattvasiddhiśāstra* and the *Songsillon-so*[13] in sixteen fascicles. The monks at Todai Monastery always consulted his commentary whenever they studied the *Tattvasiddhiśāstra*.

In this manner, the transmission of Paekche Buddhism and culture continued until Paekche was conquered by Silla. During this period many Korean monks were granted permanent residence in Japan. In addition to the study of the Buddhist texts, they performed thaumaturgic rites, such as those concerned with rain making and healing. The importance of these monks to the early development of Buddhism in Japan is made evident by the construction and naming of the Kudaradai Monastery (Great Paekche Monastery) during the eleventh year of Emperor Jomei (639).

Not only monks but nuns also were involved in this process of bringing Buddhist practice from Paekche to Japan. Three Japanese nuns Zenshin, Zensō and Eizen, travelled to Paekche in the second year of Emperor Yōmei (587) in order to study *Vinaya*. They carried on their study of the six sections of the *Vinaya* and the three levels of the *upasaṃpadā*. They pursued their studies for three years and returned to Japan and established the first formal study of the *Vinaya*. They were housed in Sakurai Monastery where other nuns were later ordained.

Some laymen such as Kuratsukuri no Tasuna who took the Buddhist name of Tokusai joined the order and took full ordination. Others who followed in this pattern were: Zensō, Zentsū, Myōtoku, Hōjōshō, Zenchisō, Zenchie, Zenkō[14], Zentoku, Zenmyō and Myōkō.

For one hundred years after the first transmission of Buddhism to Japan, the relationship with Paekche was very close. And even after the defeat of Paekche in the second year of Emperor Tenchi (663), there were numerous refugees who sought safety in Japan. Among these refugees were many monks who exerted an influence even after the fall of the kingdom. Thus, we can say with certainty that Japanese Buddhism was started by Paekche monks.

A census of the Buddhist activity during the reign of Empress Suiko, records: forty-six monasteries, 816 monks, 569 nuns. The monasteries thus had an average of thirty residents. We may assume that among these more than one thousand monks and nuns many were from Korea.

Conclusion

There have been many theories about the dates of the transmission of Buddhism to Japan, notably 538 and 552.[15] I feel that these are all too late, since Buddhism had been transmitted from China to Paekche by at least 384, if not before. If we accept the sixth century date for the start of Buddhism in Japan, it is quite removed from the time of the advent in Paekche. The established theory about the introduction of Paekche Buddhism to Japan, and later the Koguryŏ and Silla traditions, is that they first entered Yamato, where they developed into Asuka Buddhism. The initial founding of all three traditions is traditionally assumed to have occurred at the Naniwa Canal, from where it was taken to Asuka. A more probable scenario for the transmission of Koguryŏ and Silla Buddhism was that they came first to the Noto peninsula in Ishikawa Prefecture or the Niigata Prefecture, for this is where the Tsushima current would carry the vessels coming from those regions of the Korean peninsula. If we accept this route, then there is a possibility that Silla and Koguryŏ Buddhism entered Japan in the Niigata area, from where it moved southward until it finally entered northern Kantō. There is some support of this theory in the fact that northern Kantō preserves several old Buddhist monasteries, which according to legend were built by Kūkai (774-835) or Gyōgi (668-749), suggesting that the religion flourished even in such outlying areas of Japan. Traditional accounts of Buddhist history are based solely on such official records as *Nihon shoki* which tend to focus on the metropolitan culture of the capital, and thus could be expected to ignore the flourishing Buddhist cultures of these peripheral regions.

A shrine at Funagata Mountain in Miyagi Prefecture provides support for the possibility of a route via the Sea of Japan for the transmission of Buddhism. This small shrine, which is situated on a steep mountain, preserves a bronze Buddha image some fifteen centimeters in height that is ritually buried each year in the forest behind the shrine. On May first, the shrine members dig it up and install it before the shrine. Relying on the appearance of the image, the villagers divine the size of coming year's crop. This event has been witnessed and reported by an archaeologist, Mori Kōichi. According to the art historian Kuno Takeshi, this image dates from the sixth century and is considered to be the oldest extant one brought to Japan. It has been suggested that this image was brought by sea directly to Miyagi, rather than taking the route of going to the capital first and then being received by some local clans who carried it back to Miyagi.[16] Although there is no literary evidence that would corroborate this theory of transmission of Koguryŏ and Paekche Buddhism, the existence of this image gives some credence to the idea that Buddhism was introduced before the date given in the official records and that it may not have been limited to Paekche.

There are two courses through which the travel from Korea to Japan via the northern Kantō region could have taken place: one is from Niigata directly to northern Kantō and the second goes from Nagano and Usui Pass. For this latter route, we should reconsider the significance of Zenko Monastery in Nagao.

According to the archaeologist Kōichi Mori, five bronze Buddha images were excavated in Gumma Prefecture in northern Kantō from burial sites dating from the end of the sixth to the eighth centuries. These small bronze images differ from those found in Nara and Osaka, where Buddhism with the support of the court developed on a more grandiose scale. The discovery of this type of Buddha image allows us to speculate that Buddhism was transmitted to Kantō and the coastal area of the Sea of Japan, where people were independent of the state-supported Buddhism of the capitals. This latter Buddhism had been directly transmitted from Paekche to Yamato in the center of the country. We may also speculate that the transmission of Buddhism to Japan, at least on a popular level, can be pushed back before the official transmission date of 538. Thus, on the basis of archaeological discoveries in both Japan and China, we may infer that the transmission of Buddhism among the Japanese people must, like that of China and Korea, have been earlier than the official dating.

[Editor's note]
The original article, "Kudara Bukkyō no nihon denrai",

appeared in *Mahan paekche munhwa* (Mahan Paekche Culture), 7, (1984), pp. 6-71. Parts IIa and b of this article deal with recent discoveries of Buddhist images at Mount K'ung-wang and the tomb of Ho-lin-ke-erh. As this material is available from numerous sources, it was felt that due to considerations of space these two sections should be dropped from the present translation. For those readers who wish to pursue this topic further the footnote material from these two sections has been preserved in note 2 below.

NOTES

1. The original article in Japanese suffers from numerous misprints, which were corrected in preparing the English translation. Additional notes, indicated by the square brackets, have been supplied by the translator. Abbreviations: SS: *Samguk sagi;* NS: *Nihon shoki.*

2. See the study by Yen Wen-ju, who believes that the scenes found at Mt. K'ung-wang in Shantung include depictions of the Buddha's parinirvāṇa and the story of the bodhisattva offering his body to a hungry tigress. "Kung-wang shan fo-chiao tsao-hsiang te t'i-t'sai" (On the Motifs of Buddhist Images at Mt. Kung-wang), *Wen-wu* 7:302 (1981), pp. 16-9. See also Lien-yün kang shih po-wu-kuan, "Lien-yün shih kung-wang shan mo-ya tsao-hsiang tiao-ch'a pao-kao" (A Report on the Relief Images at Mt. Kung-wang at the City of Lien-yün-kang) in *Wen-wu* 7:302 (1981), pp. 1-7. See also Kamata, "Bukkyō bunka no hatten" (Development of Buddhist Culture) in his *Chūgoku bukkyōshi* vol. 2 (Tokyo: Tokyō daigaku shuppankai, 1983).) These images have been dated to the period of the Latter Han by Hsin Wen-hsiang, Yu Wei-ch'ao and Hsin Li-hsiang. "Kung-wang shan mo-ya tsao-hsinag te nien-tai k'ao-ch'a" (An Examination of the Dating of Relief Images at Mt. Kung-wang), *Wen-wu* 7: 302 (1981), pp. 8-15. See also Kamata, "Chūgoku saiko no magai-butsu: Kōbōzan magai sekizō" (The Oldest Relief Images: Lithic Relief Images at Mt. Kung-wang), *UP* 11 & 12 (122) (1982). Images with nimbuses have also been found in the Stone tomb at I-nan in Shantung. Li Tso-chih believes that in a wall painting found at Ho-lin-ke-erh in Inner Mongolia there can be seen a group worshipping

relics. The tomb is dated to the middle of the second century A.D.
Yu Wei-ch'ao in his "Tung-han Fo-chiao t'u-hsiang k'ao" (A Study
of Buddhist Images of the Eastern Han), (*Wen-wu* 5 (1980), pp.
68-77), mentions the appearance of a six-tusked white elephant in a painting
from Shen-hsien. In Szechwan the cliff tombs of Ma-hao and Shih-
tzu-wan on Mt. Lo have carvings of Buddhas outlined with nimbuses.
At Mt. P'eng, also in Szechwan, there is a triad: a Buddha flanked
by two bodhisattvas. In Chinese Turkestan a bodhisattva image, on
a strip of cotton cloth, has been found at Ni-ya north of Fang-hsien.

3. [T'ang Yung-t'ung, *Han Wei Liang-Chin Nan-pei ch'ao fo-
chiao shih* (History of Buddhism of the Han, Wei, Liang-Chin, Nan-
pei ch'ao Periods) (Ch'ang-sha: Commercial Press, 1938), pp. 53-54.]

4. [The rhapsody was composed by Chang Heng (78-139), and
is found in the *Wen hsüen, chüan* 2.]

5. Cho Myŏn-ggi, *Silla pulgyo ŭi inyŏm kwa yŏksa* (The Ideology
and History of Silla Buddhism) (Seoul: Sint'aeyang-sa, 1962), p. 52.

6. [Ienaga Saburō, ed., *Nihon bukkyōshi* (History of Japanese
Buddhism) vol. 1 (Kyoto: Hōzōkan, 1967), pp. 50-64. George Sansom,
A History of Japan to 1334 (Stanford: Stanford University Press,1958),
pp. 49-51.]

7. [For this date, I have followed the text used in the Japanese
translation of NS (*Nihon shoki*, Nihon koten bungaku taikei vol. 68
(Tokyo: Iwanami shoten, 1965), pp. 209-211). Kamata instead gives
the thirty-first year of the Empress Suiko (623).]

8. [For the circumstances under which Illa was assassinated,
see NS 20, *Honchō kōsōden* (Biographies of Eminent Japanese
Monks) 69, *Dai Nihon bukkyō zensho* vol. 103, p. 865.]

9. [I have followed the Japanese translation of *Nihon shoki*
(vol. 68, p. 169) in construing the two names given here. Kamata instead reads three names, i.e., T'aeryang, Malt'aemun, and Kagoja.]

10. [*Dai Nihon bukkyō zensho* vol. 102, p. 61.]

11. [For this date, I have followed the text used in the Japanese
translation (vol. 68, p. 211). Kamata instead gives the thirty-first
year of Empress Suiko (623).]

12. [A Paekche monk, biography in NS 30; see *Han'guk pulgyo*

ch'ansul munhŏn ch'ongnok (Seoul: Tongguk University Press, 1976), p. 272.]

13. *Han'guk pulgyo ch'ansul munhŏn ch'ongnok*, p. 5; nonextant.

14. [I have followed the Japanese translation of *Nihon shoki* (vol. 68, p. 169) in construing seven names given here. Kamata reads instead eight names, i.e., Zensō, Zentsū, Myōtoku, Hōjō, Shōzen, Chisō, Chie, and Zenkō.]

15. Obayashi Taryō, Kamata Shigeo, Mori Kōichi, "Bunka no keisei to bukkyō no denpan" (Formation of Culture and Transmission of Buddhism), *Rekishi to jinbutsu*, February 1983.

16. [Kamata also gives the date, 548, along with 538 and 552. I have omitted this date from the translation because the article does not contain any other reference to it. Perhaps another misprint?]

Early Silla Buddhism and the Power of the Aristocracy

by Lee Ki-baek

Introduction

In one of my previous works entitled "The Introduction of Buddhism in the Three Kingdoms and its Social Repercussions", I considered the process and significance of the adoption of Buddhism into the Three Kingdoms with a special look at Silla.[1] In my conclusion, I stated that: "The introduction of Buddhism was an ideological expression of the formation of centrally administered ancient states, based on absolute royal authority.[2]

Now I believe that this conclusion must be, in part, reconsidered. For example, the word "introduction" should more accurately be "adoption". The more important point to be discussed here is my statement "*absolute* royal authority" (emphasis added). While I still have no doubt that the monarch had a leading role in the "adoption" of Buddhism, it has occurred to me that I may have neglected the influence of the aristocrats.[3] During the Silla period, the *chin'gol* aristocrats were a dominent group within the governing body of the state. In this paper, I wish to expand and change some of the focus of my earlier one.

The Silla of the Three Kingdoms period was an aristocratic society structured according to the "Bone-rank" system (*kolp'um*). Important government policy was decided by the Hwabaek Council, which is believed to have been under the control of the aristocrats of "Bone-rank". This being the case, it is not possible to conclude that the Silla was under "absolute royal authority". Rather it was simply that royal authority was more consolidated than during the Confederated Kingdoms period. If we assume that through the Hwabaek Council the aristocrats were in a position to have a strong voice in the government, then we must search for some reason to account for their adoption of Buddhism. Rather than minimizing the role of the aristocrats when discussing the advent of Buddhism in Silla, we should rather look for the positive aspects of the relationship between these aristocrats and the Buddhists.

Aristocratic Power and the Adoption of Buddhism

In my first paper on this subject (mentioned above), I contended that the date of the official Silla recognition of Buddhism was not the 14th year of King Pŏphŭng's reign (527) as has been commonly believed, but either its 21st (534) or its 22nd (535).[4] The question of the adoption of Buddhism hinges on the establishment of the first monastery, Hŭngnyun. If we hold to the date of 527, assuming that the martyrdom of Ich'adon led to the official adoption of Buddhism, then the building of the monastery should have been continuous from that date. But, in fact, the building was suspended after the death of Ich'adon and was not resumed until 534 when lumber was obtained from the Ch'ŏn'gyŏng forest. This hiatus in the construction confirms my opinion of the later dating. The tradition that Buddhism was officially approved because of the miracles that followed Ich'adon's death, must have been adopted to give him added luster in history. Previously, I left the date of official adoption as either 534 or 535, but now I consider the latter one to be correct. I follow the sixty year cycle system rather than ordinary chronology for this period. By this method of calculation, I am able to fix the death of Ich'adon at 527 and the official approval of Buddhism as eight years after that event in 535.

This means that even though Buddhism may have been widely known in Silla during this period, it still had to undergo a period of opposition. The time between the death of Ich'adon and the official recognition and adoption of the religion, is a crucial one for our understanding of how it came to finally receive the support of the ruling group. Since the literary evidence is lacking for the study of the opposition to Buddhism, we must turn to the *Samguk sagi* and look at some of the events which are described therein.

517/(4th month)	The Military Bureau was established.
520/(1st month)	The Administrative Law Code was promulgated and dress requirements were set for officials.
521	Envoys were sent with tribute to the court of the Liang dynasty.
531/(4th month)	Ch'ŏbu was appointed to the position of chief minister (Sangdaedŭng), and was asked to take charge of the affairs of state.
534	Sangdaedŭng Ch'ŏlbu died.
536	The independent reign name of Kŏnwŏn was announced for the first time.
538	Permission was granted for officials appointed to posts in the outlying regions to take their families with them.

These records provide us with evidence that there was the formation of a political system based on royal authority. The first military department in the government, the Administrative Law Code, and the control of dress codes for the aristocrats are indications of the power of the court. The sending of envoys to the Chinese court was yet another sign of this growth of royal authority. The diplomatic gesture in 521 of sending representatives to the Liang court, which was 140 years after the dispatching of envoys to the Former Ch'in in 318 through the mediation of Koguryŏ, was also symbolic of the growing power of the monarch. In return, the Liang sent a Buddhist monk Yuan-piao to Silla.[5] From the report of the Liang group to the Silla court we catch a glimpse of the political system developing in this part of Korea.

> A village within the Capital is called a *ch'akp'yŏng*, and a village outside it is called *ŭmnŭk*. This is roughly approximate to the Chinese method of dividing the nation into prefectures and districts. In Silla there are six *ch'ak-p'yŏng* and fifty-two *ŭmnŭk*.[6]

In 538, provincial officials were given permission to take their families with them when they took up posts away from the capital. Hence, we can infer that officials were dispatched from the capital to the fifty-two *ŭmnŭk* in the country, reported in the record quoted above. Such activities indicate that some type of centralized political structure had been instituted. It is against this background of the increasing power of the central government that we can view with some understanding the process by which the Hŭngnyun Monastery was constructed.

The records tell us the efforts to construct the monastery failed because of the opposition of the aristocratic council. Ich'adon was in charge of the construction and when the project failed, he took the full responsibility. Originally, King Pŏphŭng appointed Ich'adon, his favorite official, to the post on his own initiative. However, when faced with the opposition of the aristocrats the king could not but sentence him to death, even though Ich'adon may have wanted to sacrifice himself by taking on the responsibility for this failure. This is an important event because it gives us a glimpse of the conflict between the sovereign and the aristocratic Hwabaek Council. Whatever the situation may have been, it was serious enough to put the rule of the king in danger and only the death of Ich'adon managed to save the situation.

If the opposition to Buddhism from the aristocrats was so severe, how did it come about that the religion gained official approval in 535. To understand this we must pay attention to the position of Chief Minister (*Sangdaedŭng*) which was created by King Pŏphŭng in 531. Here the Chief Minister was the chairman of the Hwabaek Council composed of ministers called *Taedŭng*. This post seems to have taken over matters that had previously been left to the king. On this problem, I once made the point that the creation of the position of Chief Minister suggests that royal power had become more and more autocratic, but on the other hand, it indicates that the exercise of this power by the king was substantially limited by the power of the aristocrats.[7] The fact that the post of Chief Minister was established four years after the martyrdom of Ich'adon when the rule of the king was insecure, indicates that this post was an attempt to deal with the conflict between the king and the aristocracy through some institutional structure. It would appear that the Chief Minister came into being as a result of political compromise between the two sides and only after this time was official recognition of Buddhism achieved.

The first of these Chief Ministers was Ch'ŏlbu who died in 534. Since we do not have a biography of Ch'ŏlbu dating from this period, there is no way to know the circumstances of his death. There is no indication that another Chief Minister was appointed to take his place until the end of the reign of the next ruler, King Chinhŭng (r.540-576). The position was of such importance that it was said that his "death or replacement was duly recorded in history."[8] The lack of any record of appointment after Ch'ŏlbu raises questions about the events which were transpiring. The fact that no one was appointed in this post suggests that the friction between the king and the council had developed into a new stalemate. If this supposition is true, it proves that there was a victory for royal authority. The initiation of a Chinese style reign name, Kŏnwŏn (Establishing the Origin), in 536, would support this notion of great power for the king. This success of the king in appropriating power may have been of decisive importance in the declaration of the official acceptance of Buddhism in 535.

This was not to be a final victory for absolute royal

authority. We have only to look at King Chinji (r. 576-579), who followed Chinhŭng, and was driven from the throne by the aristocrats.[9] It is commonly argued that the official recognition of Buddhism came about because of the support of the king, but it might be truer to say that it was made possible only by some type of compromise between the two sides.

The Cultic Practices Associated with Śākyamuni, Maitreya and the Cakravartin King

When we study the relationship between royal authority and aristocratic power in terms of Buddhism, the belief in Śākyamuni and Maitreya is of major significance. During the Three Kingdoms period, these two were the most important cultic figures and images of them dominated Buddhist art of that time.[10] Such images are more than pieces of art; they played a part in ritual practice and are a major type of artifact that allow us to study the religious characteristics of those who commissioned them.[11]

The veneration of Śākyamuni, the most recent Buddha to appear in the world, was an ancient practice in Buddhism. Often Śākyamuni came to be regarded as a representative of all Buddhas, and in this capacity was sometimes symbolically likened to royalty. The metaphor of kingship in the Buddhism of the Silla was not applied only to Śākyamuni. Earlier, it was compared to the concept of an ideal king within India; that is the Cakravartin King. A king who deserved this epithet was said to be one who ruled over the entire world composed of the Four Continents. It was said that the term "cakra (wheel) vartin (turner)" refers to the fact that the whole world submits to him as he turns the "wheel of life". There are four wheels that he turns: golden, silver, copper and iron.[12] It is important to note that the two sons of King Chinhŭng were given the names of Tongnyun (copper) and Saryun (or Kŭmnyun: golden).[13] Saryun (or Kŭmnyun) succeeded to the throne after his father's death and had the reign name of Chinji. Chinhŭng was a sovereign who extended the boundaries of Silla through conquests. Because of this, as Professor Kim Yŏng-t'ae points out, he was considered by his subjects to be a cakravartin.[14]

By the time of King Chinp'yŏng, however, the identification of the king had shifted from that of cakravartin to Śākyamuni. We can spot this shift in the names of the royal family. Instead of being named after the four wheels of the cakravartin, King Chinp'yŏng had the same name as the father of Śākyamuni; his queen the name of Śākyamuni's mother. The names of his two brothers, Paekpan and Kokpan, were also taken from those of Śākyamuni's uncles.[15] Following this method of naming, we may assume that any son born to King Chinp'yŏng and Queen Māyā would correspond to Śākyamuni, but they had only daughters. This identification with Śākyamuni must have been a part of the circumstances which surrounded the ascension of Queen Sŏndŏk to the throne.

Given what they knew about Śākyamuni's caste background, the Silla kings also identified themselves as belonging to the kṣatriya class. When Chajang made pilgrimage to Mt. Wu-t'ai in China, he met the Bodhisattva Mañjuśrī who told him:

> The queen of your country belongs to the kṣatriya class, and has already received a prediction that she shall become a Buddha. Because of this special destiny, his family is not like the rest of the eastern barbarians.[16]

This identity between the royal house of Silla and Śākyamuni may be interpreted as an attempt to strengthen the royal authority. Professor Kim Ch'ŏl-jun has pointed out that the Silla court was influenced by the concept of royality which was prevalent in the northern kingdoms of China, where it was held that "the King is a Buddha"; the Silla probably received this idea through the intermediary of the Koguryŏ tradition.[17] Earlier, I had taken issue with the assertion that the concept of "the King is a Buddha" came from the Buddhism found in the northern kingdoms,[18] but now I think it is necessary to revise my previous view. The prevalent idea of the protection of the country in Silla Buddhism, of which the representative exponent was the monk Chajang, should be properly seen as having been influenced by the concept of "the King is a Buddha," current in the Northern Kingdoms. It is true that we do have a different view expressed by Wŏn'gwang that "a monk should not pay homage to a king". This is a form of Buddhism which was found in the southern Chinese tradition. Even though this idea was being expressed, we must remember that Wŏn'gwang, from the sixth head-rank, which was not a top aristocratic class, held a unique position in contemporary Silla Buddhism with respect to his status, origin and thought.[19] It was Buddhist faith, which included the idea of the protection of the country with close ties between the King and the Buddha, which was accepted in Silla during the Three Kingdoms period.

It might be assumed that if the royalty of Silla was compared to either a cakravartin model of the king, or to Śākyamuni, then the authority of the king could be made absolute through reliance on Buddhism. But this was not necessarily the case, especially when we think of the relationship between the cakravartin and Maitreya, or Śākyamuni and Maitreya. The studies which have been made so far on Maitreya have shown that the Maitreya cult in Silla was based on the *Mi-le hsia-sheng ching* (T.453) rather than the *Mi-le shang-sheng ching* (T.452) and the Bodhisattva Maitreya was believed to have been incarnate as a *hwarang* in Silla.[20] This notion can be seen in the legends associated with the *hwarang* Chukchir and Kim Yu-sin or in the legend of Mirŭk sŏnhwa.

An important link between Maitreya and the Silla beliefs is spelled out in the teaching that Maitreya will come into the world when a cakravartin king is ruling.[21] This relationship between the king and Maitreya provides us with a complementary system of political and religious life. In Silla, the cakravartin was the king, and the *hwarang* represented Maitreya. The *hwarang* were the children of aristocrats, most probably sons of Chin'gol aristocrats. They were the flower of Silla aristocracy and were symbolic of the power of this social class. By using the relationship between Maitreya and the cakravartin as a model, the royalty and the aristocrats of Silla were able to have a certain harmony based in part on religious faith.

It is not only the relationship between the cakravartin king and Maitreya which could be called upon, but also that existing between Śākyamuni and Maitreya. Maitreya, a bodhisattva, like Śākyamuni, was an object of veneration. There were, however, cases in which he was considered to be already a Buddha. For example, it is recorded that on the third day of the third month and the ninth day of the ninth month each year, the monk Ch'ungdam made offerings of tea before the Maitreya figure at Samhwaryŏng on Mt. Nam in Kyŏngju. In this instance he was mentioned as a full-fledged Buddha. Professor Hwang Su-yŏng maintains that the Buddha triad image taken from Mt. Nam to the Kyŏngju National Museum is that associated with Ch'ungdam. Hence, if he is correct, we may have here an actual example of the cult of Maitreya in a Buddha form.[22]

It has been shown in recent studies, however, that most Maitreya images of the Three Kingdoms period were of the type of a seated bodhisattva figure with one foot on the ground, the other crossed over the knee.[23] Professor Tamura Enchō has made a table of twenty-one of these extant "cross-legged" images of Maitreya. They span a period from the Three Kingdoms up to the Unified Silla. Except for the one at Sinsŏnam in Kyŏngju, all of the sculptures were made within the last half of the 6th century and the first half of the 7th.[24]

One wonders if this seated bodhisattva figure of Maitreya was not the major object of worship in the Three Kingdoms, and as such was enshrined as the central figure of the main hall of monasteries. Perhaps this was true for the very first Silla monastery, Hŭngnyun. We have a record which states that the monk Chinja went before the great image of Maitreya and entreated him to incarnate as a *hwarang*. It was after this that Maitreya did appear on earth as a *hwarang* named Misi. Then, it is proper to say that the Maitreya image, the incarnation of which eventually appeared as a *hwarang*, was in the form of a bodhisattva, not a Buddha.[25] We know that Kim Yang-do constructed a Maitreya image with attending bodhisattvas to the left and right of it, a common arrangement in which the central figure was usually a Buddha.[26] However, during the latter part of the Six dynasties period in China, it was a fashion to arrange a triad with the central figure seated on a dais with one foot on the floor and the other crossed over the knee. Professor Hwang Su-yŏng has used this Chinese model to suggest that the traid images in the Mirŭk Monastery of Paekche must have been similar.[27] It has also been pointed out that the central figure in the Japanese Kōryū Monastery, thought to have been influenced by Silla, was a similar seated cross-legged Maitreya figure.[28] Based on the above, we can argue that the main image of Hŭgnyun monastery was a bodhisattva image even though it had flanking images on its sides. It should also be called to mind that a Maitreya bodhisattva image excavated in Ponghwa also seems to have been seated in the main hall.[29]

It is possible to think that the seated figure of Maitreya in the Silla of the Three Kingdoms period was depicted as a bodhisattva not a Buddha, even though in the central position of the altar. Once again, we can see a complementary relationship between Śākyamuni and Maitreya. The King likened to the Buddha and the *hwarang*-aristocrats to the transformed Maitreya who appears in the world as a bodhisattva. Just as in the case of the cakravartin and Maitreya, Śākyamuni and Maitreya came to symbolize the harmony between the royalty and the aristocracy.

A rock-cut Buddha triad image of the Paekche period in Sŏsan, South Ch'ungch'ŏng Province, is noteworthy. The central figure was a Buddha; to the right was probably a seated Maitreya Bodhisattva with one foot on the floor and the other crossed over the knee, and to the left was a standing bodhisattva. The name of the Buddha in this relief has yet to be identified.[30] This arrangement is at variance with the usual one for such trinities. But judging from the iconography of the two *mudrās* displayed by the Buddha figure, *varada* and *abhaya* we assume that the main figure is Śākyamuni.[31]

Here we have Śākyamuni and Maitreya placed side by side in a sacred Buddhist carving, symbolic of the harmony between the king and the *hwarang*, or rather the king and the aristocrats. Even though this example is from Paekche and there may be questions about using this as applicable to the Silla, there are relationships which should be considered. First, it is believed that there was a youth organization similar to the *hwarang* in Paekche. We are coming to see that it is a mistake to believe that such organizations of young men were limited to Silla. The Kyŏngdang of Koguryŏ has been cited as a specific example of such an organization.[32] In a Chinese description of the Kyŏngdang we read that "Here they study books and practice archery".[33] Although we have no direct statement about an organized structure in Paekche, we read in another Chinese reference regarding Paekche: "Their custom was to value archery and to respect ancient books and histories".[34] The striking similarity of these descriptions gives us strong support for the idea that an organization like the *hwarang* of Silla or the K'yŏngdang of Koguryŏ did exist in Paekche. It is not unreasonable to assume that this organization was related in some way to the worship of the Bodhisattva Maitreya.

Second, there are indications that the connection between the *hwarang* and Maitreya in Silla was influenced by Paekche. The reference given above to Chinja has a connection with Paekche. This is to say, Chinja went to Ungju (Present-day Kongju) in Paekche to meet a boy who was believed to be the incarnation of Maitreya. This would indicate the possibility that Paekche and Silla had in common a young men's organization and the worship of Maitreya.[35]

Third, the scenic spot in the valley lying northwest of Mt. Kaya, where the Sŏsan triad was carved, is just the sort of place where the *hwarang* of Silla might be found. Mt. Kaya was strategically important to the national defence of Paekche, located as it is on the tip of Paekche where there was exposure to sea invasion from China or Koguryŏ. During the Unified Silla, Mt. Kaya became one of the Four Fortresses which along with the Five Mountain Peaks were used for religious rituals.[36]

The above points leads one to believe that the information gathered from the Sŏsan triad can be applied to the Silla

situation as well. I, therefore, believe that Śākyamuni Buddha
and Maitreya as a bodhisattva were the major objects of Buddhist worship in Silla of the Three Kingdoms period and that
these two were symbolic of the king and the aristocracy; Silla
Buddhism grew out of this harmony between the two parties.[37]
The dominance of the king can be seen clearly in the relationship
between Śākyamuni as a Buddha and Maitreya as a bodhisattva. It is more difficult to ascertain which is greater in a
comparison between the cakravartin king and Maitreya. The
symbolic shift from the king as a cakravartin to identification
with Śākyamuni, does not imply "absolute royal authority",
rather the Buddha and bodhisattvas are in harmony with each
other, there is no confrontation nor dominance of one over
the other.

The Concept of Transmigration
and the Aristocracy

We have seen that Buddhism in Silla was not the exclusive
possession of royalty; it also was embraced by the aristocracy
adding to their status and reflecting the power of this group
within Silla. This being the case, we need to look at the way
in which these Silla aristocrats perceived Buddhism as being
of special value to themselves.

The concept of transmigration and rebirth (saṃsāra)
deserves particular attention. While it is true that we cannot
neglect the importance of such practical matters as healing or
having sons, these were secondary when compared to the aristocrat's concern about their future births. Our source for information about this can be found in the inscriptions on images
that were commissioned by the wealthy. The following examples
have been translated from the Chinese character inscriptions
published Hwang Su-yong:[38]

(1.) During the fourth year (cyclical *sinmyo*) of Kyŏng
(unidentified region name) the monk Tosu and his intimate
friends (*Kalyāṇamitra*, Naru, Ch'ŏ, Awang and Ago built

[this] statue of Amitāyus and pray that their deceased masters and parents will always remember the Buddhas and *Kalyāṇamitra*s (religious councellors) in every birth, and that they will meet Maitreya. They also wish to be born together with them in the same place, see the Buddha and hear the Dharma.

(2.) During the fifth year (cyclical *pyŏngjin*) of Kŏnhŭng, a follower of Buddhism, Sangbu Aam, who was a pure devoted woman, made an image of Śākyamuni. With every birth may she meet the Buddha and hear the Dharma and may all sentient beings share in this.

(3.) On the first day of the eleventh month of the year (cyclical) *kyemi*, Pohwa built [three Buddhist images] for her deceased father, Cho.

(4.) Chŏng Chi-wŏn built a gold image in memory of his dead wife, Cho Sa, in the hope that she will leave the lowest three destinies quickly.

(5.) During the year of (cyclical) *kapsin* . . . an image of Śākyamuni was built, [with the] wish of meeting the Buddhas and being delivered from suffering forever . . .

(6.) During the seventh year (cyclical *kimi*) of Yŏn'ga Kyŏng, the Abbot of Tong Monastery in Nangnang (P'yŏngyang), together with his disciple Yŏn and forty other followers built statues of the Thousand Buddhas of Bhadrakalpa and distributed them. The 29th of those of the present age is now being made and offered by the monk Toyong.

(7.) In the seventh year of Yŏnggang, a statue of Maitreya has been made for the benefit of his dead mother . . . Pray that the deceased may [hear] the Three Lectures of Maitreya . . . Pray that if she committed sins, then let them be removed . . . May all who believe join in this prayer.

(8.) On the 26th day of the third month of the year of (cyclical) *kabin* the disciple Wang Yŏn-son made a gilt-bronze image of Śākyamuni on behalf of his parents in this present life. By this good deed may his parents enjoy peace in this life and, without going through the cycle of the lowest births and the Eight Difficulties in every life, may they be reborn into the Pure Land, see the Buddha and hear the Dharma.

It is clear from these inscriptions that all wish to be released from rebirth in the lowest three destinies, that of being born as a hell-being, a hungry ghost or as an animal. Example inscriptions 4 and 8 are representative of this idea. Number 5 probably refers to the same when it begs to release the individual from "suffering forever". Number 7 which asks for the removal of all bad karma is undoubtedly intended to achieve this same result. In many of the cases, we see that the request implies a fortunate rebirth as a human.[39] Second, these inscriptions ask for an opportunity to meet with the Buddhas and to hear the Dharma and consequently, we assume, achieve the state of enlightenment (1, 2, 5, 7, 8). Sometimes the name of the Buddha to be met with is not given (2, 8); in others we have the idea of a multitude of Buddhas (1, 5) and in two we find the request for a meeting with Maitreya (1, 7). In inscription 7 we find the wish to meet Maitreya—an encounter made possible through the merit of the making of an image of this bodhisattva. In inscription (1) the fulfillment of the same wish was hoped for by making an image of Amitāyus.[40] This desire to meet Maitreya when he comes into the world in the future also implied the wish to be reborn as a human. Third, the inscriptions give much emphasis to the happiness of the deceased. We find prayers for parents (1), for a father (3), for a wife (4), and for a mother (7) who are already dead, and hope for good rebirths for living parents (8) and for donors (1, 2, 5, 6). While there is reference to the living, the intention of these inscriptions is primarily a concern for the next life and a desire to have it as a human.

The extant inscriptions which have been translated here are usually attributed to Koguryŏ and Paekche, but I believe that they are applicable to Silla as well. In the *Samguk yusa* we find a description of the notion of incarnation held by Silla Buddhists.

> Upon receiving notice of the death of his mother, Chinjŏng sat in seated meditation for seven days. Someone said that since his longing and sadness was so extreme and he could not bear it, therefore he washed himself with the "water of meditation". Another one said: "By means of meditation he could look at her place of rebirth." Yet another, "he offered prayers for the dead according to duty". Emerging from his meditation he went to Uisang. Uisang, accompanied by all his disciples, went to Mt. Sobaek and built a thatched roof cottage and assembled over 3000 people. For 90 days he taught the *Avataṃsaka-sūtra* . . . When the lectures were completed, Chinjŏng's mother appeared to him in a dream and said: 'I have already been born in heaven'.[41]

Here we read that the mother of Chinjŏng went to heaven after her death by virtue of her son's meditation. Even though the place of rebirth mentioned here is in a heavenly paradise, not in the human world, nevertheless, it is still the case that meritorious deeds performed for the sake of the deceased led to rebirth in a better state.

Chinjŏng was a disciple of Uisang, which would place his date as approximately the time of the unification of the Three Kingdoms. Another account from the Unified Silla period reveals to us the view of transmigration and wish for rebirth in a better destiny current at the time. The monk Sŏnnyul of the Mangdŏk Monastery died in the middle of his meritorious work of copying sūtras, but was released from the underworld to finish his work. On his way back to this world, he met a woman who told her story of being reborn in that place of torment:

> "I am from Namyŏmju of Silla. My mother and father took riceland from the Kŭmgang Monastery without permission and for this reason I am bound up in this hell and

have suffered great pain for a long time. When you return home, please tell my parents to give the land back. When I was still living in the world, I hid some sesame seed oil beneath a table and stored a beautifully woven cloth under my mattress. Would you take that oil and light the Buddha's lamp and sell the robe to pay for the copying of the sūtras, that I might be delivered from my suffering." When he went to the house of that woman, he found the oil and cloth were still there fifteen years after her death. He did just as she had instructed him and the spirit of the girl came to him and said, "Monk, because of your king deed, my suffering has already been lifted."[42]

The Mangdŏk Monastery was built after the unification and thus the tale is from that period. Such concepts of transmigration and rebirth must have existed in the Silla of the Three Kingdoms period and indeed it must have been so from the earliest period of the adoption of Buddhism.

The doctrine of rebirth in the future encouraged believers to earn merit while living in this world. Since the concept of transmigration and rebirth links the present life with future rebirth and with past karma of previous births, the situation in the present, while dependent on the past, determines the future. They believed that their previous lives could have been in any one of the Six Destinies, and that their present birth as a human indicated past meritorious action. There are a number of legends which assume that reincarnation had meant moving from the Destiny of an animal rebirth to the present one of human birth.

(1.) One day, Sabok's mother died. At that time Wŏnhyo, who was staying at Kosŏn Monastery, greeted him. But instead of responding to the greeting, Sabok said "the cow that we used in carrying the sūtras in the past is dead, why don't we bury them together?" Wŏhyo agreed.[43]

Another example of this rebirth pattern:

(2.) One of the group of monks who could not keep his vows fell to the level of rebirth as an animal and came back to this world as a bull at Pusŏk Monastery. Once, the bull was used to carry the sūtras on his back and because of the good karma which resulted from this act, rebirth occurred as a servant girl by the name of Ungmyŏn in the house of Kwijin.[44]

The first legend is from the time of the unification and the second is much later, but both tell of individuals who had lived as animals in a previous life.[45] There are also tales of humans who remained in this same destiny.

(3.) Hyegong saw the *Chao-lun* by Seng-chao and said: "I compiled this myself many years ago." In this way everyone knew that he was a reincarnation of the monk.[46]

(4.) When Sŏlchong was appointed governor of Sakchu, he set out to assume his post. Because there was a war, he was escorted by 3000 horsemen. When they came to Chukchi pass there was a lay-practitioner building a mountain road. When the governor saw this, he was much impressed and the lay-practitioner in turn was awed by the procession of the official and his retinue. After the governor had been in his new post a few weeks, he had a dream in which he saw the lay-practitioner entering his room. His wife had the same dream and they were alarmed by this coincidence. They sent a man the next day to inquire after him. The messenger set out and when he arrived at the lay-practitioner's place he was told that the latter had died a few days earlier. When the messenger reported this to the governor, it was determined that the lay-practitioner had died on the night of the dreams. The governor announced that "This lay-practitioner will be reborn here in our household." . . . From the day of the dreams, the wife knew that she was pregnant and when a son was born, he was named Chukchi.[47]

(5.) A poor woman name Kyŏngjo of Moryang-ri had a son who was given the name Taesŏng (Great Wall) because he had a large head and a broad forehead which resembled a wall. Because she was so poor, it was difficult to raise the child. She went to work for a rich man named Pogan, and she was given a small plot of land to provide her with the necessities of life. At that time, the monk Chŏmgye was about to hold a religious service at Hŭngnyun Monastery and he solicited offerings. Pogan gave fifty bolts of cloth and Chŏmgye blessed him . . . Taesŏng saw this and ran to his mother crying "I heard a monk say that offerings given now will be rewarded 10,000 fold. I think we are poor because we didn't perform good deeds in our former lives. If we don't give now, we will have even more difficulty in our next lives. What would you say to donating our land for the preparation of a ceremony and hope for a later reward?"

His mother agreed to his request and donated the land to Chŏmgye. Soon after this Taesŏng died and on that night a voice was heard in the house of Minister Kim Munyang saying: "Take care of a boy from Moryang-ri named Taesŏng." The people of the house were surprised. They made inquiries in the village and learned that the child Taesŏng had died. That day Kim's wife conceived a child and when it was born, the baby kept his left fist clenched. On the seventh day he finally opened his hand and there was a thin sheet of gold inscribed with the word 'Taesŏng'. The new parents named the child Taesŏng and brought his (former) mother to their house and cared for her along with the baby.[48]

This last story is from a period later than the Silla of the Three Kingdoms, but it also probably indicates the general conception of reincarnation current in earlier times. All of the stories provide information about the former lives of individuals who were living in the world at the time of telling the tale. As we have already seen, rebirth as a human being was the most desirable of the Six Destinies of Rebirth. These stories provide proof of the importance of merit produced in previous lives. This merit had been generated by carrying sūtras on their backs when they had lived as cattle (stories 1 and 2), by writing treatises (3), building a road (4), or by donating land to the Buddha (5). These stories all point out that the current life of an individual is not merely chance, it is determined by the actions in former lives. The characters in these stories: Sabok's mother was was widowed, living in poverty; Ungmyŏn, who suffered in the life of slavery; Hyegong, a monk of outstanding virtue; Chukchi, born into the home of a Chin'gol aristocrat becoming a *hwarang;* and Kim Tae-sŏng born into the house of Minister Kim Mun-yang, all can be understood as the results of action in previous lives. This theme is made particularly clear in the life of Kim Tae-sŏng, one was urged to accept life as it is for this is the result of former deeds.

Based on the idea that good deeds yield rewards because of the operation of cause and effect, the teachings about transmigration and rebirth provided a theoretical foundation which affirmed the strict status system known as the "Bone-Rank". It is easy to see how the ruling aristocrats of Silla could have accepted reincarnation as a doctrine which could give justification for their high positions. They believed that they were born as aristocrats in reward for meritorious deeds of their previous lives and this concept of just reward should be accepted by the whole society. Is it any wonder that the Chin'gol aristocrats warmly welcomed the doctrine of transmigration and rebirth which so strongly supported the "Bone-Rank" system of Silla?

Later, we can see the reaction from those groups in society which held lesser rank: the *yuktup'um* aristocrats, commoners and the lowly classes. Perhaps this is why Confucian scholars from the ranks of the *yuktup'um* such as Kangsu and Sŏl Ch'ong were critical of the Buddhist world view and stood behind the principles of merit which results from moral actions in this life. According to these two, a man's worth ought to be determined not by birth but solely on the basis of moral action and even the king is not exempt from this principle.[49]

Among the lower classes, the Pure Land teachings were taken up as a protest against the concept of transmigration and rebirth. The goal of the Pure Land followers was to overcome the cycle of birth and death inherent in this scheme. They sought to be released from the world of suffering and to find eternal life and bliss in the Pure Land. The majority of those who believed in this form of Buddhism were those who suffered under the "Bone-Rank" system. This would have included Ungmyŏn, the slave girl. In this way the lower classes challenged the concept of transmigration and rebirth and indirectly the social order of the "Bone-Rank" system that ruled their lives.

While it must be admitted that no literary reference can be given which states explicitly that the *Chin'gol* aristocrats accepted reincarnation as a doctrine useful in defending their high status, I believe that the stories presented above give us sufficient ground for such a conclusion.

Conclusion

This study has been a reconsideration of my earlier work "The Introduction of Buddhism in the Three Kingdoms Period and its Social Repercussions". In that article, I saw the adoption of Buddhism as an affirmation of royal authority and as a denial of the power of the aristocracy. I have in this present work reconsidered the role of the aristocracy and sought for those aspects of Buddhism which would have been positive ones for them. Focusing on Silla, because we have relatively more material for this period, I have reached the following new conclusions:

First, the sovereign was the first to push for the adoption of Buddhism and the aristocrats were initially opposed to it. The execution of Ich'adon in 527 was a result of this opposition. The official recognition of Buddhism in 535, on the other hand, was brought about by cooperation between royalty and aristocracy, as is evidenced by the establishment of the office of Chief Minister.

With reference to the comparison of the king to the Cakra-vartin or to Śākyamuni and the belief that the *hwarang* were incarnations of Maitreya, I have pointed out that the royalty and the aristocracy were able to establish a harmonious relationship on a basis provided by Buddhism. Thus, I have concluded that the aristocracy was not left out of the decision to officially adopt Buddhism as the religion of the state. On the contrary, I now believe that Buddhism of this early period of Silla developed in an atmosphere of cooperation between the king and the upper levels of the aristocracy.

My last point has been to consider the value of Buddhism for these aristocrats. Here it seems that a doctrine such as transmigration and rebirth which justified their privileges, must have been seen as one such positive factor. While it is clear that the aristocrats were interested in both the benefits which accrued in this birth and the bliss of the expected in the next, I emphasize that they would have focused on an idea that justified their privileged position in society.

The discussion presented above has not been a thorough examination of the Buddhist doctrines found in the writings of monks. Rather, I have tried to look into the social significance of the Buddhist faith. At times, I have been forced to make some bold conjectures, but in doing so, I hope that we can better understand Buddhism in its true historical perspective.

NOTES

1. *Yŏksa hakpo* (Journal of History; hereafter YH), vol. 6 (1954), p. 128-205; also compiled in my *Sila sidae ŭi kukka pulgyo wa yugyo* (State Buddhism and Confucianism during the Silla period; hereafter SKPY) (Seoul, 1978), pp. 2-54.

2. YH, vol. 6, p. 204; SKPY, p. 54.

3. In this work I will call the *chin'gol* aristocrats who dominated Silla society simply "aristocrats" except when it is necessary to distinguish them from *yuktup'um* aristocrats.

4. YH, vol. 6, p. 45; SKPY, p. 12.

5. "Liang sent an emissary, a monk by the name of Yuan-piao, with incense, sūtras and statues." SY, III, "Ado brings Buddhism to Silla."

6. Liang shu, vol. 54.

7. Lee Ki-baek, "Sangdaedŭng ko" (A Study of the Sangdaedŭng), YH, vol. 19 (1962), pp. 9-10; see also Silla chŏngch'i sahoesa yŏn'gu (A Study of the Political and Social History of Silla), (Seoul, 1974), p. 96.

8. Kim Chŏng-hŭi, "Chinhŭng ibi ko" (A Study of the Two Stelae of Chinhŭng), in the Wandang sŏnsaeng chŏnjip (The Complete Works of Wandang), chapter 1, p. 9.

9. The Samguk sagi does not mention Chinji's dethronement, but the Sumguk yusa says, "He reigned for four years. Because of his misgovernment and sexual indulgence, he was dethroned by his people." SY I, "Tohwanyŏ and Pihyŏngnang."

10. Lee Ki-baek, "Samguk sidde ŭi pulgyo chŏllae . . .", YH, vol. 6, pp. 161, 168-171; and SKPY pp. 28-29.

11. Recently Professor Mun Myŏng-dae, in his series of essays, has attempted an approach to the history of Silla sculpture from this viewpoint; see, for example, "Kyŏngdŏkwangdae ŭi amit'a chosang munje" (Amitabha Images During King Kyŏngdŏk's Reign), in Yi hongjik paksa hwagap kinyŏp han'guk sakak nonch'ong (Festschrift for Dr. Yi Hongjik) (1969), pp. 647-86.

12. See the entry on cakravartirāja in Mochizuki Shinkō, Bukkyō daijiten (Dictionary of Buddhism).

13. The "sa" of Saryun is presumably a transliteration of "soe" meaning "iron". Since the older brother of the crown prince represents the copper wheel, it is appropriate to refer to the younger brother as the iron wheel. See Kim Ch'ŏl-jun, "Silla sangdae sahoe ŭi dual organization" (Dual Organization in the Early Silla Period, part 2), YH, vol. 2 (1952), p. 91.

14. Kim Yŏng-t'ae, "Mirŭk sŏnhwa ko" (On Mirŭk Sŏnhwa), Pulgyo hakpo (Journal of Buddhist Studies), vol. 3/4 (1966), p. 145.

15. Kim Ch'ŏl-jun, p. 92.

16. SY, vol. 3, "Nine-story pagoda of Hwangnyong Monastery."

17. Kim Ch'ŏl-jun, p. 191.

18. Lee Ki-baek, YH, vol. 6, p. 190; SKPY, p. 43.

19. For Wŏ'gwang see Lee Ki-baek, "Wŏn'gwang kwa kŭ ŭi sasang" (Wŏn'gwang and His Thought), *Changjak kwa pip'yŏng*, vol. 10 (1968).

20. A pioneering work on the Maitreya cult is Yaotani Takayasu "Shiragi shakai to Jōdokyō" (Silla Society and Pure Land Buddhism), *Shisho*, vol. 7 (1937). Later works include: Mishima Shoe, *Shiragi karo no kenkyu* (Study of the Hwarang in Silla), (1934); Hwang Su-yŏng, *Silla namsan samhwaryŏng mirŭk sejon* (Silla Maitreya Image from Samhwaryŏng on Mt. Nam), in *Kim chewon paksa hoegap kinyŏm nonch'ong* (Festschift for Kim Chewon) (1969); and Kim Sanggi, *Hwarang Kwa mirŭk sinang e taehayŏ* "On the Hwarang and the Maitreya Cult", in *Festschift for Yi Hong-jik.*

21. According to the *Ch'ang e-han-ching* (*Dirghāgama*), vol. 6, when Maitreya comes forth, the cakravartin will also appear (see Mochizuki).

22. Hwang Su-yŏng, *op. cit.* As Mr. Hwang has pointed out, we should note the fact that this Maitreya Buddha image is seated in a "European style" which may be close to the posture described *infra.*

23. Hwang Su-yŏng, "Paekche pan'ga sayusang sugo" (On the Contemplating, Half Cross-legged Images of Paekche), YH, vol. 13 (1960); also Hwang Su-yŏng, "Silla pan'ga sayu sŏksang sogo" (On the Contemplating, Half Cross-legged Images of Silla), *Festschift for Kim Chewon*, (1969); Nakagiri Isao, *Chōsen gakuhō*, vol. 48 (1968); Tamura Enchō, "Pan'ga sayusang kwa sŏngdŏk t'aeja sinang" (The Half Crossed-legged Images and the Cult of Prince Shōtoku"), in *Hanil kodae munhwa kyosŏpsa yŏn'gu* (Studies in the History of Cultural Associations between Korea and Japan in Ancient Times) (Seoul: 1974).

24. Tamura Enchō, pp. 54-55.

25. SY, vol. 3, "The Mirŭk sŏnhwa and the monk Chinja."

26. "Because of this Yang-do embraced Buddhism for the rest of his life. He had three statues made for the main hall in the Hŭngyun

Monastery: Maitreya and two bodhisattvas, one on each side." SY, vol. 5, "Milbon the exorcist."

27. Hwang Su-yŏng, "On the half Cross-legged images of Paekche," YH, vol. 13 (1960).

28. Tamura Enchō, p. 66.

29. Mun Myŏng-dae, "Silla pŏpsangjong ŭi sŏngnip munje wa kŭ misul" (The Formation of the Dharmalakṣaṇa School of Silla and its Art), YH, vol. 63, (1974), p. 158.

30. Mr. Hwang Su-yŏng has deferred this for further study in his "Sŏsan Paekche maae samjon pulsang" (Rock-cut Buddha Triad from Paekche in Sŏsan), *Chindan hakpo*, vol. 20, (1959), p. 115. Tamura Enchō has noted that, "there is no other instance of such a traid form, composed of a Buddha in the middle and two bodhisattvas—one standing and one half cross-legged. Therefore, it is difficult to identify." *op. cit.* pp. 52-53.

31. *Varada* and *abhaya* were the most common mudrās used by Śākyamuni Buddha. Even though they were sometimes employed for the images of Amitābha or Bhaiṣajyaguru Buddha, unless specifically indicated, it is natural to identify the image exhibiting those mudrās with Śākyamuni.

32. Lee Ki-baek, "Koguryŏ ŭi kyŏngdang" (The Kyŏngdang of Koguryŏ), YH, vol. 35/36, (1967).

33. *Chiu t'ang shu*, vol. 199.

34. *Chou shu*, vol. 49.

35. Hwang Su-yŏng, in his "On the contemplating, half cross-legged bodhisattva images of Paekche," argued that "towards the end of the Three Kingdoms period the Maitreya cult began in the region around Kongu and prospered in that area."

36. *Samguk sagi*, vol. 32, "Rituals".

37. Tamura Enchō argued that in China the cross-legged figure with one foot touching the floor was originally conceived as Siddhārtha and in Japan as Prince Shōtoku (*op. cit.*, pp. 51, 80). However, it would be appropriate to assume that in Silla the image first transmitted to Korea was Maitreya and in Silla it was from the beginning looked

upon, not as prince Siddhārtha, but rather as Maitreya, who Śākyamuni had predicted would become a Buddha.

38. Hwang Su-yŏng, *Han'guk kŭmsŏk yumun* (Extant Inscriptions of Korea) (1976).

39. There is some question concerning the use of "Pure-land (*chŏngt'o*)" in inscription 8. Judging from the sentiment expressed that, "in every life . . ." one hopes "to see the Buddha and hear the Dharma," it is difficult to identify this Pure Land as that of Amitābha.

40. It has been pointed out that such instances existed in China as well. See Tsukamoto Zenryū, "Ryūmon sekkutsu ni arawaretaru Hoku-gi bukkyō" (The Nature of Buddhism of the Northern Wei as Evidenced in the Lung-men Cave) in *Shina bukkyōshi kenkyū: Hoku-gi* (A Study of Chinese Buddhism: Northern Wei), (1942), pp. 581-584.

41. SY, vol. 5, "The virtues of filial piety and good deeds of the monk Chinjŏng".

42. SY, vol. 5, "Sŏnnyul coming back to life".

43. SY, vol. 4, "Sabok did not speak".

44. SY, vol. 5, "The servant Ungmyŏn ascending to the Western Pure Land by reciting the Buddha's [name]".

45. In story (1) and the next one (3) where one would expect to read "former life", we find "in olden times" instead. However, from the context it should be understood as "former life."

46. SY, vol. 4, "Two Hyes (Hyesuk and Hyegong) joined in the dusty world".

47. SY, vol. 2, "Chukchirang during King Hyoso's reign".

48. SY, vol. 5, "Taesŏng's filial piety to his parents in two lives".

49. Lee Ki-baek, "Silla kolp'umje ha ŭi yugyojŏk chŏngch'i inyŏm" (Confucian political ideology under the "Bone-rank" system of Silla), *Taedong munhwa yŏn'gu*, vol. 6/7, (1970), pp. 142-149.

* The original article is Lee Ki-baek (Yi Ki-baek), "Sill ch'ogi pulgyo wa kwijok seryŏk," *Chindan hakpo* 40 (1975), pp. 21-39; also compiled in his *Silla sidae ŭi kukka pulgyo wa yugyo* (State Buddhism and Confucianism during the Silla Period, hereafter SKPY) (Seoul, 1978), pp. 2-54.

Silla Buddhism:
Its Special Features

by Rhi Ki-yong

Buddhism from the period of its earliest introduction has exerted an enormous influence on Korea. It arrived during the period of the Three Kingdoms before the peninsula was united into a single nation. Buddhism helped bring people together; it was the spiritual support which united them. Officially adopted as the state religion in the sixth century, it remained so for nearly eight hundred years, up to the fourteenth century. Even after this time, during the Chosŏn dynasty when it was persecuted by the government which favored Confucianism, Buddhism remained a powerful religion in both relief and moral principle.[1]

Buddhism in the Silla dynasty had an especially significant place in society, deeply influencing philosophy, art and literature. This essay will examine the special features of Silla Buddhism which played such an important role in unifying the kingdom.

The Different Forms of Buddhism in the Three Kingdoms

There was a great difference in the form that Buddhism took in Silla as compared to the other two kingdoms,[2] Koguryŏ and Paekche. At the time when the three kingdoms on the peninsula were in opposition to one another, Koguryŏ was the most advanced. Silla seems to have been least developed from all points of view, in part due to its geographical isolation from China, the center of East Asian civilization. Also, the Silla people were of a southern nature; they were pliable and made political decisions through consensus. This was quite different from the northern tough minded military disposition found among the people of Koguryŏ. The kings of Koguryŏ and Paekche held absolute power and were in close cultural contact with China. Such tendencies were weak in Silla. In Silla, Buddhism was first officially recognized by King Pŏphŭng in 527, but this was not the result of his decision alone. In Koguryŏ and Paekche, on the other hand, official recognition followed immediately upon its introduction into their courts. The martyrdom of Ich'adon, a kinsman and official at the court, and the consequent reorientation by the aristocrats made this recognition possible. Prior to this time, there were individuals in Silla who knew about Buddhism and the king himself was supportive of the new teaching. It was only the opposition by many aristocrats that delayed official acceptance. Ich'adon decided to offer his life for the cause. After committing the crime of starting to build a monastery on the pretext of following the king's command, his execution was demanded by the aristocrats who were in conflict with the throne. Ich'adon wanted above all else for his sacrifice to aid in the propagation of the Dharma of the Buddha among the people of Silla. He was convinced that a miracle would occur because of his firm belief in Buddhism. At his execution, as the story goes, when his head was severed, the sky became dark, the earth rumbled and white milk flowed from his wound rather than blood. His head flew away to the summit of Mt. Kŭmgang (a mountain north of Kyŏngju). It is said that the aristocrats were astonished and repenting of their action, prostrated themselves before the king. The king and aristocrats acting together, thus recognized Buddhism as the state religion for the first time. Later King Pŏphŭng, whose name means "making the Buddha's Dharma flourish", abdicated, relinquishing the throne to his young son, King Chinhŭng, and became a monk while his wife joined the order of the nuns. Thus they lived in retreat for the rest of their lives.

Let us consider the impact Buddhism had on the thinking of the people of the Three Kingdoms. It seems probable that, until unification in 668 under the Unified Silla, understanding of the texts remained at an elementary state. According to extant historical records, a higher level of Mahāyāna thought was known in Koguryŏ than in the other two kingdoms. For example, Podŏk and his ten disciples gave lectures on the *Mahāparinirvāṇasūtra*. There were monasteries named after important doctrines and persons found in the texts: monasteries such as Yuma (Vimalakīrti) and Taesŭng (Mahāyāna); a monk called Ilsŭng (Ekayāna in Sanskrit, the One Vehicle). Uiyŏn, a Koguryŏ monk stayed in Ch'ang-an from 576-591 and brought back to Korea such texts as the *Shih-ti ching-lun* (*Daśabhūmikasūtraśāstra*), the *Ta-chih'tu lun* (?*Mahāprajñāpāramitāśāstra*), the *P'u-sa-ti ching* (*Bodhisattvabhūmiśāstra*) and the *Chin-kang pan-juo ching lun* (*Vajracchedikaprajñāpāramitā* commentary). Hyeryang, a Koguryŏ monk who travelled to Silla and became the highest ranking cleric in King Chinhŭng's reign (540-576) seems to have been quite learned in the Mahāyāna texts.

In 643, Taoism which had been introduced in Koguryŏ in 624, was raised to the level of state religion with the support of a powerful minister of state Yŏn Kaesomun. In this northern kingdom some opposition to Buddhism probably began in the late sixth century, as evidenced by Hyeryang's move to Silla and the many Buddhist monks who went to Japan. The Japanese sources report on the large number of Koguryŏ monks teaching from the late sixth until the early seventh century: Hyep'yŏn, Hyeja, Sŭngnyung, Tamjing, Hyegwan, Tojŭng and Tosun. On the whole Koguryŏ Buddhism seems to have been, as a tradition, dominated by a scholastic emphasis on Mahāyāna doctrine practiced in a monastic setting; it does not seem to have reached a stage where it could be practiced or understood by the general population.

The situation of Buddhism in Paekche was similar to that of Koguryŏ. There are few remaining literary sources, but those we have indicate an emphasis on ritual, and the *Vinaya;* the theoretical studies of the doctrine may have lagged behind that of Koguryŏ. Although Buddhism was introduced in 384, none of our sources for a study of Paekche date before the sixth century; the oldest artifacts of Buddhism in this kingdom were found in the tomb of King Muryŏng (r. 501-522). Among the items in that tomb are lotus patterned tiles and other artifacts of Buddhist origin, along with objects of other popular religious traditions.[3] It was not until King Sŏng's reign (523-553) that we find a record of attempts being made to achieve a more profound understanding of Buddhism. In 526, later historical sources report, Kyŏmik returned to Paekche after studying in India for five years. He brought with him texts such as the five recensions of the *Vinaya* (*Wu-pu-lü*) and the *Abhidharma* which he translated into Chinese. We are not sure about the exact nature of the texts which he brought since his name does not appear in the colophons of any of the translations of the *Vinaya* nor do we find it in Uich'ŏn's catalogue, the *Sinp'yŏn chejong kyojang ch'ongrok*. Early Paekche Buddhism may have been strongly influenced by that of Koguryŏ; the political events that resulted in monks from the northern kingdom moving to Japan or Silla, would have also caused them to travel to Paekche.

Lacking a deep understanding of Buddhist practice, followers in Koguryŏ and Paekche probably understood the doctrine on a limited level from examining a few of the texts of the canon. Evidence for this is the fact that monks were used as political and military spies. This same situation also held true for Silla before unification; however, as Buddhism became the officially recognized religion and monks were given high status, there developed a considerable difference between the practice of the religion in Silla as compared to the other two kingdoms.

Special Features of Silla Buddhism

Silla Buddhism had the following characteristics:

(1.) All Silla kings after Pŏphŭng were ardent Buddhists, some even renouncing the world and becoming monks.

(2.) Monks enjoyed a high social status and were influential in the affairs of society. There were special ranks of recognition such as that of *kuksa* (National Teacher) and *wangsa* (King's Teacher). The *hwarang* youth organization peculiar to Silla was spiritually guided by Buddhist monks.[4]

(3.) The Buddhist spirit deeply penetrated the political ideology. For example, many kings took Buddhist names: Pŏphŭng (Promoting the Dharma) and Chinhŭng (Truly Promoting). King Chinhŭng named his two sons after two of the four wheels of the cakravartin king in Buddhist lore from India: Kŭmnyun ("Golden Wheel") and Unnyun ("Silver Wheel"). Queen Sŏndŏk was called by the name "Tŏngman" (S. Gṇamālādevī) and Queen Chindŏk by the name, "Sŭngman (S. Śrīmālādevī). Place names were also taken from Indian Sanskrit ones such as the capital of Silla: Sillabŏl or Sŏrabŏl, a transliteration of Śrāvastī, the site of many stories about the life of the Buddha.

(4.) The scholastic study of Buddhism was active. Korean monks began to write their own commentaries on the sutras, even before unification.[5]

(5.) Ethics for daily life were emphasized and followed in Silla before and after unification. These ethics were, in part, based on the spirit of the rules of conduct for bodhisattvas (*bodhisattvasīla*). We can see this influence in the *Sesok ogye* (Five Modes of Lay Conduct) which were given to the *hwarang* youth by monk Wŏn'gwang. However, Chajang put great emphasis on the *Vinaya* and also taught on the rules of conduct for the bodhisattvas. Wŏnhyo (617-686) wrote commentaries on texts which dealt with the actions of the bodhisattva such as the *Fan-wang ching* and the *Yu-chia shih-ti lun* (*Yogācārabhūmiśāstra*).[6]

(6.) Except for the later period of the dynasty, Silla Buddhists tried to synthesize the various traditions into one tradition, avoiding sectarianism. This extended even to other religions, and they tried to include important parts of the teachings of all Buddhist schools in China, as well as Confucianism and Taoism in their belief structure. Wŏnhyo's concept of *hwajaeng* (peaceful integration of disputes by harmonization) was the philosophical manifestation of this tendency.[7]

(7.) Buddhism provided a new philosophy to deal with duality, whether in subject-object relations or such important problems as life and death. This was based on the Mahāyāna teaching that saṃsāra and nirvāṇa are not different from each other.[8]

(8.) Silla Buddhism displayed three very distinct periods of development.

1) Early Period (From King Pŏphŭng [514-540] to the first half of King Munmu's reign [661-681]).

2) Prospering Period (after unification—the last half of King Munmu's time until King Hyegong [r. 765-780]).

3) Declining Period (lasting until the fall of the dynasty).

These special characteristics of Silla Buddhism were prevalent in the Early Period but from the Prospering Period onward, there were major changes in the tradition. The bodhisattva ideals faded away and were replaced by a dependence on rituals and ceremonies which were performed by rote without the spirit of the Mahāyāna teachings. During the Declining Period, scholastic study of the Dharma had less support.

(9.) During the Declining Period, a new form of Buddhism emerged based on the *Ch'an* (K. *Sŏn*) from China. Nine divisions of this school developed in Korea and became known as the "Nine Mountains of *Sŏn*". But this *Sŏn* Buddhism was not easy for the masses to understand; it reflected more closely the tastes of the aristocracy. Social upheaval which marked the decline of the dynasty brought about a return to popular religious practices and until the stability of the Koryŏ the ruling classes lost their role of leadership in the society.

(10.) Silla Buddhism provided the spiritual basis for the kingdom during its time of greatest development and prosperity, the decline of Buddhism also marked the decline of the kingdom.

The main philosophical leader of Silla Buddhism was Wŏnhyo who was both practical and original in his thinking.[9] He was an outstanding scholar whose writings display a profound understanding of the important doctrines of Mahāyāna. An examination of his writings shows that he was deeply absorbed in the thought of the *Ta-ch'eng ch'i-hsin Lun* (Awakening of Faith) and using this text as a basis showed a profound understanding of various *Mahāyāna* sūtras, such as the *Lotus Sūtra*, the *Chin-kuang-ming*, the *Ta-sheng tonghsing*, the *Nirvāṇa Sūtra*, the *Avataṃsakasūtra*, the *P'u-sa ying-luo pen-yeh*, the *Mahāprajñāpāramitāsūtra*, the *Ta-chi*, the *Yao-shih pen-yuan*, and śāstras such as the *Chung-kuan*, the *Twelve-gate Treatise*, the *Yu-chia lun* and the *Mahāyānasaṃgraha*. Before becoming a monk, it is conceivable that he was a member of the *hwarang* youth organization which was so important for the aristocrats of Silla. In any case, he became a teacher of these young men. A free spirit, he stood beyond the notion of sacred and profane. He made use of both sword and pen during his life and in following the principles of Mahāyāna at its most profound level, he is said to have remained unaffected by his surroundings and never made improper use of his status as a leader and teacher.[10] He gave up the opportunity to study in T'ang China and turned away from a life course which could have led him to the highest posts of National Teacher or King's Teacher. He remained a man of the people and went out to wander among men of all classes. He had talent in music, writing and teaching, but was not limited by any particular discipline, nor was he confined by the words of the scripture or obsessive involvement with ritual and chanting. He responded to the desires of ordinary people who wished for a fortunate rebirth in the Pure Land. He also gave support to the beliefs in the bodhisattvas Maitreya, Avalokiteśvara and Kṣitigarbha. And yet at the same time he taught that being concerned about rebirth in either paradise or hell was the result of inferior belief.[11]

Wŏhnyo's aim was the attainment of "Oneness" that comes from the perfection of wisdom. In Korean this also means "being large". His ideal was, in other words, the realization of a Higher Self (*tae-a*). This "oneness" was to be understood within the context of the teachings found in the Buddhist texts, such as that of "one" (*il*) and "all-embracing circle" (*wŏn*), the major doctrines of the *Avataṃsakasūtra*. He described this as the "great" (*tae*) of the *Ta-ch'eng ch'i-hsin lun*. The "one" was conceived by Wŏnhyo as the integration of every kind of power and wisdom; we might even say it was a *dharaṇi* in a Buddhist sense. As such, the "one" was seen as the source of all values, the "source of the one mind" and as the source it brought about the extinction of all conflicts. The focus on "one" cannot be considered apart from the social situation of Silla before unification. This ideal of total harmony was taught to the political leaders and the young elite and served as a doctrine which could promise peace and prosperity through the uniting of the Three Kingdoms.

Uisang, an intimate friend of Wŏnhyo approached the problem of unity through the teaching of One Vehicle (*ekayāna*), the major theme of the *Avataṃsakasūtra*. Uisang had studied under Chih-yen in China and later held the title of National Teacher. His thought which was in agreement with the spirit of Wŏnhyo's teachings, was given a pictoral form: a meander design made up of a poem consisting of 210 Chinese characters entitled the *Hwaŏm ilsŭng pŏpkyedo*.[12] The meander begins with the word *pŏp* (Dharma) and the remaining characters weave their way until the final word near the center which is *pul* (Buddha). The design is composed of 54 turns and is in the shape of a square. This poem taught one to go forward through the right path firmly holding the Dharma. "In one there is all, in all there is one; one is all, all is one." There is another famous meander made by a Silla monk, the *Haein sammaedo* (The Ocean Seal Samādhi Meander), which follows this format used by Uisang.[13]

Among the disciples of Uisang, there was P'yohun, who wrote a poem urging the realization of *pratītya-samutpāda*.

The self is a dharma produced from conditions.

Conditions become as they are because of the self.

The self is produced by means of conditions, [but] the self has no foundation.

Conditions are produced because of self, [but these] conditions have no [self-]nature.

The being or non-being of all dharmas is originally one.

The dharma of being and non-being are not originally two.

When it exists, it is not existing, but non-existing.

When it does not exist, it is not non-existing, but existing.

The dharmas originally do not move.

The mind of subjective conception also does not arise.

From the teaching of these distinguished monks, the people of Silla learned that these doctrines could be applied in the realm of social activity. They saw that the individual and the group are not separated, but are interrelated to one another. The rulers and people were also subject to this same notion of "being one" because there is no difference between self and others.

The ethical side of Buddhism also influenced the values of the Silla kingdom, the idea that humans must live with a generous and compassionate attitude and with a mind of wit and humour in accord with the ideal of wisdom (*prajñā*) was emphasized.[14] We find one statue which conveys these teachings —the eleven-headed Avalokiteśvara image in the cave near Kyŏngju called Sŏkkuram. The eleven faces which appear on the top of the head of this bodhisattva, which is located just behind the main Buddha image in the cave, were held to represent the Buddhist ideal of a human being. The *Shih-i-mien shen-chou ching i-shu* (Commentary on the Eleven-headed Incantation Sutra) by Hui-chao of the T'ang, which was popularly known in Silla, gives us the meaning of the eleven faces.[15] The three faces on the right represent compassion in its three aspects (1) providing ease to those who experience pain (2) helping those who have virtue acquire wisdom (3) helping those who have wisdom gain divine power. The three faces on the left have the aspect of force of anger in its three forms (1) anger toward deluded beings who seek to escape suffering but perform those very acts which produce it. (2) anger toward those who search for pleasure without any knowledge of the cause of it. (3) anger toward those who hold onto the state of confusion with calm acceptance. According to the *I-shu* these faces of compassion and of anger represent "civilian" and the "military" respectively. In the center between the triads of the other faces, is an image of the Buddha in his Transformational body (*nirmāṇakāya*). This Buddha figure signifies the ultimate goal of the practice of Mahāyāna Buddhism. On the second level in the center there are three faces which are characterized as "the faces that show all their teeth during laughter." These represent the praise of those beings who cultivate good karma. On the top level in the center we find three more faces who are designated "the faces of great explosive laughter." This is the distinctive mark of broadmindedness which accepts all sentient beings, making no distinction between good and evil. For the bodhisattvas who possess wisdom, neither purity nor impurity can be objects of attachment.

One other doctrinal grouping, called the Four All Embracing Virtues (*catussaṃgraha*) was a part of the Buddhist tradition which gave support to the Silla spirit. These four are: (1) giving the desired gifts to others (*dāna*), (2) using affectionate speech (*priyavacana*), (3) performing actions which profit others (*arthakṛtya*), (4) cooperating with others (*samanārthatā*). All of these virtues were stressed in Wŏnhyo's writings and in Uisang's meander. The practice of such virtues could produce protection and power. Wŏnhyo likened these practices to the invincibility of the ocean and sky, when he taught "The ocean cannot be destroyed by poison and the sky cannot be injured by a sharp sword." Such promises of power must have been great support to the kingdom as it strove for the goal of unification.

NOTES

1. Cf. Takahashi Tōru, *Richō bukkyō* (Buddhism in the Chosŏn Dynasty (Osaka, 1929); *Chōsen Zenkyōshi* (History of Ch'an Buddhism in Korea) (Tokyo: 1930); Yi Nŭng-hwa, *Chosŏn pulgyo t'ongsa* (History of Buddhism in Korea) (Seoul, 1918).

2. Rhi Ki-yong, "Pulgyo sasang ŭi suyong kwa kŭ pyŏnmo" (The Reception of Buddhism and its Transfromation), in *Han'guk minjok sasangsa taegye* (History of the Thought of the Korean People) vol. 1 (Seoul: *Asea haksul yŏn'guhoe*, 1971), pp. 89-135.

3. Cf. Munhwajae kwalliguk, (Cultural Property Preservation Bureau), ed., *Muryŏng wangnŭng palgul chosa pogosŏ* (Excavation Report of the Tomb of King Muryŏng). (Seoul, 1974).

4. Yi Sŏn-gŭn, *Hwarangdo yŏn'gu* (Study of Hwarangdo), (Seoul, 1954).

5. Min Yŏng-gyu, "Silla changsorok changp-yŏn" (A List of Buddhist works by Silla monks) in *Paek sŏnguk paksa songsu kinyŏm pulgyohak nonmunjip* (Festschrift in honor of Dr. Paek Sŏnguk) (Seoul, 1957), pp. 345-402.

6. Rhi Ki-yong, "Wŏnhyo ŭi posalgye kwan" (Wŏnhyo's view of the *bodhisattvaśīla*), (Tongguk taehakkyo nonmunjip, vol. 3.4 (1968), and *Pulgyo hakpo*, vol. 5, (1967); also compiled in his *Han'guk pulgyo yŏn'gu* (Study of Korean Buddhism, hereafter HPY), (Seoul: *Han'guk pulgyo yŏnguwon ch'ulp'anbu*, 1982), pp. 305-43.

7. Rhi Ki-yong, "Han'gukjŏk sayu ŭi il chŏnt'ong" (A Tradition in the Korean Way of Thought) *Tongbang hakchi*, vol. 10; in HPY, pp. 127-62.

8. *Hwaŏm ilsŭng pŏpkyedo* by Uisang, which will be discussed

later, is a good example of such a thought.

9. Cf. *Wŏnhyo chŏnjip* (The Complete Works of Wŏnhyo), (Seoul, 1973); Rhi Ki-yong, *Wŏnhyo sasang* (Thought of Wŏhyo), (Seoul, 1967).

10. The biography of Wŏnhyo in *Sung Kao-seng chuan* and the section "Wŏnhyo, the unbound one" in the *Samguk yusa*.

11. Wŏhyo, *Amit'agyŏng so* (Commentary on the *Amitābhasūtra*).

12. *Taishō* no. 1887a.

13. *Taishō* no. 1889.

14. The section of "the Monk Hyegong" in *Samguk yusa* (vol. 4) is a good example.

15. *Taishō* no. 1802, vol. 39, p. 1005 b, c.

This is originally a lecture given at the first symposium on Korean-Japanese Culture in Tokyo in 1969. It was later published in *Han*, vol. 2 (1972) in Japanese under the title, "Shiragi bukkyō no seikaku to sono gendaiteki igi" (Characteristics of Silla Buddhism and its meanings for today), and again compiled in Korean translation in Rhi's *Han'guk pulgyo yŏn'gu* (Study of Korean Buddhism), Seoul, 1982, pp. 453-463. We cut its fourth chapter "The Meanings for Today" and edited it for the purpose of the present volume.

Glossary for Korean Words

Ado 阿道
Agō 阿琚
Ajikki 阿直岐
Aryŏng 闕英
Awang 阿王
Chajang 慈藏
Ch'akp'yŏng 啄評
Chang 丈
Chesŏk 帝釋
Chihwang 智晃
Chihye 智惠
Chimyŏng 智明
Chin'gol 眞骨
Chinja 眞慈
Chinji 眞智
Chinjŏng 眞定
Cho Sa 趙思
Ch'ŏlbu 哲夫
Chŏmch'albo 占察寶
Chŏng Chi-wŏn 鄭智遠
Ch'ŏngam-ri 清岩里
Chŏngnim 定林
Ch'ŏn'gyŏng 天鏡
Chŏnmil 轉密
Ch'ŏnno 賤奴
Chukchi 竹旨
Ch'ungch'ŏng 忠清
Ch'ungdam 忠談
Haktong 學童
Han'gŭl 한글
Hansan 漢山
Hansŏng 漢城
Hoguk sasang 護國思想
Hose-rang 好世郎
Hŭksan 黑山
Hŭngnyun 興輪
Hwabaek 和白
Hwajaeng 和靜

Hwangnyong 皇龍
Hwangnyong 黃龍
Hwarang 花郎
Hyech'o 慧超
Hyegong 惠空
Hyegwan 惠灌
Hyehyŏn 惠現
Hyein 惠仁
Hyeja 惠慈
Hyejung 惠衆
Hyemi 慧彌
Hyep'yŏn 惠便
Hyeryang 惠亮
Hyesik 惠宿
Hyesuk 惠宿
Hyet'ong 惠通
Hyŏn'gwang 玄光
Hyŏnil 玄一
Hyŏnt'o 懸吐
Ibullan 伊弗蘭
Ich'adon 異次頓
Igyŏndae 利見臺
Iksan 益山
Il 一
Illa 日羅
Ilsŭng 一乘
Imgang 臨江
Imin 壬寅
In 印
Inwang paekchwahoe 仁王百座會
Iryŏn 一然
Kabin 甲寅
Kagoja 賈古子
Kaktŏk 覺德
Kamŭn 感恩
Kangnŭng-kun 江陵郡
Kapcha 甲子
Kapsin 甲申

Kaya 伽倻
Kim Mun-yang 金文亮
Kim Tae-sŏng 金大城
Kim Yang-do 金良圖
Kim Yu-sin 金庾信
Kimi 己未
Kiwŏn 祇園
Koguryŏ 高句麗
Kokpan 斛飯
Koksan 谷山
Kŏnbok 建福
Kongju 公州
Kŏnwŏn 建元
Kosŏn 高仙
Kuji 龜旨
Kuksa 國師
Kukt'ong 國統
Kulbul 掘佛
Kŭmgang 金剛
Kŭmgang kyedan 金剛戒壇
Kŭmnyun 金輪
Kunsu-ri 軍守里
Kwijin 貴珍
Kyemi 癸未
Kyeyu 癸酉
Kyŏmik 謙益
Kyŏndŭng 見登
Kyŏng 敬
Kyŏngdang 扃堂
Kyŏngjo 慶祖
Kyŏngju 慶州
Malgal 靺鞨
Malt'aemun 末太文
Mangdŏk 望德
Manp'asikchŏk 萬波息笛
Maranant'a (Mālānanda) 摩羅難陀
Milbon 密本
Mirŭk 彌勒
Mirŭk sŏnhwa 彌勒仙花
Misi 未尸

Mit'a 彌陀
Moryang-ri 牟梁里
Muae 無㝵
Muning 文仍
Munmyŏng 文明
Munno-rang 文弩郎
Muyong 舞踊
Myŏnggwan 明觀
Myŏnghyo 明晶
Namyang 南陽
Namyŏmju 南閻州
Nangdo 郎徒
Nansŭng 難勝
Naru 那婁
Norisach'igye 奴利斯致契
Odae 五臺
Ojak-pi 塢作碑
Paedalta 倍達多
Paegyŏ 白如
Paekche 百濟
Paekchŏng 白淨
Paekpan 白飯
Paengnyul 栢栗
P'ajinch'an 波珍湌
Palchŏng 發正
P'algwanhoe 八關會
P'ayak 波若
Pŏbun 法雲
Podŏk 普德
Pogan 福安
Pohwa 寶華
Ponghwa 奉化
Pŏp 法
Pŏpchŏng 法定
Pul 佛
Pulgasaŭi 不可思議
Punhwang 芬皇
Pusŏk 浮石
Puyŏ 扶餘
P'yohun 表訓
P'yŏngch'ŏn-ri 平川里

Pyŏngjin 丙辰
P'yŏngyang 平壤
P'yowŏn 表員
Sabi 泗沘
Sabok 蚊福
Sabul 四佛
Sach'ŏnwang 四天王
Saja 師子
Sakchu 朔州
Samhan 三韓
Samhwaryŏng 三花嶺
Sangbu Aam 上部 兒奄
Sangdaedŭng 上大等
Saryun 舍輪
Sesok ogye 世俗五戒
Sil 實
Silche 實際
Silla 新羅
Sillabŏl 室羅伐
Sinbang 神昉
Sinmi 辛未
Sinsŏnam 神仙庵
Sŏkkuram 石窟庵
Sŏndo 仙桃
Sŏngmun 省門
Sŏngnam 城南
Sŏnnyul 善律
Sonyŏnsŏsŏng 少年書省
Sŏrabŏl 徐羅伐
Sŏsan 瑞山
Ssangyong 雙龍
Suda 水多
Sudŏk 修德
Sulchong 述宗
Sundo (Shun-tao) 順道
Sŭngman 勝曼
Sŭngnang 僧朗
Sŭngnyung 僧隆
Sŭngt'ong 僧統
Suwŏn 水源
Tae-a 大我

Taean 大安
T'aean 泰安
Taedong 大同
Taedoyuna 大都維那
Taedŭng 大等
T'aehak 太學
Taehŭngnyun 大興輪
T'aehyŏn 太賢
T'aemun'ga 太文賈
T'aeryang 太良
T'aeryangmal 太良末
Taesa 大師
Taesŏsŏng 大書省
Taesŭng 大乘
Taet'ong 大通
Taewang-am 大王岩
Tamhye 曇慧
Tamjing 曇徵
Tamsi 曇始
Tamuk 曇旭
Tamyuk 曇育
Tan'gun 檀君
T'o 吐
Todŭng 道登
Tohŭm 道欽
Tojang 道藏
Tojo 道祖
Tojŭng 道證
Tokpohasŏ 都維那娘
Tŏkch'ang 德昌
Tŏkchŏk 德積
Tong 東
T'ongdo 通度
Tŏngman 德曼
Tongnyun 銅輪
Toŏm 道嚴
Toryun 道倫
Tosu 道須
Tosun 道順
Tu 斗
Tu-pu Ho-si 獨步河西

Ŭich'ŏn　義天
Ŭigak　義覺
Ŭijŏk　義寂
Ŭisang　義湘
Ŭiyŏn　義淵
Ŭlch'uk　乙丑
Ŭmnŭk　邑勒
Ung　熊
Ungju　熊州
Uugmyŏn　郁面
Ŭnnyun　銀輪
Wang In　王仁
Wang Ko-dŏk　王高德
Wang Yŏn-son　王延孫
Wanghŭng　王興
Wangsa　王師
Wŏn　圓
Wŏnch'ŭk　圓測

Wŏlch'ung　月忠
Wŏn'gwang　圓光
Wŏnhyo　元曉
Yang　兩
Yŏktŏk　亦德
Yŏn Kaesomun　淵蓋蘇文
Yŏn'ga　延嘉
Yŏnggae　令開
Yŏnggŭn　令斤
Yonghwa hyangdo　龍華香徒
Yŏn'gi　燕岐
Yŏngjo　聆照
Yŏngt'ap　靈塔
Yŏngwi　令威
Yosŏk　瑤石
Yuktup'um　六頭品
Yuma　維摩

BIBLIOGRAPHY

BUDDHIST CANONICAL WORKS

Amit'agyŏng so 阿彌陀經疏 by Wŏnhyo 元曉. *T.* 1759.

Amit'agyŏng ŭigi 阿彌陀經義記 by Chajang 慈藏 (not extant).

Ch'ang e-han ching 長阿含經 [*Dīrghāgamasūtra*]. *T.* 1, *K.* 647.

Chao-lun 肇論 by Seng-chao 僧肇. *T.* 1858.

Ch'eng-shih lun 成實論 [*Satyasiddhiśāstra*]. *T.* 1646, *K.* 966.

Chi shen-chou san-pao kan-t'ung lu 集神州三寶感通錄 by Tao-hsüan 道宣. *T.* 2106, *K.* 1069.

Chieh-t'o-chieh ching 解脫戒經 [*Pratimokṣasūtra*]. *T.* 1460, *K.* 910.

Chin-kāng pan-jo lun 金剛般若論 [*Vajracchedikāprajñapāramitāsūtraśāstra*] by Asaṅga. *T.* 1510, *K.* 555.

Chin-kang pan-jo (po-lo-mi) ching lun 金剛般若(波羅密)經論 [*Vajracchedikāprajñāpāramitāsūtraśāstra*] by Vasubandhu. *T.* 1511, *K.* 558.

Chin-kuang-ming ching 金光明經 [*Suvarṇaprabhāsa-(uttamarāja) sūtra*]. *T.* 663, *K.* 1465. Cf. *T.* 664, 665, *K.* 127, 128.

Ch'u san-tsang chi-chi 出三藏記集 by Seng-yu 僧祐 *T.* 2145, *K.* 1053.

Chung-ching-lu 衆經錄 by Fa-shang 法上.

Chung(-kuan)lun 中(觀)論 [*(Mūla)madhyamakaśāstra*] by Nāgārjuna. *T.* 1564, *K.* 577.

Chūron shoki 中論疏記 by Anchō 安澄. *T.* 2255.

Chung-kuan-lun shu 中觀論疏 by Chi-tsang 吉藏. *T.* 1824.

Erh-ti i 二諦義 by Chi-tsang 吉藏. *T.* 1854.

Fa-hua-ching hsüan-i shih-ch'ien 法華經玄義釋籤 by Chan-jan. *T.* 1717.

Fa-yuan chu-lin 法苑珠林 by Tao-shih 道世. *T.* 2122, *K.* 1406.

Fan-i ming-i chi 飜譯名義集 by Fa-yün 法雲. *T.* 2131.

Fan-wang ching 梵綱經 [*Brahmajālasūtra*]. *T.* 1484, *K.* 527.

Fo-hsing-lun 佛性論 by Fa-shang 法上

Fo-shuo fan-chieh tsui-pao ch'ing-chung ching 佛說犯戒罪報輕重經. *T.* 1467, *K.* 932.

Fu-mu en-chung ching 父母恩重經. *T.* 2887.

Haedong kosŭng chŏn 海東高僧傳 by Kakhun 覺訓. *T.* 2065. (Also see Peter Lee in the Secondary Literature)

Haein sammaeron 海印三昧論 by Myŏnghyo 明皛. *T.* 1889.

Hokkekyō shigi 法華經私記   by Ryōchū 良忠.
Honchō kōsōten 本朝高僧傳.
Hsu kao-seng chuan 續高僧傳   by Tao-hsüan 道宣.   *T.* 2060, *K.*
1075.
Hwaŏm ilsŭng pŏpkyedo 華嚴一乘法界圖   by Uisang 義湘.
T. 1887(a).
I-ching yuan-ch'i 譯經緣起   by Seng-fang 僧昉.
Jen-wang pan-jo po-lo-mi ching 仁王般若波羅密經.   *T.* 245, *K.* 19.
Ju leng-ch'ieh ching 入楞伽經   [*Laṅkāvatārasūtra*].
T. 671, *K.* 160. Cf. *T.* 670, 672, *K.* 159, 161.
K'ai-yüan shih-chiao lu 開元釋敎錄   by Chih-sheng 智昇.
T. 2154, *K.* 1062.
Kao-seng chuan 高僧傳   by Hui-chiao 慧皎.   *T.* 2059, *K.* 1074.
Kuang hung-ming chi 廣弘明集   by Tao-hsüan 道宣.
T. 2103. *K.* 1081.
Kwanhaengbŏp 觀行法   by Chajang 慈藏   (not extant).
Li-tai san-pao chi 歷代三寶記   by Fei Ch'ang-fang 費長房.
T. 2034, *K.* 1055.
Mi-le hsia-sheng ching 彌勒下生經.   *T.* 453, *K.* 197.
Mi-le shang-sheng ching 彌勒上生經.   *T.* 452, *K.* 194.
Miao-fa lien-hua ching 妙法蓮華經   [*Saddharmapuṇḍarīkasūtra*]. *T.*
262, *K.* 116. Cf. *T.* 263, 264, *K.* 117, 118.
Mo-ho seng-ch'i lü 摩訶僧祇律   [*Mahāsanghikavinaya*]. *T.* 1425, *K.*
889.
Naiden jinroshō 內典塵露章   by Gyōnen 凝然.   In *Dai nihon buk-*
kyō zensho, vol. 3.
Pai lun 百論   [*Śata(ka)śāstra*] by Āryadeva. *T.* 1569, *K.* 581.
Pei-Wei seng Hui-sheng shih hsi-yu-chi 北魏僧惠生使西域記   by Hui-
sheng. *T.* 2086.
Pi-ch'iu-ni ta-chieh 比丘尼大戒   (v. *Shih-sung pi-ch'iu-ni po-lo-t'i*
mu-ch'a chieh-pen 十誦比丘尼波羅提木叉戒本. *T.* 1437, *K.* 899.
P'u-sa-ti(-ch'ih) ching 菩薩地(持)經   [*Bodhisattvabhūmi*]. *T.* 1581,
K. 523.
P'u-sa ying-lo pen-yeh ching 菩薩瓔珞本業經.   *T.* 1485, *K.* 530.
Sabunyul kalma sagi 四分律羯磨私記   by Chajang 慈藏
(not extant).
Samnon chongyo 三論宗要   by Wŏnhyo 元曉   (not extant).
San-lun hsüan-i 三論玄義   by Chi-tsang 吉藏.   *T.* 1852.
San-tsung lun 三宗論   by Chou-yung 周顒.
Seng-chi chieh-hsin 僧祇戒心.
She-li-fu wen ching 舍利弗問經   [*Śāriputraparipṛcchā*]. *T.* 1465, *K.*

907.

She ta-ch'eng lun 攝大乘論 [*Mahāyānasamgraha*] by Asaṅga. *T.* 1592, 1593, 1594, *K.* 588, 591, 592.

Sheng-man shih-tzu hou i-cheng ta fang-pien fang-kuang ching 勝鬘師子吼一乘大方便方廣經 [*Śrīmālā(devī)simhanādasūtra*]. *T.* 353, *K.* 54.

Shih-erh-men lun 十二門論 [*Dvādaśanikāyaśāstra*] by Nāgārjuna. *T.* 1568, *K.* 579.

Shih-i-mien shen-chou hsin-ching i-shu 十一面神呪心經義疏 by Hui-chao 慧沼. *T.* 1802.

Shih-sung lü 十誦律 [*Sarvāstivādavinaya*]. *T.* 1435, *K.* 890.

Shih-sung pi-ch'iu po-lo-t'i mu-ch'a chieh-pen 十誦比丘波羅挽木叉戒本 [(*Sarvāstivāda*) *Prātimokṣasūtra*]. *T.* 1436, *K.* 902.

Shih-ti-ching lun 十地經論 [*Daśabhūmikasūtraśāstra*] by Vasuban-dhu. *T.* 1522, *K.* 550.

Sinp'yŏn chejong kyojang ch'ongrok 新編諸宗敎藏總錄 by Ŭich'ŏn 義天 *T.* 2184.

Sipsongyul mokch'agi 十誦律木叉記 by Chajang 慈藏 (not extant).

Sŏngsillon so 成實論疏 by Tojang 道藏 (not extant).

Ssu-fen lü 四分律 [*Dharmagupta(ka)vinaya*]. *T.* 1428, *K.* 896.

Sung kao-sung chuan 宋高僧傳 by Tsan-ning 贊寧 *T.* 2061.

Ta-ch'eng ch'i-hsin lun 大乘起信論 [*Mahāyānaśraddhotpādaśāstra*] by Aśvaghoṣa. *T.* 1666, 1667, *K.* 616, 623.

Ta-ch'eng hsüan-lun 大乘玄論 by Chi-tsang 吉藏. *T.* 1853.

Ta-ch'eng i-chang 大乘義章 by Fa-shang 法上.

Ta-ch'eng t'ung-hsing ching 大乘同性經 [*Mahāyānābhisamaya(sūtra)*]. *T.* 673, *K.* 151.

Ta-chi ching 大集經 (v. *Ta-fang-teng ta-chi ching* 大方等大集經) [*Mahāvaipulyamahāsannipātasūtra*]. *T.* 397, *K.* 56.

Ta-chih-tu-lun 大智度論 [*Mahāprajñāpāramitāśāstra*] by Nāgārjuna. *T.* 1509, *K.* 549.

Ta chou k'an-ting chung-ching mu-lu 大周刊定衆經目錄 by Ming-ch'üan 明佺. *T.* 2153.

Ta-fang-kuang-fo hua-yen ching 大方廣佛華嚴經 [(*Buddha*)*avataṃsaka-sūtra*]. *T.* 278, *K.* 79. Cf. *T.* 279, *K.* 80.

Ta pan-jo po-lo-mi-to ching 大般若波羅密經 [*Mahāprajñāpāramitā-sūtra*]. *T.* 220, *K.* 1.

Ta-pan nieh-p'an ching 大般涅槃經 [*Mahāparinirvāṇasūtra*]. *T.* 374, 375, *K.* 105, 1403.

Ta pi-ch'iu san-ch'ien wei-i 大比丘三千威儀 *T.* 1470, *K.* 940.

Ta-p'i-p'o-sha lun 大毘婆沙論   (v. *A-p'i-ta-mo ta-p'i-p'o-sha lun* 阿毘達磨大毘婆沙論) [(*Abhidharma*)*mahāvibhāṣā*(*śāstra*)]. *T.* 1545, *K.* 971.

Ta-p'in pan-jo ching 大品般若經   (v. *Mo-ho pan-jo po-lo-mi ching* 摩訶般若波羅密經   [*Pañcāviṃśatisāhasrikāprajñāpāramitāsūtra*]. *T.* 223, *K.* 3. Cf. *T.* 221, *K.* 2.

Ta-t'ang hsi-yü chi 大唐西域記   by Hsüan-tsang 玄奘. *T.* 2087, *K.* 1065.

Ta-t'ang hsi-yu ch'iu-fa kao-seng chuan 大唐西域求法高僧傳   by I-ching 義淨. *T.* 2066, *K.* 1072.

T'an-wu-te chieh-mo 曇無德竭磨   (v. *Ssu-fen pi-ch'iu-ni chieh-mo-fa* 四分比丘尼竭磨法) [*Dharmaguptabhikṣṇnīkarman*]. *T.* 1434, *K.* 919.

Ti-lun shu 地論疏   (v. *Shih-ti lun i-shu* 十地論義疏) by Fa-shang 法上. *T.* 2799.

Tseng-i a-han ching 增一阿含經   [*Ekottarāgama-*(*sūtra*)]. *T.* 125, *K.* 649.

Tseng-i-shu-fa 增一述法   by Fa-shang 法上.

Wei-mo-chieh so-shuo ching 維摩詰所說經   [*Vimalakirtinideśasūtra*]. *T.* 475, *K.* 119. Cf. *T.* 474, 476-479, *K.* 120-124.

Yŏraejanggyŏng so 如來藏經疏   by Wŏn'gwang 圓光 (not extant).

Yoraejang sagi 如來藏私記   by Wŏn'gwang 圓光 (not extant).

Wu-fen lü 五分律   (v. *Mi-sha-sai-pu ho-hsi wu-fen lü* 彌沙塞部和醯五分律) [*Mahīśāsakavinaya*]. *T.* 1421, *K.* 895.

Wu-liang-shou ching 無量壽經   [*Sukhāvatīvyūhasūtra*]. *T.* 360, *K.* 26.

Yao-shih-ju-lai pen-yuan ching 藥師如來本願經   [*Bhaiṣajyagurupūrva praṇidhānaviśeṣavistara*(*sūtra*)]. *T.* 449, *K.* 176.

Yu-chia shih-ti lun 瑜伽師地論   [*Yogācārabhūmiśāstra*] by Maitreya. *T.* 1579, *K.* 1579, *K.* 590.

Yuan-jen lun 原人論   by Tsung-mi 宗密. *T.* 1886.

CLASSICAL WORKS

Gankōji garan engi narabini ryūki shizaichō 元興寺伽藍緣起幷流記資財帳 [History of the Gankō Monastery and Ledger of Property and Income].

"Hsi-ching fu" 西京賦 [Rhapsody of the Western Capital] by Chang Heng 張衡

Jōgū shōtoku hō teisetsu 上宮聖德法王帝說   [Biography of Prince Shōtoku, King of Dharma].

Miruk pulgwangsa sajŏk 彌勒佛光寺事蹟.

Nihon shoki 日本書記.

Pohanjip 補閑集 by Ch'oe Cha 崔滋 Also see Yi Sangbo in the Secondary Literature

Samguk yusa 三國遺事 by Iryŏn 一然. Also see T. Ha, H. Hayashi, K. Tsuboi in the Secondary Literature.

Samguk sagi 三國史記 by Kim Pu-sik 金富軾. Also see H. Inoue, S. Kim, in the Secondary Literature.

Sinjŭng tongguk yŏji sŭngnam 新增東國輿地勝覽 [Revised Survey of Korean Geography] by Yang Song-ji and No-sa-jin

Zoku Nihongi 續日本記.

SECONDARY LITERATURE

Ahn Kye-hyŏn 安啓賢. "Wŏnhyo ŭi mit'a chŏngt'o wangsaeng sasang" 元曉의 彌陀淨土往生思想 [Wŏnhyo's View of the Rebirth in Amitābha's Pure Land]. *Yŏksa hakpo* 歷史學報 17/18 (1962): 245-275; 21 (1963): 1-32.

———. "Pulsari sinang kwa han'guk pulgyo" 佛舍利信仰과 韓國佛敎 [Buddha's Relic Cult in Korean Buddhism]. *Pulgyo sasang* 佛敎思想 13 (1963).

———. "Koguryŏ pulgyo ŭi chŏn'gae" 高句麗佛敎의 展開 [The Development of Koguryŏ Buddhism]. *Han'guk Sasang* 韓國思想 7 (1964): 65-76.

———. "Han'guk pulgyosa, sang, kodaep'yŏn" 韓國佛敎史(上), 古代篇 [History of Korean Buddhism, Part 1: Ancient Period]. In *Han'guk munhwasa taegye* 韓國文化史大系 vol. 4, pp. 171-220. Seoul: Korea University Press, 1970.

Best, Jonathan W. "Diplomatic and Cultural Contacts between Paekche and China". *Harvard Journal of Asiatic Studies* 42, no. 2 (1982): 443-501.

Bukkyō geijutsu 佛敎藝術 [Buddhist Art] 83 (1972). (Special volume on the Korean Buddhist Art.)

Buswell, Robert. *The Korean Approach to Zen: The Collected Works of Chinul.* Honolulu: University of Hawaii Press, 1983.

Chin Hong-sŏp 秦弘燮. "Kyeyu myŏng samjon ch'ŏnbul pisang e taehayŏ" 癸酉銘三尊千佛碑像에 對하여 [On the Buddha-triad Stele with the Inscription of the Year K*yeyu*]. *Yŏksa hak'po* 19 (1962), pp. 83-109.

———. "Kudara jiin no garan seido" 百済寺院の伽藍制度 [Monastic Structures of Paekche]. In Kudarashi Kenkyukai 百済史研究會 ed., *Kudarashi no kenkyū* 百済史の研究, pp. 325-360.

Cho Myŏng-gi 趙明基. *Silla pulgyo ŭi inyŏm kwa yŏksa* 新羅佛敎의 理念과 歷史 [The Ideas and History of Silla Buddhism].

Seoul: Sint'aeyang-sa. 1962.

Ch'oe Kwŏn-muk 崔權黙. "Kudara no chūgoku kankei ni kansuru shokō" 百濟の中國關係に關する小考 [A Note on the Ties between Paekche and China]. In *Kudarashi no Kenkyū*, pp. 193-219. Tokyo: Kokusho kankōkai, 1979.

Chŏng Chung-hwan 丁仲煥. "Silla ŭi pulgyo chŏllae wa kŭ hyŏnse sasang" 新羅의 佛敎傳來와 그 現世思想 [Introduction of Buddhism in Silla and its Realistic Nature]. In *Cho Myŏnggi paksa hwagap kinyŏm pulgyo sahak nonch'ong* 趙明基博士華甲紀念佛敎史學論叢 [Festschrift in Honor of Dr. Cho Myŏng-gi], pp.173-195. Seoul, 1965.

———. "Silla sŏnggol ko" 新羅聖骨考 [Study of *Sŏnggol* of Silla]. In *Yi Hongjik paksa hoegap kinyŏm han'guk sahak nonch'ong* 李弘植博士回甲紀念韓國史學論叢 [Festschrift in Honor of Dr. Yi Hong-jik], pp. 35-52. Seoul, 1969.

Chōsen kinseki sōran 朝鮮金石總覽 [Collections of Korean Metal and Lithic Inscriptions]. Keijō (Seoul): Chōsen sōtokufu, 1919.

Eda Toshio 江田俊雄. "Shiragi no Jizō to Godaisan" 新羅の慈藏と五臺山 [Chajang of Silla and Mt. Wu-t'ai]. *Bunka* 文化 21, no. 5 (1957): 44-55.

Fujita Toyohachi 藤田豊八. *Tōzai kōshōshi no kenkyū: nankai hen* 東西交渉史の研究：南海篇 [A Study of the History of Contacts between East and West: The South Seas]. Tokyo: Oka shoin, 1932.

———. "Zenkan ni okeru seinan kaijō kōtsu no kiroku" 前漢に於ける西南海上交通の記錄 [Record of the Routes on the South-Western Sea during the Former Han Period]. In *Tōzai kōshōshi no kenkyū* pp.95-135.

Fukada Kyūya 深田久稱. *Chūō ajia tankenshi* 中央アジア探險史 [History of the Exploration of Serindia]. Special volume in the series *Seiiki tanken kikō zenshū* 西域探險紀行全集 [Explorations of the Western Regions]. Tokyo: Kosuisha, 1971.

Funaki Katsuma 船木勝馬. "Hokugi no seiiki kōtsu ni kansuru shomondai" 北魏の西域交通に關する諸問題 [Issues Conerning the Routes through Serindia during the Northern Wei Period]. *Nishi nihon shigaku* 西日本史學 4 (1950).

Gard, Richard A. "The Mādhyamika in Korea". *Indogaku bukkyōgaku kenkyū* 印度學佛教學研究 7, no. 2 (1959): 50-78.

Ha Tae-hŭng and Grafton K. Mintz. *Samguk Yusa: Legends and History of the Three Kingdoms of Ancient Korea*. Seoul: Yonsei University Press, 1972.

Han'guk pulsang sambaek sŏn 韓國佛像三百選 [Three Hundred

Selected Works of Korean Buddhist Sculpture]. Sŏngnam: Academy of Korean Studies, 1982.

Hayashi Hideki 林英樹 trans. *Sangoku ishi* 三國遺事. 2 vols. Tokyo: Sanichi shobō, 1975, 1976.

Hirai Shunei 平井俊榮 "Sanron gakuha no genryū keifu" 三論學派の源流系譜 [The Origin and Lineage of the San-lun School]. *Tōhōgaku* 28 (1964): 52–65.

Hirakawa Akira 平川彰. "Kanyaku ritten honyaku no kenkyū" 漢譯律典飜譯の研究 [Study of the Chinese Translation of the *Vinaya*]. In *Ritsuzō no kenkyū* 律藏の研究 [Study of *Vinaya*], pp. 155–289. Tokyo: Sankibō busshorin, 1960.

Hong Yun-sik 洪潤植. "Chūgoku nanhokucho to Kudara no bukkyō" 中國南北朝と百濟の佛教 [Buddhism during the Nan-Pei Ch'ao Period in China and Paekche]. *Bukkyōshi kenkyū* 佛教史研究 18 (1983).

Hsin Wen-hsiang 信立祥, et. al. "Kung-wang shan mo-ya tsao-hsiang te nien-tai k'ao-ch'a" 孔望山磨崖影像的年代考察 [An Examination of the Dating of Relief Images at Mt. Kung-wang]. *Wen-wu* 文物 7, no. 302 (1981): 8–15.

Hwang Su-yŏng 黃壽永. "Sōsan Paekche maae samjon pulsang" 瑞山百濟磨崖三尊佛像 [Rock-Cut Buddha Triad from Paekche in Sōsan]. *Chindan hakpo* 震檀學報 20 (1959).

——. "Paekche pan'ga sayusang sogo" 百濟半跏思惟像小考 [On the Contemplating Half Cross-legged Images of Paekche]. *Yŏksa hakpo* 13 (1960): 1–22.

——. "Ch'ungnam t'aean ŭi maae samjon pulsang" 忠南泰安의 磨崖三尊佛像 [The Rock-Cut Buddha Triad Image in T'aen, South Ch'ungch'ŏng Provinice]. *Yoksa hakpo* 17/18, (1962): 51–63.

——. "Ch'ungnam yŏng'gi sŏksang chosa kaeyo" 忠南燕岐石像調査概要 [An Examination of Stone Steles in the Yŏn'gi Region, South Ch'ungch'ŏng Province]. *Yesul nonmunjip* 藝術論文集 3 (1964).

——. "Silla namsan samhwaryŏng mirŭk sejon" 新羅南山三花嶺彌勒世尊 [Silla Maitreya Image from Samhwaryŏng on Mt. Nam]. In *Kim Chewŏn paksa hoegap kinyŏm nonch'ong* 金載元博士回甲紀念論叢 [Festschrift for Dr. Kim Che-won], pp. 909–941. Seoul, 1969.

——. *Han'guk kŭmsŏk yumun* 韓國金石遺文 [Extant Inscriptions of Korea]. Seoul: Ilchisa, 1978.

Ienaga Saburō 家永三郎, ed. *Nihon bukkyōshi* 日本佛教史 [History of Japanese Buddhism]. Vol. 1. Kyoto: Hōzōkan, 1967.

Ikeuchi Hiroshi 池內宏. *Mansenshi kenkyū* 滿鮮史研究 [Studies

in the History of Manchuria and Korea]. Vol. 2: Medieval Period.
Kyoto: Sokokusha, 1951. Reprint. Yoshikawa kōbundō, 1960.

Imanishi Ryū 今西龍. "Shiragi koku Enkō hōshiden" 新羅國圓光
法師傳[Biography of Wŏn'gwang of Silla]. In his *Shiragishi kenkyū*
新羅史の研究　[Study of the History of Silla]. Keijō (Seoul):
Chikazawa shoten, 1933.

——. *Kudarashi kenkyū* 百濟史研究　[A Study of the History of
Paekche]. Tokyo: Chikazawa shoten, 1934. Reprint. Tokyo: Kokusho kankōkai, 1970.

Inoue Hideo 井上秀雄. *Higashi ajia minzokushi.* 東アジア民族史
[History of Peoples in East Asia]. 2 vols. Tōyō bunko series, nos.
264 and 283. Tokyo: Heibonsha, 1974, 1976.

——. "Chōsen ni okeru bukkyō juyō to shinkan'nen" 朝鮮における
佛教受容と神觀念　[The Reception of Buddhism in Korea and
the Conception of Spirits]. *Nihon bunka kenkyūsho kenkyū hōkoku*
日本文化研究所研究報告　[Research Bulletin of the Japanese Cultural Research Center] vol. 13 (1977): 45-69.

——, trans. *Sangoku shiki* 三國史記. Vols. 1-2. Tōyō bunko series,
nos. 372 and 425. Tokyo: Heibonsha, 1980-1984. [Still in progress].

Ishida Mikinosuke 石田幹之助. *Nankai ni kansuru shina shiryō* 南
海に關する支那史料　[Chinese Sources on the South Seas]. Tokyo:
Seikatsusha, 1945.

Kamata Shigeo 鎌田茂雄. "Chūgoku saiko no magaibutsu: kōbōzan
magai sekizō" 中國最古の磨崖佛：孔望山磨崖石像　[The Oldest
Relief Images: Lithic Relief Images at Mt. Kung-wang]. *UP*, vol.
11, no. 12 (1982): 1-5.

——. *Chūgoku bukkyōshi* 中國佛教史　[History of Chinese Bud-
dhism]. Vols. 1-2. Tokyo: Tokyo daigaku shuppankai, 1982, 1983.

——. "Bukkyō bunka no hatten" 佛教文化の發展　[Development
of Buddhist Culture]. In *Chūgoku bukkyōshi*, vol. 2.

——. "Kudara bukkyō no nihon denrai" 百濟佛教の日本傳來　[The
Transmission of Paekche Buddhism to Japan]. *Mahan paekche munhwa* 7 (1984): 61-71.

Karube Jion 輕部慈恩. *Kudara iseki no kenkyū* 百濟遺蹟の研究
[A Study of the Historical Monuments of Paekche]. Tokyo: Yoshikawa kōbundō, 1971.

Katsuragi Sueji 葛城末治. *Chōsen kinsekikō* 朝鮮金石攷 [Korean
Epigraphy]. Keijō (Seoul): Osaka yago shoten, 1935.

Kim Chŏl-jun 金哲埈. "Silla sangdae sahoe ŭi dual organization"
新羅上代社會의 dual organization　[Dual Organization in the
Early Silla Period]. *Yŏksa hakpo* 1 (1952): 15-48; 2 (1952): 85-

114.

Kim Chŏng-hŭi 金正喜. "Chinhŭng ibi ko" 眞興二碑考 [A Study of the Two Stelae of Chinhŭng]. In *Wandang sŏnsaeng munjip* 阮堂先生文集 [Complete Works of Wandang]. Seoul: Sinsŏng munhwasa, 1972.

Kim Ing-sŏk 金芿石. "Koguryŏ sŭngnang kwa samnon hak" 高句麗僧朗과 三論學 [Sŭngnang of Koguryŏ and his Study of the *San-lun*]. In *Paek Sŏnguk paksa songsu kinyŏm pulgyohak nonmunjip* [Festschrift in Honor of Dr. Paek Sŏng-uk] 41-68. Seoul, 1959.

Kim Sa-yŏp 金思燁, trans. *Sangoku shiki* 三國史記 2 vols. Tokyo: Rokko shuppan, 1980, 1981.

Kim Sang-gi 金庠基. "Hwarang kwa mirŭk sŏnhwa" 花郞과 彌勒仙花 [Hwarang and Mirŭk Sŏnhwa]. In *Yi Hongjik paksa hwagap kinyom han'guk sahak nonch'ong* [Festschrift in Honor of Dr. Yi Hong-jik], pp. 647-686. Seoul, 1969.

Kim T'aek-kyu 金宅圭. "Silla oyobi nihon kodai no shinbutsushūgōni tsuite" 新羅及び日本古代の神佛習合について [The Integration of Spirits and Buddhas in Silla and Japan during Ancient Times]. In Tamura Enchō 田村圓照 and Hong Sun-ch'ang 洪淳昶, eds., *Shiragi to Asuka, Hakuhō no bukkyō bunka* 新羅と飛鳥白鳳の佛教文化 [Silla and Buddhist Culture of Asuka and Hakuhō], pp. 201-263. Tokyo: Yoshikawa Kōbunkan, 1975.

Kim Tong-hwa 金東華. "Koguryŏ sidae ŭi pulgyo sasang" 高句麗時代의 佛教思想 [The Buddhist Thought of the Koguryŏ Period]. *Asea yŏn'gu* 亞細亞硏究 2, no. 2 (1959): 1-44.

——. "Paekche sidae ŭi pulgyo sasang" 百済時代의 佛教思想 [Buddhist Thought in Paekche Period]. *Asea yŏn'gu* 5, no. 1 (1962): 57-85.

——. *Pulgyo ŭi hoguk sasang* 佛教의 護國思想 [The National Protection Ideology of Buddhism]. Seoul: Pulgyo sinmunsa, 1976.

Klm Tong-uk 金東旭. "Silla chŏngt'o sasang ŭi chŏn'gae wa wŏnwangsaengga" 新羅淨土思想의 展開와 願往生歌 [The Development of Pure Land Thought in Silla and the "Wŏnwangsaengga"]. *Chungang taehakkyo nonmunjip* 中央大學校論文集 2 (1957).

——. "Tosolga yŏn'gu" 兜率歌硏究 [Study of "Tosolga"]. *Seoul-taehakkyo nonmunjip*: *inmun sahoe kwahak p'yon* 서울大學校論文集 人文社會科學篇 6 (1957).

Kim Won-yong 金元龍. "Koguryŏ kobun pyŏkhwa e issŏsŏ ŭi pulgyojŏk yoso" 高句麗 古墳壁畵에 있어서의 佛教的 要素 [Buddhist Elements Appearing on Koguryŏ Tomb Murals]. In *Paek Sŏnguk paksa songsu kinyŏm pulgyohak nonmunjip*, pp. 199-224. Seoul: 1959.

Kim Yŏng-su 金映遂. "T'ongdosa ŭi kyedan e taehayŏ" 通度寺의 戒壇에 對하여 [On the *Śila* Altar in T'ongdo Monastery]. *Ilgwang* 一光 9 (1933).

Kim Yŏng-t'ae 金煐泰. "Mirŭk sŏnhwa ko" 彌勒仙花考 [On Mirŭk Sŏnhwa]. *Pulgyo hakpo* [Journal of Buddhist Studies] 3/4 (1966): 135-149.

──. "Silla chinhŭngwang ŭi sinbul kwa kŭ sasang yŏn'gu" 新羅 眞興王의 信佛과 그 思想研究 [Study of King Chinhŭng's Faith in Buddhism and his Thought]. *Pulgyo hakpo* 5 (1967): 53-83.

──. "Sŭngryŏ *nangdo* ko" 僧侶郎徒考 [Study of the Monk *Nangdo*]. *Pulgyo hakpo* 7 (1970): 255-274.

──. "Silla ŭi chŏmch'al pŏphoe wa chinp'yŏ ŭi kyobŏp yŏn'gu" 新羅의 占察法會와 眞表의 教法 研究 [A Study of Chanch'a Dharma-Assemblies in Silla and Chinp'yo's Doctrinal Teachings]. *Pulgyo hakpo* 9 (1972): 99-136.

──, ed. "Ilbon sasŏ e poinŭn han'guk pulgyo saryo" 日本佛教에 보이는 韓國佛教史料 [Historical Sources on Korean Buddhism Found in Japanese Historical Documents]. *Han'guk pulgyohak* 韓 國佛教學 4 (1979): 130-152.

Ko Yu-sŏp 高裕燮. *Chosŏn t'appa ŭi yŏn'gu* 朝鮮塔婆의 研究 [Study of Korean Pagodas]. Seoul. 1948.

Kodama Daien 小玉大圓. "Chūo ajia to Kudara bunka" 中央ア ジアと百濟文化 [Central Asia and Paekche Culture]. *Mahan paekche munhwa* 7 (1984): 85-105.

Kudarashi Kenkyūkai 百濟史研究會, ed. *Kudarashi no kenkyū* 百 濟史の研究 [A Study of the History of Paekche]. Tokyo: Kokusho kankōkai, 1979.

Lee Ki-baek 李基白. "Samguk sidae ŭi pulgyo chŏllae wa kŭ sahoejŏk sŏnggyŏk" 三國時代의 佛教 傳來와 그 社會的 性格 [The Introduction of Buddhism in the Three Kingdoms and its Social Repercussions]. *Yŏksa hakpo* [Journal of History] 6 (1954): 128-205. Later compiled with slight revision in his *Silla sidae ŭi kukka pulgyo wa yugyo*, pp. 2-54.

──. "Sangdaedŭng ko" 上大等考 [A Study of the *Sangdaedŭng*]. *Yŏksa hakpo* 19 (1962): 1-51. Also compiled in *Silla chŏngch'i sahoesa yŏn'gu* 新羅政治社會史 研究 [A Study of the Political and Social History of Silla]. Seoul: Ilchogak, 1974.

──. "Koguryŏ ŭi kyŏngdang" 高句麗의 扃堂 [The Kyŏngdang of Koguryŏ]. *Yŏksa hakpo* 35/36 (1967): 42-54.

──. "Wŏn'gwang kwa kŭ ŭi sasang" 圓光과 그의 思想 [Wŏn'gwang and His Thought]. *Ch'angjak kwa pip'yŏng* 創作과 批評

[Creation and Criticism] 10 (1968). Also compiled in *Silla sidae ŭi kukka pulgyo wa yugyo*, pp. 103-120.

———. "Silla kolpumje ha ŭi yugyojŏk chŏngch'i inyŏm" 新羅 骨品 制下의 儒敎的 政治理念 [Confucian Political Ideology under the "Bone-rank" System of Silla]. *Taedong munhwa yŏn'gu* 6/7 (1970).

———. "Silla ch'ogi pulgyo wa kwijok seryŏk" 新羅初期 佛敎와 貴族 勢力 [Early Silla Buddhism and the Power of the Aristocracy]. *Chindan hakpo* 40 (1975): 21-39. Compiled in *Silla sidae ŭi kukka pulgyo wa yugyo*.

———. *Silla sidae ŭi kukka pulgyo wa yugyo* 新羅時代의 國家佛敎와 儒敎 [State Buddhism and Confucianism during the Silla Period]. Seoul: Han'guk yŏn'guwŏn, 1978.

Lee, Peter. *Lives of Eminent Korean Monks: The Haedong Kosŭng Chŏn*. Harvard Yenching Institute Studies, no. 25. Cambridge: Harvard University Press, 1969.

Lien-yun kang shih po-wu-kuan 連雲港市博物館. "Lien-yun shih kung-wang shan mo-ya tsao-hsiang tian-ch'a pao-kao" 連雲港市孔 望山磨崖造像調査報告 [A Report on the Relief Images at Mt. Kung-wang at the City of Lien-yun-kang]. *Wen-wu* 7, no. 302 (1981): 1-7.

Makita Tairyō 牧田諦亮. *Rikuchō koitsu kanzeon ōkenki no kenkyū* 六朝古逸觀世音應驗記の研究 [Study of Records of Spiritual Responses of Avalokiteśvara of the Six Dynasties Period]. Tokyo: Heirakuji shoten, 1970.

Matsuda Tōshō 松田壽南. *Hanboku to nankai: Ajiashi ni okeru sabaku to kaiyō* 漢北と南海：アジア史における砂漠と海洋 [Northern China and the South Seas: Desert and Ocean in Asian History]. Tokyo: Shikai shobō, 1942.

Mikami Tsugio 三上次男. "Kodai ni okeru kōeki to bunka kōryū" 古代史における交易と文化交流 [Trading and Cultural Exchange in Ancient Times]. In *Kodaishi Kōza*, vol. 13. Tokyo: Gakuseisha, 1966.

Min Yŏng-gyu 閔泳珪. "Silla changsorok changp'yŏn" 新羅章疏 錄長編 [List of Buddhist Works by Silla Monks]. In *Paek sŏnguk paksa songsu kinyŏm pulgohak nonmunjip* [Festschrift in Honor of Dr. Paek Sŏnguk], pp. 345-402. Seoul, 1957.

Mishina Akihide 三品彰英. "Chōsen ni okeru bukkyō to minzoku shinkō: Bukkyō no juyō keitai" 朝鮮における佛敎と民俗信仰：佛敎 の受容形態 [Buddhism and Folk Beliefs in Korea: The Form of Reception of Buddhism]. *Bukkyō shigaku* 佛敎史學 [Buddhist Historical Studies] 4, no. 1 (1954): 9-33.

——. *Mishina Akihide ronbunshū* 三品彰英論文集 [Collected Essays of Mishina Akihide]. Vols. 3, 4, 5. Tokyo: Heibonsha, 1971-73.

——. *Sangoku ishi kōshō* 三國遺事 考證 [Investigation of the *Samguk yusa*]. 2 vols. Tokyo: Asahi Shinbunsha, 1976. Reprint.

Miyamoto Shōson 宮本正尊. "Daijō to shojō" 大乘と小乘 [Ma-hāyāna and Hīnayāna]. In *Bukkyō no konpon mondai* 佛敎の根本問題, vol. 3, pp. 278-279, 492-496. Tokyo: Yagumo shoten, 1944.

Mun Myŏng-dae 文明大. "Kyŏngdŏkwangdae ŭi amit'a chosang munje" 景德王代의 阿彌陀 造像 問題 [Amitābha Images during King Kyŏngdŏk's Reign]. In *Yi Hongjik paksa hwagap kinyŏm han'guk sahak nonch'ong* [Festschrift in Honor of Dr. Yi Hong-jik], pp. 649-86. Seoul 1969.

——. "Silla pŏpsangjong ŭi sŏngnip munje wa kŭ misul" 新羅 法相宗의 成立 問題와 그 美術 [The Formation of the Dharmalakṣaṇa School of Silla and its Art]. *Yŏksa hakpo* 62 (1974): 75-105; 63 (1974): 133-162.

Munhwajae kwalliguk 文化財管理局 [Cultural Property Preservation Bureau], ed. *Muryŏngwangnŭng palgul chosa pogosŏ* 武寧王陵發掘調查報告書 [Excavation Report of the Tomb of King Muryŏng]. Seoul: 1974.

Nagasawa Kazutoshi 長澤和俊. *Hōkenden Sōun koki* 法顯傳・宋雲行記 [Biography of Fa-hsien and the Travelogue of Sung-yün]. Tōyō Bunko series, no. 194. Tokyo: Heibonsha, 1971.

——. "Iwayuru *Sōun kōki* ni tsuite" いわゆる宋雲行記について [On the So-called *Travelogue of Sung-yun*]. In *Shiruku rōdoshi kenkyū* pp. 459-480. Tokyo: Kokusho kankōkai, 1979.

Naitō Shumpō 內藤雋轉. "Chōsen shinakan no kōro oyobi sono suii ni tsuite" 朝鮮支那間の航路及其推移に就て [Sea Routes Between Korea and Chin and their Changes]. In *Naito hakushi shoju kinen shigaku ronsho.* 內藤博士頌壽記念史學論叢 Tokyo: Kobundo, 1930.

Nagakiri Isao 中吉功. "Dōzō bosatsu hankazō shōzon" 銅造菩薩半跏像鈔存 [On Bronze Half Cross-legged Images]. *Chōsen gakuhō* 朝鮮學報 48 (1968): 193-206.

Ninomiya Keinin 二宮啓任. "Kankoku no busshari shinkō ni tsuite" 韓國の佛舍利信仰について [The Buddha's Relic Cult in Korea]. *Chōsen gakuhō* 45 (1969): 39-55.

Nukariya Kaiten 忽滑谷快天. *Chōsen zenkyōshi* 朝鮮禪敎史 [History of Ch'an Buddhism in Korea]. Tokyo: Shunjusha, 1930.

Obayashi Taryō 大林太良, et. al. "Bunka no keisei to bukkyō no

denpa" 文化の形成と佛教の傳播 [Formation of Culture and Transmission of Buddhism]. *Rekish to jinbutsu* 歴史と人物 (February 1983).

Ōchō Enichi 横超 慧日. "Kōritsu denrai izen no chūgoku ni okeru kairitsu" 廣律傳來以前の中國における戒律 [*Vinaya* in China before the Transmission of the Complete *Vinayas*]. In *Chūgoku bukkyō no kenkyū* 中國佛教の研究 [Study of Chinese Buddhism], pp.11-189. Kyoto: Hōzōkan, 1958.

——. "Kumarajū no honyaku" 鳩摩羅什の飜譯 [The Translations of Kumārajīva]. *Otani gakuhō* 大谷學報 39, 4 (1958): 1-25.

Ōchō Enichi and Suwa Yoshizumi 諏訪義純. *Rajū* 羅什 [Kumārajīva]. Chūgoku no jinbutsu 中國の人物 series. Tokyo: Daizō shuppan, 1982.

Ogawa Kiyoshi 大川清, ed. *Kudara no kōkogaku* 百濟の考古學 [Archaelogy of Paekche]. Tokyo: Yuzankaku, 1972.

Renondeau, G. "La date de l'introduction du bouddhisme au Japon" *T'oung Pao* 47 (1959): 16-29.

Rhi Ki-yong 李箕永. *Wŏnhyo sasang* 元曉思想 [Thought of Wonhyo]. Seoul: Wonŭmgak, 1969.

——. "Wonhyo ŭi posalgye kwan" 元曉의 菩薩戒觀 [Wŏnhyo's View of the *Bodhisattvaśila*]. *Tongguk taehakkyo nonmunjip* 3/4 (1968). Compiled in his *Han'guk pulgyo yŏn'gu*, pp. 305-403.

——. "Han'gukjŏk sayu ŭi il chŏnhyŏng" 韓國的 思惟의 一典型 [A Type in the Korean Way of Thought]. *Tongbanghakchi* 東方學志 10 (1969). Compiled in his *Han'guk pulgyo yŏn'gu*, pp. 129-162.

——. "Pulgyo sasang ŭi suyong kwa kŭ pyŏnmo" 佛教思想의 受容과 그 變貌 [The Reception of Buddhism and its Transformation]. In *Han'guk minjok sasangsa taegye* 韓國民族思想史大系 [History of the Thought of the Korean People], vol. 1, pp.89-135. Seoul: Asea haksul yŏn'guhoe, 1971.

——. "Silla pulgyo ŭi sŏngkyŏk kwa kŭ hyŏndaejŏk ŭiŭi" 新羅佛教 의 性格과 그 現代的 意義 [Characteristic of Silla Buddhism and its Meanings for Today]. Originally published in Japanese in *Han*, 韓 2 (1972); compiled in his *Han'guk pulgyo yŏn'gu*, pp.453-463.

——. "Inwang panya-kyŏng kwa hoguk pulgyo: kŭ ponjil kwa yŏksajŏk chŏn'gae" 仁王般若經과 護國佛教 : 그 本質과 歷史的 展開 [The Sūtra of Benevolent Kings and National-protection Buddhism: Its Sources and Historical Development]. *Tongyanghak* 東洋學 5 (1975). Compiled in his *Han'guk pulgyo yŏn'gu*, pp.163-193.

——. *Han'guk pulgyo yŏn'gu* 韓國 佛教 研究 [Study of Korean

Buddhism]. Seoul: Han'guk pulgyo yŏn'guwŏn ch'ulp'anbu, 1982.

Rogers, Michael C. *The Chronicle of Fu Chien: A Case of Exemplar History*. Chinese Dynastic Histories Translations, no. 10. Berkeley and Los Angeles: University of California Press, 1986.

Saito Tadashi 齊藤忠. "Fuyo gunshūri haiji iseki ni mirareru garan haichi to sono genryū" 扶餘軍守里廢寺遺蹟に見られる伽藍配置とその源流 [The Layout of the Monastery in the Puyŏ Kunsu-ri Temple Ruins and its Origin]. In Tamura and Hwang, ed. *Kudara bunka to asuka bunka*, pp. 83–105.

Sakaino Tetsu 境野哲. *Shina bukkyōshi kōwa* 支那佛教史講話 [History of Chinese Buddhism]. 2 vols. Tokyo: Kyōritsusha, 1927–29.

Sakamoto Yoshitane 坂元義種. *Kudarashi no kenkyū* 百濟史の研究 [Studies in the History of Paekche]. 2 vols. Tokyo: Hanawa shobō, 1978.

——. *Kodai higashi ajia no nihon to chōsen* 古代東アジアの日本と朝鮮 [Japan and Korea in Ancient East Asia]. Tokyo: Yoshikawa Kōbundō, 1978.

Shiratori Kurakichi 白鳥庫吉全集. *Shiratori Kurakichi zenshū* [Collected works of Shiratori Kurakichi], Vols. 3 and 5. Tokyo: Iwanami shoten, 1970.

Suematsu Yasukazu 末松保和. "Shiragi bukkyō denrai densetsu ko" 新羅佛教傳來傳說考 [On the Legends Concerning the Transmission of Buddhism to Silla]. In *Shiragishi no shomondai* 新羅史の諸問題 [Issues in Silla history]. pp. 207–234. Tokyo: Tōyō bunkō, 1954.

——. *Seikyu shiso* 靑丘史草 [Miscellaneous Essays on Korean History]. Tokyo: Kasai shuppansha, 1965, 1966.

Sugimoto Naojirō 杉本直沿郎. "Indoshina kodai shakai no shiteki seikaku: tokuni funan no baai" インドシナ古代社會の史的性格：特に扶南のばあい [Historical Characteristics of the Ancient Societies of Indo-China, with Special Reference to Fu-nan] in *Tōnan ajiashi kenkyū*, 東南アジア史研究, vol. 1, pp. 308–526. Tokyo: Nihon gakujutsu shinkōkai, 1956.

Szczesniak, Boleslaw. "The Kōtaiō monument". *Monumenta Nipponica* 7, no. 5 (1951): 242–68.

Takahashi Toru 高橋亨. *Richō bukkyō* 李朝佛教 [Buddhism in the Chosŏn Dynasty]. Osaka, 1929.

Takashi Hataka. "An Interpretation of King Kwanggaet'o's Inscription", translated by V. Dixon Morris, *Korean Studies* 3 (1979): 1–18.

Tamura Enchō 田村圓澄. "Pan'ga sayusang kwa sŏngdŏk t'aeja

sinang" 半跏思惟像斗 聖德太子信仰 [The Half Cross-legged Images and the Cult of Prince Shōtoku] In *Hanil kodae munhwa kyosŏpsa yŏn'gu* 韓日古代文化交涉史硏究 [Studies in the History of Cultural Associantions between Korea and Japan in Ancient Times], pp. 43–100. Seoul: Ŭryu munhwasa, 1974.

——, and Hwang Su-yŏng, ed. *Kudara bunka to Asuka bunka* 百濟文化と飛鳥文化 [Cultures of Paekche and Asuka]. Tokyo: Yoshikawa kōbundō, 1978.

——. "Kudara bukkyōshi josetsu" 百濟佛教史序說 [Preliminary Investigation of the History of Buddhism in Paekche]. In Tamura and Hwang, ed. *Kudara bunka to Asuka bunka* pp. 304–357.

——. *Kodai chōsen bukkyō to nihon bukkyō* 古代朝鮮佛教と日本佛教 [Ancient Korean Buddhism and Japanese Buddhism]. Tokyo: Yoshikawa kōbundō, 1980.

T'ang Yung-t'ung 湯用彤. "She-shan chih san-lun-tsung-shih luehk'ao" 攝山之三論宗師略考 [Short Study of the History of the San-lun School on Mt. She]. *Shih-hsueh tsa-chih* 史學雜誌 2, no. 5, (1931).

——. *Han-wei liang-chin nan-pei ch'ao fo-chiao shih* 漢魏兩晋南北朝佛教史 [History of Buddhism during the Han, Wei, Western and Eastern Chin, and Nan-pei ch'ao periods]. Ch'ang-sha: Commercial Press, 1938.

Tongguk taehakkyo pulgyo munhwa yŏn'guso 東國大學校 佛教文化硏究所, ed. *Han'guk pulgyo ch'ansul munhŏn ch'ongnok* 韓國佛教撰述文獻總錄 [A Comprehensive Catalogue of Korean Buddhist Works]. Seoul: Dongguk (Tongguk) University Press, 1979.

——. *Kankoku bussho kaidai jiten* 韓國佛書解題事典 [Annotated Bibliography of Korean Buddhist Books]. Tokyo: Kokusho kankōkai. 1982.

Tsuboi Kumezo 坪井九馬三, and Kusaka Hiroshi 日下寛, trans. *Genbun wayaku taishō sangoku ishi* 原文和譯大正三國遺事. Chōsen kenkyūkai, 1915.

Tsuda Shōkichi 津田左右吉. *Tsuda Shōkichi zenshū* 津田左右吉全集 [Collected Works of Tsuda Shokichi], vols. 11 and 12. Tokyo: Iwanami Shoten, 1964.

Tsukamoto Zenryū 塚本善隆. "Ryūmon sekkutsu ni arawaretaru hokugi bukkyō" 龍門石窟に現れたる北魏佛教 [The Nature of Buddhism of the Northern Wei as Evidenced in the Lung-men Cave]. In his *Shina bukkyōshi kenkyū: hokugi* 支那佛教史研究：北魏 [A Study of Chinese Buddhism: Northern Wei]. Tokyo: Kōbundō, 1942.

——. "Kumarajū ron" 鳩摩羅什論　[On Kumārajīva], 1 and 2. In *Yuki kyōju shoju kinen bukkyō shisōshi ronshū* 結城教授頌壽記念佛教思想史論集　pp. 359-378. Tokyo: Daizo shuppan, 1964.

——. *Chūgoku bukkyō tsushi* 中國佛教通史　[History of Chinese Buddhism]. Tokyo: Suzuki gakujutsu zaidan, 1968.

Uchida Ginpu 內田吟風. "Gogi sōun shaku esho seiiki gukyōki konin josetsu" 後魏宋雲釋惠生西域求經記考認序說　[Historical Investigation of the *Hsi-yu ch'iu-ching chi* by Sung-yun and Shih Hui-sheng of the Eastern Wei, a Preliminary Study] in *Tsukamoto hakushi shoju kinen bukkyō shigaku ronshū* 塚本博士頌壽紀念佛教史學論集,　pp. 113-124. Kyoto 1961.

Wŏnhyo chŏnjip 元曉全集　[The Complete Works of Wŏnhyo]. Seoul: Tongguk yŏkkŏngwŏn, 1973.

Yabuki Keiki 矢吹　慶輝. *Meisha yoin kaisetsu* 鳴沙餘韻解說. Tokyo: Iwanami shoten, 1933.

Yamamoto Tatsurō 山本達郎. "Indoshina no kenkoku setsuwa" 印度支那の建國說話　[Foundation Legends of Indo-China] in *Tōzai kōshō shiron* 東西交渉史論, vol. 1. Tokyo: Tōyama shobō, 19339.

——. "Kodai nankai kōtsū to funan no bunka" 古代南海交通と扶南の文化　[Routes through the Ancient South Seas and the Cultures of Fu-nan]. In *Kodaishi kōza* 古代史講座, vol. 13, pp. 124-144. Tokyo: Gakuseisha, 1966.

Yaotani Takayasu 八百谷孝保. "Shiragi shakai to jōdokyō" 新羅社會と淨土教　[Silla Society and Pure-land Buddhism]. *Shisho* 史潮 7, (1937).

Yen Wen-ju 閻文儒. "Kung-wang shan fo-chiao tsao-hsiang te t'i-t'sai" 孔望山佛教造像の題材　[On the Motifs of Buddhist Images at Mt. Kung-wang]. *Wen-wu* 7 : 302 (1981) : 16-19.

Yi Hong-jik 李弘稙. "Silla sŭnggwanje wa pulgyo chŏngch'aek ŭi munje" 新羅 僧官制와 佛教政策의 問題　[On the *Saṃgha* System of Silla and its National Policy Concerning Buddhism]. *Paek Sŏnguk paksa songsu kinyŏm pulgyohak nonmunjip*, pp. 659-680. Seoul, 1959.

Yi Nŭng-hwa 李能華. *Chosŏn pulgyo t'ongsa* 朝鮮佛教通史　[History of Korean Buddhism]. 3 vols. Keijō(Seoul): Sinmun'gwan, 1918. Reprint, Seoul: Poryŏn'gak, 1979.

Yi Sang-bo 李相寶, trans. *P'ahanjip, Pohanjip, Yŏgong p'aesŏl* 破閑集, 補閑集, 櫟翁稗說. Seoul: Taeyang sŏjŏk, 1972.

Yi Sŏn-gŭn 李瑄根. *Hwarangdo yŏn'gu* 花郎道研究　[Study of the Hwarangdo]. Seoul: Tongguk munhwasa, 1954.

Yi Sung-nyŏng 李崇寧. *Silla sidae ŭi p'yogibŏp ch'egye e kwanhan siron* 新羅時代의 表記法 體系에 關한 試論　[An Essay on Silla-

Period Writing Systems]. Seoul: T'ap ch'ulp'ansa, 1978.

Yoneda Miyoji 米田美代治. *Chōsen jōdai kenchiku no kenkyū* 朝鮮上代建築の研究 [Study of the Architecture of Ancient Korea]. Osaka: Osaka Akitaya, 1944.

Yu Sŏk-u 柳奭祐. "Koguryŏ ŭi hŭngmang kwa chonggyo kwan' gye" 高句麗의 興亡과 宗敎關係 [Rise and Fall of Koguryŏ and their Religious Reasons]. *Kyŏngbuk taehakkyo nonmumjip* 慶北大學校論文集 [Journal of Kyŏngbuk Unversity] 1–4 (1956–58).

Yu Wei-ch'ao 俞偉超. "Tung-Han fo-chiao t'u-hsiang k'ao" 東漢佛敎圖像考 [A Study of Buddhist Images of the Eastern Han]. *Wen-wu* 5 (1980): 68–77.

Yun Chang-sop 尹張爕. *Han'guk kŏnch'uksa* 韓國建築史 [History of Korean Architecture]. Seoul: Tongmyŏngsa, 1973.

Yun Mu-byŏng 尹武炳. *Puyŏgun ŭnsanmyŏn kŭmgongri paekche saji palgul chosa pogo* 扶餘郡恩山面琴公里百濟寺址發掘調査報告 [Excavation Report of a Monastery Site of Paekche in Kumgong-ri, Unsan-myon, Puyo-gun]. Seoul: National Museum of Korea, 1969.

Index